SWITZERLAND

THE Michael's NEW GUIDE

SWITZERLAND

Managing Editor

Michael Shichor

Series Editor

Amir Shichor

INBAL TRAVEL INFORMATION LTD.

Inbal Travel Information Ltd.
P.O.Box 1870 Ramat Gan 52117
Israel

The publishers have done their best to ensure the accuracy and currency of all information contained in this guide; however, they can accept no responsibility for any errors and/or inaccuracies found.

Intl. ISBN 965-288-119-8

Text: Shlomo Papirblat
Graphic design: Michel Opatowski
Cover design: Bill Stone
Photography: Sharon Bentov
Swiss National Tourist Office
Office du Tourisme de Genève, Basel Tourist Board, Tourismusverband St. Gallerland, Lausanne Tourist Office, Lugano Tourist Office, Tourist Office of Berne
Photo editor: Yoel Sitruk
Editorial: Sharona Johan, Or Rinat, Lisa Stone
D.T.P.: Irit Bahalul, Michael Michelson
Printed by Havatzelet Press Ltd.

Sales in the UK and Europe:
Kuperard (London) Ltd.
9 Hampstead West
224 Iverson Road
London NW6 2HL

Distribution in the UK and Europe:
Bailey Distribution Ltd.
Learoyd Road
New Romney
Kent TN28 8X

U.K. ISBN 1-85733-113-3

CONTENTS

TABLE OF MAPS

Preface

Switzerland is the jewel of the Alps and the capital of European tourism. Its breathtaking beauty cannot be matched. The taste of its chocolate, the accuracy of its clocks and the secrecy of its banks, are legendary. It is this Switzerland that we set out to discover, to experience and to enjoy.

Shlomo Papirblat visited Switzerland's cities and villages, tasted all the wonders of the land and left no stone unturned to provide us with the wealth of information that is contained in this book.

The variety of sightseeing spots in Switzerland, from its beautiful ancient cities to the enchanting landscapes of the Alps and fabulous mirror-like lakes, make Switzerland a joy to visit, and a guide like this – an essential traveling companion.

A great deal of work has been put into this guide by a great many people. We gratefully acknowledge the assistance extended by the Swiss Tourist Offices, Swissair, and of course, the editorial staff at Inbal Travel Information Ltd., who compiled and edited the material.

We are certain that visiting and touring Switzerland with this guide will open new doors to its treasures and will be an unforgettable experience.

Have a pleasant trip!

Michael Shichor

Using this Guide

In order to reap maximum benefit from the information in this guide, we advise the traveler to carefully read the following passage. The facts contained in this guide were compiled to help the tourist find his or her way around and to ensure that he enjoys his stay to the upmost.

The Introduction provides details which will help you make the early decisions and arrangements for your trip. We suggest that you carefully review the material, so that you will be more organized and set for your visit. Upon arrival in Switzerland, you will feel more familiar and comfortable with the country.

The suggested routes are arranged according to geographical areas, a system that allows for an efficient division of time and ensures a thorough knowledge of each region. More so, this guide will direct you to unexpected places that you may not have heard of and did not plan to visit.

Many languages are spoken in the different parts of Switzerland. In this guide we have used the local name for the places mentioned. The Graubünden Canton, for instance, is called Grisons in French, but here, it is referred to by its local German name – Graubünden.

The chapters on main cities include maps and indexes of sites that will help you find your way. On reaching each city, the guide will direct you to recommended accommodation and restaurants.

The rich collection of maps covers the tour routes in great detail. Especially prepared for this book, they will certainly add to the efficiency and pleasure of your exploration of Switzerland.

To further facilitate the use of this guide, we have added a detailed index. It includes all the major sites mentioned throughout the guide. Consult the index to find something by name and it will refer you to the place where it is mentioned in greatest detail.

During your visit you will see and experience many things – we have therefore left several blank pages at the back of the guide. These are for you, to jot down those special experiences from people and places, feelings and significant happenings along the way.

Because times and places are dynamic, an important rule of thumb when traveling, and especially when visiting a country like Switzerland, should be to consult local sources of information. Tourists are liable to encounter certain inaccuracies in this guide, and for this we apologize.

In this guide we have tried to present updated information in a way which allows for an easy, safe and economical visit. For this purpose, we have included a short questionnaire and will be most grateful to those who will take the time to complete it and send it to us.

Have a pleasant and exciting trip – Bon Voyage!

PART ONE – A GENERAL VIEW

History

In the year 58 BC, the legions of Julius Caesar overcame the Helvetians in the western part of what is today Switzerland and annexed it to the Roman colony of Belgium Gallia. Some 50 years later, they conquered Eastern Switzerland and added it to the Roman Empire as the colony of Rhaetia.

The Roman conquest, like all conquests, brought with it a new culture and language, as well as a process of urbanization. Many remains from that period can still be seen today. In the Augusta Rauraca colony near Basel, the amphitheater, the baths and the forum from the period of the Roman rule still stand.

In the third, fifth and sixth centuries, Switzerland was invaded by various tribes who seized as much land as they could and annexed it. These invasions laid the basis for the ethnic differences between the German-speaking and the French-speaking Swiss of today.

These differences deepened under 9th century Frankish rule, when the eastern part of Switzerland was transferred to Ludwig the German in 843 AD, the southern area to Italian Lombardy in 879 AD and the western section to the Kingdom of Burgundy in 888 AD.

European politics continued to develop dynamically. In the 11th century, the entire area of today's Switzerland was incorporated into the Holy Roman-German Empire. The feudal era took hold of the country, which was controlled by nobles and princes of the church and whose fortressed castles became the foundation for the development of cities and trade centers. The city of Fribourg was established in 1157 and Bern in 1191.

With the weakening of the Roman-German giant, local rule gained in strength, a natural process encouraged by several feudal dynasties. Toward the end of the 13th century, two of these dynasties, Hapsburg and Savoy, defeated the others in internal struggles and divided the lands between them – the east went to Hapsburg and the west to Savoy. It was then that the "Swiss process" began.

Along the shores of the Lake of the Four Cantons in the "forest regions" of Uri, Schwytz and Unterwald, local feudal rule was oppressive; the citizens wanted to alleviate this situation. They decided to recognize the supreme authority of the distant Roman Emperor only, thus granting themselves a certain degree of autonomy.

On August 1, 1291, representatives of the three regions made an "eternal pact" for mutual assistance in the joint struggle for freedom against the Hapsburgs, who were threatening their relative autonomy. This historic pact was the birth of the Helvetian Confederation which was later renamed after the Swiss (Schwyz) area.

Concrete evidence of this unusual development in feudal Europe emerged in the Battle of Morgarten in 1315, when the fighters of the "alliance" defeated the Hapsburg army of Leopold of Austria. Against the background of this historic battle emerged the legend of William Tell, the daring archer, who split an apple that had been placed on his son's head. The folklore revolving around the character of Tell began to gather force only in the 15th century, and it was in the 19th century, when Schiller created his literary masterpiece based on this legend, that it became an intrinsic part of Swiss culture.

The alliance gained further victories in the 14th century and the union between them was very successful. Various cities and regions began to join the alliance. Luzern joined in 1332, Zürich in 1351, Glarus and Zug in 1352 and Bern in 1353. In the same period, the union was known by the name of "The Eight Cantons." As their power grew, so did their courage. They overran the Aarau region, where the Hapsburg family castle was located; they annexed the Ticino area in the south, as well as the Thurgau region in the north. Charles, Count of Burgundy, was defeated by the Swiss army in 1477 when he himself fell in battle.

At this stage, when it was no longer possible to ignore the growing alliance, Emperor Maximilian decided to try to regain what was actually part of his empire. However, the spirit of the Swiss grew stronger, in battles that erupted in 1499 and they were victorious again.

Stories of the courage of the alliance fighters soon spread throughout Europe and the abilities of the Swiss soldier became legendary. The strength of these fighters actually lay in their simplicity. These were courageous soldiers, city dwellers and farmers, unable to equip themselves with the heavy armor of the knights of their day. Their ease of movement, bravery and long spears (for they were skilled in using pitchforks) gave them a decisive advantage over the heavily armed they fought against.

The rulers of Europe began to hire the services of the legendary Swiss soldiers and mercenaries, by order of princes and kings. They fought for money and part of the booty, which was sent home to Switzerland. To this day this military tradition is maintained at the Vatican in Rome, where the watchmen of the Vatican and the Pope's bodyguards are all Swiss Guards.

A different aspect of the military success was less positive. In many of the alliance settlements where the men had become soldiers, the land was neglected. Easy money led to arguments and dishonesty, and internal conflicts erupted between the cantons. In 1481, when matters seemed about to erupt into a full-fledged civil war, a recluse monk called Saint Klaus intervened with a compromise, by which all the cantons in the alliance were declared equal. An arrangement was made for division of the land, and intervention in the internal affairs of another canton was forbidden.

As a result of this broad change, the last ties with the Hapsburg Empire were broken and new cantons joined the union: Fribourg, Solothurn, Basel, Schaffhausen, and Appenzell. By the early 16th century, 13 cantons belonged to the alliance, along with other cities and regions that were considered allies only, including Geneva, St. Gallen, Valais and Neuchâtel. The alliance, however, had not yet sufficiently evolved and not everyone viewed the political problems

At the main street in Vaduz

arising around them in Europe in the same way. Thus, in various struggles between neighboring rulers, Swiss cantons could sometimes be found on both sides of combat.

For a short time in the early 16th century, the Cardinal Schiner, seemed to have unified the cantons behind a single goal; assistance to the papal states in the war against France. But despite this internal success, the struggle ended in military defeat for Switzerland at the Battle of Marignano in 1515, followed by a peace treaty with France. After the last alliance members had signed the agreement, Switzerland stepped down from the European political stage for a while and renounced further territorial expansion on its part.

Among the participants in the Battle of Marignano was the military cardinal, Zwingli. In light of the state of affairs – the Swiss neglecting their land and their work to fight alongside the papal armies, for political power and influence over Europe – Zwingli began to have doubts about the path of the Catholic Church. These doubts, unlike those expressed by Luther, were based on a different approach which negated the authority of the Pope, his moral standards and his interpretation of the Holy Scriptures. These thoughts, in fact, sowed the seeds of the Reformation. Zwingli brought the reform to Zürich, disassociating the canton from the Vatican. Other cantons including Bern, Basel, Schaffhausen and Appenzell were influenced by what happened in Zürich and also cut themselves off from the leaders of the Church.

This breakaway led to harsh animosity with those cantons that remained Catholic – primarily Uri, Schwyz, Luzern, Unterwald and Zug, and eventually to a confrontation on the battlefield at Kappel in 1531, won by the Catholics. The Cardinal Zwingli met his death in battle.

Nevertheless, the desire for unification was stronger than the differences, and shortly afterwards a peace treaty was signed between the two sides. The Reformation thus remained in the cantons that had already adopted it. However, although the alliance was renewed by formal agreement, circumstances created a division within the union. The Protestant cantons maintained a political and cultural bond with England and the Scandinavian states, while the Catholic cantons developed close ties with France, Spain and Austria. Although the alliance did not disintegrate, in effect it was very limited in scope and the cantons acted as sovereign entities in domestic and foreign affairs.

The aftereffects of the religious warfare continued to leave their mark in the following years. The Appenzell canton split in two as a result of its internal battles. In the second half of the 16th century, the Catholic alliance was established and centered in Luzern, as were two Protestant alliances. In 1536,

Calvin came to one of these alliances centered in Geneva and the new revolutionary religious movement named after him (Calvinism) evolved.

The Thirty Year War reunified the cantons, in their effort to protect their independence against outside forces. In 1648, as part of the Treaty of Westphalia at the end of the war, Switzerland's independence and neutrality was recognized.

Nevertheless, it seems that one more armed battle between the cantons would be necessary in order to stabilize the religious status quo in Switzerland. The struggle took place in 1712, and this time the Protestants won. After this, all was quiet in Switzerland, until the French Revolution, which threw the country into a storm. At the beginning of the revolution, Switzerland did not intervene in what was happening beyond its border, but anti-revolutionary public sentiments were stirred by the slaughter of Swiss Guard soldiers who died in defense of Louis XVI, in August 1792. In 1794, revolutionaries took control of Geneva, inspired by the French and aided by Paris; and in 1797, after their war in Italy had ended, the French invaded Switzerland. Under the protection of their army, the invaders set up the Leman Republic in the Vaud area north of Lake Léman (Lake Geneva). In 1799, the Austrians, Prussians and Russians invaded Switzerland to fight on the side of the monarchy against the French. After a long, bloody battle, France pervaded and took control of the entire territory of Switzerland. The alliance between the cantons was declared invalid and the French-influenced Helvetian Republic was established.

The Republic's government was similar to the system that had been introduced in Paris; with a council, a senate and a ruling directorate of 50 members. The cantons became administrative regions subject to the centralized power. Life, however, did not return to normal. Serious conflicts erupted between those in favor of the new arrangement and those dedicated to the System of Federations. When things became serious, both sides turned to the strongest individual of the period, Napoleon Bonaparte, to decide the issue.

His decision was published in February, 1803; the unsuccessful Helvetian Republic was dissolved. The alliance of the cantons was returned to power and six new cantons – St. Gallen, Graubünden, Thurgau, Aargau, Vaud and Ticino – were added to the original 13.

Some other important changes were made: religion was separated from the state, a federal army

was set up, the customs charges among the cantons was abolished and an education system was established.

The "new" Switzerland was seemingly neutral regarding European policies. However, the countries leading the struggle against Napoleon regarded Switzerland as the French Emperor's ally. Many Swiss soldiers did, in fact, fight in Napoleon's wars and thousands paid with their lives, particularly in the unsuccessful attempt to occupy Russia. Thus, the countries at the front line were not convinced by Switzerland's declared neutrality, and in 1814 they invaded and conquered the country. At the Vienna Congress, held in 1815, the independence of Switzerland was officially recognized, and the groundwork was laid for its true neutral character. Corrections were also made in the marking of its borders, returning Geneva, Valais, and Neuchâtel to Switzerland. In August, 1815, when Switzerland's new constitution was approved, these areas were declared as cantons, bringing the total of cantons to 22.

The constitution of 1815 symbolized a return to the conservatism of the days predating Napoleon. Almost complete sovereignty was restored to the cantons regarding money, customs and tax collection. Freedom of religious ceremony was revoked and the right to vote was restricted to property owners. These changes and others like them stirred Swiss society and polarized the conservatives against the relatively liberal Bonapartes. The latter were inspired by France, especially by the civil rebellion of 1830 in Paris. Riots and confrontations erupted in several cantons – and eventually new changes were made in the constitution. At the same time the Basel canton split into two sovereign halves: Basel the city and Basel the village.

In addition to political disagreement, there were also religious arguments and in their wake, the alliance broke up. A union was formed of the seven conservative Catholic cantons – Schwyz, Uri, Luzern and others – called the Sonderbund ("separate alliance"). The leaders of the alliance refused to cancel their union, which was

A typical view of the Swiss Middle-lands

illegal under Swiss law, which led to the outbreak of the civil war of 1847.

General Dufour, of Geneva, a brilliant military man, talented engineer and a man of wide horizons, led the federal army in a war against the "separate alliance", winning without much bloodshed. This victory guaranteed the possibility for a common future. This was the last of Switzerland's wars, to this day.

After the liberal cantons had won on the battlefield, talks were begun which gave birth to the Constitution of 1848, dividing the rule between the cantons and the institutions of the federation. This law established a federal council of seven members, as well as legislative bodies, a supreme court and the other institutions that function, with only slight changes, to this day (for more details see the chapter on Government).

In 1874, due to political pressures, a number of changes were introduced into the constitution. The most important of which was the concept of the referendum. In addition, the civil and punitive laws of all cantons were unified; it was no longer more worthwhile to steal in a neighboring city, in a different canton.

Switzerland's declared neutrality stood up to the test in the two World Wars. Switzerland was hurt economically, but much less than its neighbors who had taken an active part in the wars. In both wars the federal army was put on a state of high alert and many of its reserves were called up to prepare against attempted invasion. Today, when the Swiss tell war stories, they recall the days when they were mobilized during World War II. Many escaped British and American POWs, managed to find sanctuary in Switzerland until the war was over.

Between the wars, a monetary economic union was made between Switzerland and the principality of Liechtenstein, which included, among other things in provision of communications, transportation, defense and other services to Liechtenstein, from Switzerland.

In a 1971 referendum on the question of suffrage for women, the men of Switzerland finally agreed to grant women the right to vote.

In another referendum in September 1978, Switzerland's 23rd canton, Jura, was added to the state, as a result of pressure from the French-speaking residents in the northern section of the Bern canton.

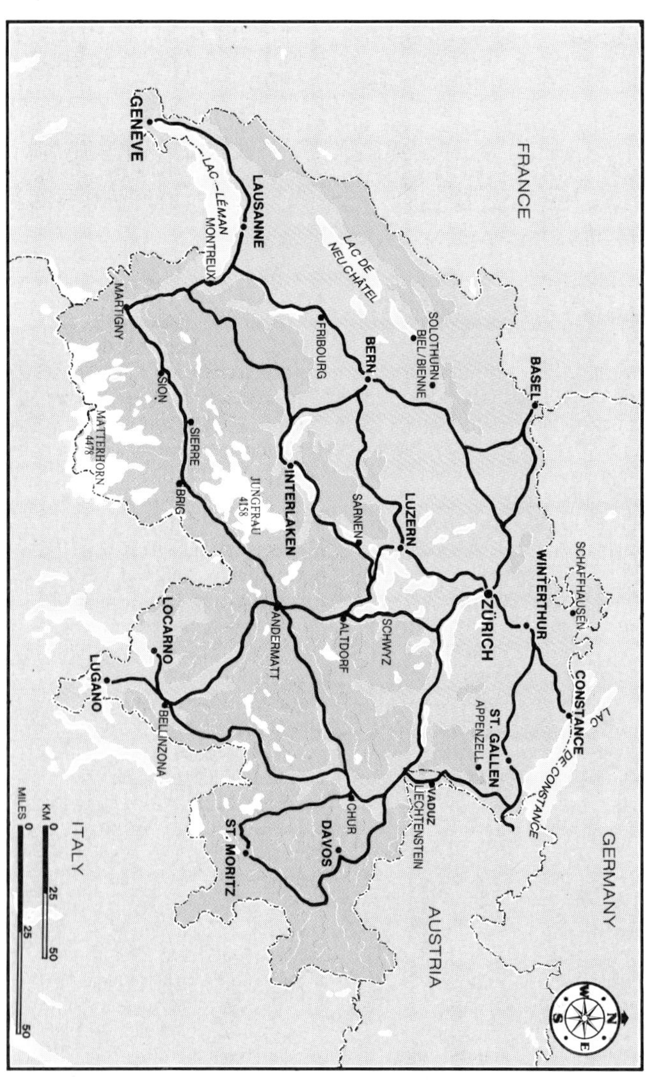

SWITZERLAND

Aletsch Glacier, the largest of its kind in Switzerland

Geography

Switzerland lies in the heart of central Europe. It covers 15,941 sq. miles. Its borders measure 1,176 miles: the border with Italy is 463 miles long; with France 357 miles; with Germany 226 miles; with Austria 102 miles, and with Liechtenstein 26 miles. Switzerland is a mountainous country in the full sense of the word; 50% of its territory is higher than 3,280 ft. and its mountain tops tower to heights of over 13,000 ft. In general, Switzerland is divided into three regions, spreading from southwest to northeast: the Alps (60% of the area of the country); the Plateau or the Middle-lands (30%); and the Jura (10%).

THE ALPS

Approximately one-fifth of the Alps mountain range is located in Swiss territory; it spreads like a giant arch, some 750 miles long. The area is very broken up because of the "cuts" from the huge glaciers, that moved through the area thousands of years ago. These long valleys, and especially the larger ones, like the Rhine and the Rhône, serve today as major arteries of transportation. The average altitude in the area is some 5,575 ft., but there are some mountain tops that reach close to 13,000 ft.

The Swiss Alps are dotted with glaciers and snowy masses covering a total area of 1,172 miles. Aletsch, with an area of 46 miles, is the largest of the Alpine glaciers. These glaciers are a reminder of the prehistoric period, in which the entire region was covered with ice.

A large number of mineral deposits, together with constant erosion, have created extraordinary landscapes that are constantly changing.

Switzerland is home to the Bernese Oberland, a set of high-reaching mountains in the Middle Alps, including the Aletschhorn, 13,754 ft., and the famous Jungfrau, 13,633 ft. To the northeast of the Bernese Oberland tower the Glarus and Appenzell

Alps, and to its south, the Valais Alps.

THE PLATEAU OR THE MIDDLE-LANDS

This region is a sort of "corridor" lying between the Alps and the Jura mountains, some 156 miles long and 38 miles wide. Its average altitude is some 2,000 ft.

The plateau spreads out between two large lakes – in the south Lake Léman (Geneva) and in the north, the Lake of Constance. This is the only flat terrain in Switzerland, and naturally, it is the most populated and built-up area, as well as being the agricultural heart of the country.

The scenery in the Middle-lands is hilly and rounded, and the height of its mountain tops ranges between 1,315 and 1,970 ft. Here and there, a few mountains (up to 3,900 ft. high) tower over the plain.

THE JURA

The Jura (in French), or Yura (in German), is a range of mountains ranging some 125 miles in western Switzerland, along the entire border with France. On the Swiss side, the Jura is an average of 12.5 miles wide.

The average altitude in the region is some 2,300 ft., which includes many mountain tops over 5,000 ft. high, like the Tendre, 5,505 ft., the Dolent, 5,498 ft. and the Chasseral, 5,300 ft.

The Jura is a mixture of meadows, forests, mountain peaks and deep valleys. At the foot of the Jura, descending toward the Middle-lands, lies the Lake of Neuchâtel. The southern Jura borders Lake Léman and Geneva.

Lots of Water

Water is one of Switzerland's most important resources. Because of the large amount of precipitation and the ridges which form watersheds, Switzerland is the birthplace of several rivers, including the largest river in western Europe – the Rhine. The sources of the Rhine are in the northern Swiss Alps; its major tributary is the

Aare River. The Rhine is 825 miles long, of which 235 miles flow through Switzerland. The Rhine is navigable beginning near the city of Basel.

Switzerland is abundant in lakes. In addition to the largest and most well known, there are hundreds of medium-sized and small lakes, so close to one another that wherever you are in Switzerland, you are never more than 10 miles from a lake.

The highest peaks in Switzerland are: the Rosa, 15,193 ft.; the Dom, 14,902 ft.; the Weisshorn, 14,774 ft.; the Matterhorn, 14,682 ft. and the Dent Blanche, 14,257 ft.

The longest rivers (in Swiss territory) are: the Rhine, 235 miles; the Rhône, 165 miles; the Aare, 184 miles; the Reuss, 98 miles; and the Linth-Limmat, 82.5 miles.

Switzerland's largest lakes are: Léman (Geneva) 227 sq. miles; Constance (Bodensee), 211 sq. miles; Neuchâtel, 85 sq. miles; Vierwaldstätter, 114 sq. miles and the Lugano, 19 sq. miles.

Switzerland's largest glaciers are: Aletsch, 46 sq. miles; Gorner, 25 sq. miles; Fiesch, 15 sq. miles; Aare, 14 sq. miles and Grindelwald, 11 sq. miles.

Climate

Switzerland is located right in the middle of Europe, and therefore its climate is extremely varied, combining many types of climates, typical throughout Europe; this combination actually constitutes a climate of its own.

Small, picturesque villages dot the Rhine Valley

Switzerland is affected by the sub-polar climate from the north, the ocean climate and the Gulf stream climate from the west, the Mediterranean climate from the south, and the continental climate from the east. The great differences in altitude also influence the climate – two spots that are relatively close geographically might have extremely sharp differences in climate. In Lugano the annual precipitation is an average of 70°, on Monte Generoso it is 80°, in the Sion mountains only 23° and in Staldenrid 21°.

Thus, it is difficult to talk about the Swiss climate – except for the area of the Middle-lands, where in recent years the rainfall has measured 21° annually, with an average annual temperature of 7-9°C. In the mountainous regions, and particularly above 12,460 ft. all precipitation is in the form of snow.

The average monthly temperature distribution (in Celsius) in Zürich is typical of the climatic conditions on the plains: January minus 1ºC; February 2ºC; March 4.2ºC; April 8ºC; May 12.5ºC; June 15.5ºC; July 17.2ºC; August 16.8ºC; September 13.5ºC; October 8.4ºC;

November 3.3°C; and December 0.2°C. These are, of course, averages: there are years when September is a balmy 25°C, and January can, at times, drop below 5°C.

Population

Beginning in 1850, a population census has been conducted every 10 years.

In the first census, some 2.4 million Swiss residents were counted. In 1900 there were 3.3 million people, in 1950 – 4.7 million, in 1980, 6.3 million, and in 1994 – 6.87 million.

The population density is 400 persons per sq. mile – one of the highest figures in Europe. Excluding the area occupied by mountains and lakes, the average density in the populated areas alone reaches 650 persons per sq. mile!

Switzerland's population is divided into politically, culturally and socially autonomous cantons.

Language

The Swiss constitution, which was approved in 1874, officially recognizes three languages: German, French and Italian. In 1938, the Romansch language was added. Territorially, the linguistic divisions more or less parallel the cantons, though there are places where "islands" of one language are surrounded by a "sea" of another. The German language is predominant in the cantons of Appenzells, Aargau, Basel, Bern, Glarus, Graubünden, Luzern, St. Gallen, Schaffhausen, Schwyz, Solothurn, Thurgau, Unterwalden, Uri, Zug and Zürich. French is dominant in Fribourg, Geneva, Jura, Valais, Vaud and Neuchâtel. Italian is spoken in Ticino and in the southern part of Graubünden. Romansch is spoken in a small part of Graubünden, though even here it is diminishing.

In the last four decades, no major changes have occurred in the language blocks. Research indicates a decline in the number of German speakers (7%), an even slighter decrease in the number of French speakers (2%) and a small rise, due to immigration, in the number of Italian speakers (4%). The linguistic division is: German, 65%; French, 18%; Italian, 10%; Romansch, 1%. The remaining 6% is divided among foreign languages.

The spoken language of the German speakers is a local dialect, known as Shwyzerdütsch, but the language of the media – radio, television and the press – as well as the German taught in the schools, is "Hoch Deutsch" – "high-level" German.

The French spoken in Switzerland has undergone changes in the last few generations, and the local Franco-Provençal dialect has almost been completely replaced by modern French. Only a few, mostly elderly, residents of the canton of Fribourg still use the Franco-Provençal French in their daily speech.

Most of the Italian-speakers of Switzerland also speak a local Lombardic dialect.

The Rhaeto-Romanic, or Romansch, speakers are not only a minority among the Swiss, they are also divided among themselves. There are five different dialects of the Romansch language in Switzerland, which naturally makes communication difficult and puts their language at a risk of extinction.

In an attempt to preserve the Rhaeto-Romanic language, the federal government provides financial resources for cultural institutions that operate in this language. It is predicted, however, that by the year 2000, there will be only a few, mostly elderly people, whose mother tongue is Romansch.

It should be noted that more and more Swiss, particularly the young, have mastered each others languages. Young citizens in the French cantons speak German fluently and vice versa. Many of them also speak English, having learned it in school.

Government

The system of government in Switzerland is not simple, and even native Swiss have trouble understanding its intricacies. Nonetheless, we will try to explain its main principles.

The entire Swiss government is located in a single building in the federation's capital. The Federal Palace in Bern houses the Council of States, the National Council (the legislature), and all the government offices. Strange? That's just the beginning.

In front of the splendid palace stand three huge statues, stone

The Church Square (Kapellplatz) at Luzern

images of the founding fathers – the leaders of the three cantons of Uri, Schwyz and Unterwald – who laid the foundation for the Confederation in 1291.

The public is permitted to attend the sessions held in the building. The 46 members of the Council of States represent their respective cantons (two from every canton). The 200 members of the National Council represent the nation, based on proportional elections. All seats are equipped with small earphones, in which simultaneous translation of the speeches presented is broadcast in the various official languages. It looks something like an international convention.

The Cabinet – that is, the government – is comprised of seven members. These high-ranking officials are not called ministers, but federal advisors. They are chosen by the Federal Assembly, consisting of the members of the Council of States and the members of the National Council.

The seven are officially appointed for four years, but according to political tradition, their term of office is almost unlimited, as they are constantly re-elected. When does an advisor, nevertheless, complete his career? When he passes away, when he retires, of when he has, heaven forbid, committed a serious legal offense. (In 1988 the one female member in charge of law and government was forced to leave her post after a financial scandal in which her husband was involved). The average term of office of an advisor is approximately 10 years. The record is held by an advisor who kept his post for 28 consecutive years. It is important to recall that these are not high-profile leaders of the type we expect in the western world; these government officials are, in fact, no more than professional managers.

Each of the advisors serves, on a rotation basis as president of the Confederation for one year. The president does not have the authority of the head of state, of course, nor of prime minister. He continues to manage the affairs of the advisory for which he is responsible (government ministries in Switzerland are known as "advisories"), and at the same time leads the meetings of "the seven". He welcomes visiting heads of state, as well as receiving diplomats who present their credentials.

Swiss conservatism is also expressed in the internal party division among the seven advisors. According to a set model, aimed at preventing unnecessary upset, a formula of 2-2-2-1 is always maintained. The group consists of two advisors who identify with the Radical party, two from the Socialist party, two from the Christian Democrats and one from the Democratic Federation.

Conservatism and caution also slow down and restrain the legislative system. Any member of the

Council of States or the National Council can oppose a law proposed by the Cabinet and implementation of laws or amendments to laws are far from easy.

Every proposal must be supported in one round of votes by a majority of the members of the two houses, although if a law has been approved, it is enough to collect 50,000 signatures of citizens to bring the matter to referendum, which can serve as a sort of public veto. Incidentally, every Swiss citizen, on reaching the age of 20, must swear an oath of allegiance to the Federation before being granted the right to vote in the elections and referendums.

However, the real political power in Switzerland is concentrated in the base of the federal pyramid. Every canton is like a sovereign state – there are in total 26 cantonal parliaments and in total 26 cantonal governments in Switzerland. Problems and disagreements between the federal government and the cantons are brought up for discussion and settlement to the federal court, located in Lausanne. This is also where conflicts between cantons are dealt with.

However, the cantonal government is not the lowest level of government. There are 3,071 local authorities in Switzerland, each selected at a public meeting for election of the local council. The area covered by a local authority varies: there are large jurisdictions like Davos, of 100 sq. miles, and tiny ones, like Fonte Teresa, of only 300 sq. yds.

It is a system, then, of many states within a state. In the small communities, where elections are held in the central square by local citizens raising their hands, democracy is directly at work.

The local authorities have a great deal of power, and decide for themselves on such subjects as education, health, transportation, and housing, sometimes with absolute disregard of federal-level decisions from Bern.

The abundance of governmental bodies imposes upon the citizens a heavy burden of elections, at every level of government. It is no wonder that the voting rate often falls below 30%.

Economics and Money

Switzerland has no seaports; it is incredibly poor in minerals; most of the raw material for its industries has to be imported from other countries; and its mountainous landscape and climatic conditions dictate a very limited type of agriculture. Switzerland was forced to develop an economy that could prosper even in these conditions. In the course of time, the limitations became advantages. Devotion and professional standards ensure that the label "Swiss-Made" is a mark of quality in banking, watches, chocolate and lace. Tourists also benefit from Swiss standards of service.

Banking

How did it all start? European rulers, willing to pay a high price to hire the services of Switzerland's finest soldiers, the Swiss Guards, bought their skills for war and for personal protection.

These Swiss mercenary units sent home large sums of money which they received for their dangerous work – as well as part of the booty from the battles they won, which was an accepted part of payment.

These treasures and monies had to be looked after and in about 1700, experts in such matters began to emerge. These men eventually became bankers. Their major activities were in Geneva, Zürich, Basel, Bern, Neuchâtel and Lausanne.

The first Swiss bankers had a natural talent for negotiation and a keen sense of business; their area had served for hundreds of years as a land bridge for trade routes between the Mediterranean and Northern Europe. In addition, because the Swiss were fluent in so many languages they could solicit clients from the neighboring countries for their emerging banking industry.

With experience and time, a strong base developed for modern banking. Switzerland's neutrality throughout both World Wars, established its reputation as a safe place for money, and the tradition developed of keeping foreign currency in its safes – and investing in the various financial channels proposed by its banks.

In 1934, the concept of confidentiality in banking was legislated. This made Switzerland an ideal place for foreign citizens and organizations harassed by their governments to keep money. Thus, for instance, when the Nazis came to power in Germany, many of its Jewish citizens deposited their money and valuables in Swiss bank safes. In addition, the method of opening an account that bears a number only – ensuring absolute anonymity – is ideal for various depositors.

A system of laws developed in Switzerland to ensure protection to the customers of the banks. It is forbidden to disclose any details whatsoever about accounts – the identity of the depositors, their origin and so forth. Foreign authorities cannot receive information from a Swiss bank, unless by special court order. The Swiss judges, loyal to this traditional concept, do not allow investigation in matters of tax evasion, financial or political suspicions, or offenses against currency laws of other countries. Immunity in such cases remains solid. Stories abound about tax inspectors whose purpose for visiting Switzerland was not acceptable to the authorities; they were put back on the first return flight after being declared undesirable guests – a purely financial matter.

At one point, these opportunities attracted many of the giants of crime – particularly members of organized crime in the U.S.
A battery of unpleasant accusations began to spread regarding the large amounts of money making their way from the U.S. to banks in Switzerland – profits of the Mafia families from gambling, prostitution, drugs and other such activities. This somewhat clouded the Swiss banks' reputation. Accordingly, in 1973, the Swiss and US governments signed an agreement allowing investigation and examination of accounts based on suspicion that the money originated in criminal activity.

It is no secret that the banks in Switzerland still serve as a shelter for many of the world's wealthy who do not wish to share their capital with the tax authorities in their countries. However, without debating the moral issue, foreign depositors should be aware of the revolutionary precedent set by the supreme court in Switzerland, in its decision of February, 1989.

It all began with a lawsuit filed by a French citizen who had opened bank accounts in Geneva, in a branch of one of the large Swiss banks; following an internal disclosure, the bank was sued by the tax authorities in his country. The depositor was forced to pay a high fine, and sued the Swiss bank for compensation of this loss.

After lengthy legal proceedings and three separate appeals, the matter eventually reached the federal supreme court, where five judges heard the case. By a majority of three to two, they decided that a foreign citizen whose account is exposed by the income tax authorities of his country is not protected by the law of confidentiality and secrecy of accounts.

This means that anyone who evades paying taxes by opening a bank account in Switzerland is taking a personal risk that may be greater than he imagined – if the tax authorities in his country succeed in obtaining proof that such an account exists.

Today, the secret of the Swiss banks lies in the stability of the Swiss franc. The national bank strongly protects the stability of its currency, and this offers depositors and business people the opportunity for long-term planning, without being influenced by the fluctuations of the international finance market, which is so vulnerable to unpredictable shocks.

The National Swiss Bank is the backbone of banking in the country. It is said, although it is difficult to check, that the huge basements under the parking lot across from the Federal Palace in Bern house the currency and gold reserves of the National Bank. The figure exceeds 11 billion dollars, a third of which is in gold.

In the past few years, operating in Switzerland have been 500 commercial banks, 29 cantonal banks, 24 private banks and 16 branches of foreign banks, with more than 4,000 branches throughout the country. The large centers, of course, are in Geneva and Zürich.

Alongside the banks, the Swiss insurance sector serves as a very important financial instrument. It holds a respected place in the front line of international insurance businesses. The Swiss themselves spend a lot of money on insurance.

Bern's 450 year old Clock Tower

Clocks

In the late 16th century, the French Protestant Huguenots fled from France to Switzerland, after a long struggle between their church and the Catholic Church. They laid the basis for the love affair between Switzerland and measured time.

The Huguenot refugees, with their precise instruments, and invaluable know-how passed down from father to son, settled first in Geneva and later in other parts of the Jura region, particularly in Neuchâtel.

As early as the beginning of the 17th century, the first clock making companies were established in Geneva. This was a real breakthrough in the industry, which until then had been managed in a few clock makers' workshops.

In the mid-19th century, there was another important breakthrough when the first precision instruments were built for production of the tiny parts of the clock's mechanism. It was then that the art of clock making became a real industry. This technical achievement put the local manufacturers at a great advantage over their competitors throughout the world and granted Switzerland predominance in this field for more than 100 years. To this day, the words "Swiss clock" and "precision" are considered synonymous in many languages.

Thanks to the large profits made from selling the clocks, an extensive research and development system was set up. The Swiss Laboratory for Clock Research was established in 1921 in Neuchâtel. In the same city, in 1962, the Electronic Center for Clock Making was established: it was here, five years later, that the first quartz clock was manufactured. However, since the discovery of the quartz clock, the Swiss clock industry has been in decline because of Japanese competition; quartz clocks have fewer parts and can be assembled mechanically and quickly. The Swiss clock, nevertheless, continues to tick, and the industry is still an important source of income to the Swiss economy.

Tourism

Not only the Swiss claim that Switzerland is the country that invented European tourism. Indeed, as an organized industry, tourism began to flourish here as early as the 18th century. The country's landscapes, Alps and the peace and quiet have always attracted tourists and vacationers.

Located in central Europe, Switzerland was an obvious transit station for traders and travelers going from southern to northern Europe and back; thus it became a classic tourist center of the Old World. Word also got around that its air was good for curing respiratory illnesses, and many visited its sanatoriums to regain their health.

This tradition continues, although in a somewhat different form. Tourism is an extremely important industry, contributing some 8% of the annual national income. Close to 260,000 people work directly or indirectly in the Swiss tourist business, with a capacity of 282,000 beds in hotels, motels, pensions and health resorts, and another 360,000 beds in youth hostels and 274,000 places in mobile camper parks. Switzerland offers its tourists some 27,000 restaurants, cafés, taverns and the like.

The main seat of The Swiss National Tourist Office is at 38 Bellaristrasse, CH-8027 Zürich, Tel. (01) 288.11.11, fax 288.12.05.

PART TWO – SETTING OUT

How to Get There

BY AIR

From the US, four airlines fly to Switzerland: *Delta*, *TWA*, *American Airlines* and *Swissair*. *Delta* and *TWA* fly from New York, *American Airlines* from Chicago and *Swissair* from New York, Chicago, Atlanta and Boston. Alternatively, you can fly to any major city in Europe and get a connection from there.

American Airlines: Equitable Building, 120 Broadway, Tel. (800) 433.73.00 (nationwide).

TWA: 605 Third Ave, New York, NY 10016, Tel. (800) 892.41.41 (nationwide).

Swissair: 608 Fifth Ave, New York, NY 10020, Tel. (800) 221.47.50 (nationwide).

From the UK you can fly to Zürich, Geneva, Basel and Bern. *Swissair* and *British Airways* fly to Zürich, Geneva and Basel from Heathrow and also to Zürich from Manchester and Birmingham. *Dan Air* flies to Geneva and Bern from Gatwick, Newcastle and Aberdeen. *British Caledonian* flies to Geneva from Gatwick.

BY RAIL

From the UK it is very easy to get to Switzerland. Trains leave from London (Liverpool St.) to Harwich, for a ferry crossing to the Hook of Holland and connections to Luzern, Basel and Zürich; and from London (Victoria) to Dover, for a ferry to Ostende and connections through Brussels to Basel; or take the hovercraft to Boulogne for the train through Paris, to Geneva, Lausanne or Bern on the same day. There is daily railroad service from every central European city to Zürich, Geneva and Basel. A line of the rapid TGV train (175 m.p.h) from Paris to Lausanne, via Geneva runs at a frequency of one train every hour, daily.

BY ROAD

You can go by bus or car on ferries from Folkstone, Harwich, Dover, Ramsgate and Sheerness. From Zeebrugge, Vlissengen, Ostend and Dunkirk, on the other side, the roads to Switzerland are good and the trip can be made in a day. The short crossings, however, from Dover and Folkestone to Calais and Boulogne, will mean a much longer drive through Paris, which you may prefer to avoid.

For entry into Switzerland, motorists require a passport (European nationals staying longer than 3 months in the country need only an identity card), vehicle registration papers and a driver's license.

Switzerland's central location has made it the crossroads of Europe; fast highways (*autostradas*) lead to this country from Italy, France, Germany and Austria.

Documents

Upon entering Switzerland you will be asked to present a valid passport in order to gain entrance for up to three months. A stay of over three months may require a visa (inquire at the Swiss consulate prior to your arrival). In order to drive a vehicle you must have a valid international driver's license which should be kept with your passport. You should also carry your original driver's license.

If you plan to stay in hostels, it is worthwhile obtaining a membership card from the Youth Hostels Association. This card entitles one to discount rates, and to priority if a hostel has few vacancies. If relevant, you should also acquire an International Student Identity Card (ISIC) for a possible discount at museums, cinemas, and concerts .

It is very important to purchase travel insurance for medical care and baggage before setting out; even treatment for a serious cold in Switzerland costs money, and insurance helps – all the more so in the case of an accident. You should also insure your baggage; although there are stories that the Swiss never lock the doors of their homes, or their cars, there is no need to take unnecessary risks.

If you decide to visit Switzerland with a dog or a cat, you must prepare a veterinary certificate confirming that the animal has been vaccinated against rabies. The vaccination must be given at least 30 days, and no more than a year, before entering Switzerland. The veterinary certificate must be written in English, French, German or Italian.

Money

There is no restriction on the amount of money that a tourist may bring into Swiss territory. The only limitations, if any, exist in the country of origin.

In general, it is recommended to change money at bank branches or at special counters in the airports and the larger train stations. You can also change money in a hotel or a major department store, but this sometimes involves extra expense. The difference between the official exchange rate and the "house" rate can be substantial.

The Swiss franc (FS) is divided into 100 centimes. The bills in circulation are for 10, 20, 50, 100, 500 and 1,000 francs, and the coins are 5 francs, 2 francs, 1 franc, 50 centimes, 20 centimes, 10 centimes and 5 centimes.

All international credit cards are accepted in most places of business, hotels and restaurants in Switzerland. The most widely recognized are Eurocard and Visa. The same is true for traveler's checks, which can also be exchanged in banks.

National Holidays

January 1 – New Year
April 1 – Good Friday
April 4 – Easter Monday (varies)
May 1 – Work Holiday
May 12 – Ascension Day (varies)
May 23 – Whit Monday (varies)
August 1 – National Day
December 25 – Christmas Day

On these dates the stores, offices and banks are closed, and there is no public transportation. In addition to the above mentioned, there are special festivals in the various districts and cantons, each according to its own religion and history, and they will be specified in the relevant chapters.

How Much will It Cost?

A few examples of a tourist's primary expenses – food and lodging – may be helpful. This will give you an idea, albeit very general, of the expenses you can expect, without, of course, accounting for personal preferences that are likely to affect your budget.

It should be emphasized that in prices, Switzerland is also a country of variety. It is true that some of its cities, such as Geneva, Zürich and Lugano are expensive by European standards, and these have given Switzerland a reputation of an expensive country. On the other hand, you will find that in other cities and country towns, the prices are as much as 20% lower than the Geneva "index."

You should also remember that in hotels and pensions (guest houses) the year is generally divided into three seasons, each with different rates. The dates vary from place to place, according to its character (a winter resort is less expensive in the summer, for instance), and the differences between seasons range from 15-25%, on the average.

In Geneva, for example, a single guest in a five-star hotel will pay about 350-600 francs for bed and breakfast, and a couple about 420-820 francs. In a four-star hotel, the prices are about 150-400 francs for a single and 200-520 for a double. The prices in a two-star hotel are 50-170 francs for a single and 70-

220 francs for a couple. Bed and breakfast in a one-star hotel costs 45-120 francs for a single and 70-150 for a couple.

At youth hostels in Geneva, a bed for a night costs about 20 francs, with breakfast about 30 francs.

Restaurants for lunch and supper can be divided into three categories: expensive – 100-150 francs; moderately priced – 70-120 francs; inexpensive – 40-70 francs. These prices are per person and do not include drinks.

A very interesting and favorably priced option is available at the restaurants and cafeterias of *MIGROS* and *CO-OP* supermarket nets throughout Switzerland. For example, a pack of film costs about 7 francs in the Migros chain, while its price in a regular store is about 15 francs.

Customs

Bringing items other than those mentioned below into Switzerland is considered "importation," with all the procedures associated with that term. However, don't worry too much; the authorities are not unreasonable, and might even be flexible.

A complete exemption from any customs fee is granted for personal effects such as clothes, toiletries, books, personal sports equipment, video and photographic equipment (non-professional), musical instruments and camping gear.

Food and light beverages may be brought into Swiss territory only in a quantity appropriate for one day's consumption. The quantity for tobacco, for example, is 200 cigarettes, 50 cigars or 250gr.

The value of gifts to local residents brought into the country may not exceed 100 francs. Gifts, which the tourist brings into the country and takes upon leaving are allowed at up to 2,000 francs.

For further information please contact, in Geneva, Tel. (022) 310.61.33; in Lausanne, Tel. (021) 342.01.11; in Basel, Tel. (061) 287.11.11.

PART THREE – WHERE HAVE WE LANDED?

Transportation

Thanks to a long tradition and extensive investment, it is extremely easy to get around Switzerland, quickly and efficiently. Don't forget the precision for which the people of this country are famous; it is an important factor in helping you plan your trip ahead of time.

BY TRAIN

The federal railroad company was founded (following a referendum, of course) in 1898 (the trains are marked with initials in the country's different languages: SBB in German, CFF in French, FSS in Italian). Railroad tracks were laid in the early days running from the north to the south and from east to west. The natural problem of the topography – the mountains – was solved with the construction of the famous tunnels. The first one to be dug was the well-known St. Gotthard Tunnel (10.5 miles long); next was Simplon, Switzerland's longest tunnel (12.5 miles long). The newest tunnel in Switzerland, completed in 1982, is the Furka Tunnel (9.5 miles long).

Traveling through these tunnels is a unique experience. Testimony to this is the special place they have been given in literature, particularly detective stories, that use the impact of the sudden transition

from daylight to absolute darkness as the setting for gruesome murders.

In addition to the federal railroad, there are also private train companies. So numerous are the special projects carried out by these private train companies that they have become part of the country's history. In the late 19th century, passage to the Jungfrau (11,330 ft. high!) was broken through and facilities for a train were installed. Another company, whose main line runs from Montreux to the Bernese Oberland, offers its travelers the opportunity to ride in cars in the original turn-of-the century design, with panoramic windows. Another company, which runs from Blonay in the Vaud canton, still uses steam engines, for the pleasure of its passengers.

Add to all these cable cars, which help reach the mountain tops and ski resorts.

The Swiss Travel System offers a variety of cards and services:

Swiss Pass: the Swiss Pass is the ideal ticket for a trip through Switzerland. It entitles the holder to unlimited travel on the entire network of the Swiss Travel System, including most private railroads, postal coaches, lake steamers, and the urban transit systems in 30 cities in Switzerland. It also allows the holder to buy an unlimited number of transportation tickets for excursions to mountain tops at a reduction of up to 25%. The Swiss Pass is valid for consecutive days only.

The Swiss Pass can be obtained outside Switzerland from the Swiss National Tourist Office branches abroad or at travel agencies. It is also available at the Swiss border railway stations and at Zürich and Geneva airports. The card should be kept with your passport while you travel in Switzerland.

Here is a list of the approximate prices:

Swiss Pass	1st class	2nd class
8-day pass	US$300	US$210
15-day pass	US$350	US$250
1-month pass	US$480	US$330

Swiss Card: this ticket entitles the holder to one free round trip plus half price tickets for all additional trips:

One free day trip from any entry point – airports or any border station – to the destination of your choice within Switzerland, and one free trip back from this location or another to any departure point. The Swiss Card also entitles its holder to locally purchase an unlimited number of tickets on all of Switzerland's scheduled services by train, postal coach and lake steamer at half price (with a reduction of 25% on some mountain railroads).

A 1st class Swiss Card costs about US$130; a 2nd class one – about US$118. The cards are valid for one month.

Swiss Flexipass: the Swiss Flexipass is similar to the Swiss Pass, but is valid on 3 non-consecutive days within a 15-day period.

Swiss Rail 'n Drive: the Swiss Rail 'n Drive combines a 3/15-day Flexipass with car rental for 3 non-consecutive days. You can purchase up to 5 additional car rental days in North America, but they must be purchased before departing to Switzerland.

The interior of a Swiss TGV express train

Fly-Rail Baggage: for visitors who arrive and depart by air, Switzerland's railways offer a unique baggage service, namely: Fly-Rail Baggage: You can direct baggage to be transported from your departure point abroad to any Swiss railway line offering baggage services.

Inquire at the Swiss National Tourist Office, or at *Swissair*. Ask for the pamphlet *Unique Switzerland* which contains many interesting rail offers.

BY BUS

The "postbus," called *postauto* in German, *cars postaux* in French and *autopostali* in Italian, is an institution that originated in 1849; along with the letters and packages, the yellow horse-drawn mail carriages began picking up hitchhikers. Even then this was a serious transportation system, encompassing 955 lines, covering some 2,900 miles. In the early 20th century, this service reached its peak, exceeding 1.8 million passengers a year, with a fleet of about 2,250 carriages and 2,500 horses.

After World War I, two significant changes took place in the postal service: first, many of the longest and most important lines were taken over by the train, and the mail carriages were left with mainly the mountainous routes. Second, when motorized buses arrived on the scene, the era of the horse-drawn carriage died. Today, the postbus goes wherever the train doesn't. It is still yellow, and thanks to the bus, mountains and remote valleys are accessible.

One-fourth of all the passenger bus lines are part of the postbus service. The other three quarters are buses belonging to private companies who work for and are directly supervised by the postal service. The schedules and rates are set by the postal service.

Some 1,600 towns, villages and other points are included in the extensive network connecting them with the large cities and train stations, covering 7,000 collection and departure points. About 70 million passengers use this service very year.

The postbus service also organizes tours, some guided, some combined with hikes, to tourist sights, mountains and village routes. Pamphlets with a detailed description of the routes for every area are available in the bus stations.

BY CAR

Every tourist over 18 years of age with a valid international driver's license is permitted to drive a vehicle in Switzerland.

It is compulsory to wear seat belts, in the city as well as on inter-city roads.

Children under 12 may sit in the back seat of the car only.

The speed limit within the cities is

50 km.p.h; on highways (*autostradas*) – 80 km.p.h. (50 m.p.h.). The speed limit, however, is seldom respected; be careful!

A car registered in another country is charged (once a year) for use of the *autostradas*.

It is compulsory to turn on your headlights when driving through a tunnel.

On some roads, it is compulsory, by order of the local police, and as noted on special signs placed by the side of the road, to use snow-chains on the tires in the winter.

In case of a breakdown or accident, you can call the Swiss Touring Club (TCS) for assistance by dialing 140.

Information on road conditions during stormy weather is available at Tel. 160.

It is recommended not to set out late Friday afternoon or evening, or late Sunday, because of traffic jams created by weekend vacationers.

CAR HIRE

Most of the international car hire companies have at least one outlet located in Switzerland; their addresses and telephone numbers will be specified in the relevant chapters.

LIMOUSINES

There are three major companies in Switzerland which can offer Limousine services: LCCS (Limousines and Chauffeured Car Services), LCR (Luxury Car Rental) and SCR (Sports Car Rental).

Zürich (all three):
European Chauffeured Car Associates/ ECCA

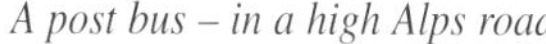

A post bus – in a high Alps road

11 Hammerstrasse,
Tel. (01) 383.92.92,
fax (01) 383.92.90.

Geneva (all three):
Executive Car Service,
59 Rue des Paquis,
Tel. (022) 732.79.77,
fax (022) 731.42.71.

Lausanne (all three):
Beau-Rivage Palace's Limousine Service,
Place du General Guisan, Ouchy,
Tel. (021) 613.33.33,
fax (021) 613.33.34.

Basel (LCCS/ LCR):
Limousinen Service Basel,
72 Grellingerstrasse,
Tel. (061) 311.21.21,
fax (061) 311.22.22.

Luzern (LCCS/ LCR):
Bucher Travel Inc.,
11 Haldenstrasse,
Tel. (041) 50. 11.66,
fax (041) 51.74.50.

A welcoming hostel and restaurant in Appenzell

Accommodation

In the cities, towns and villages of Switzerland, the tourist will find a very wide variety of accommodation. The conditions vary, as do the prices. Each to his own, according to taste and pocketbook. One comment: It is always worth taking a peek at the room offered to see for yourself where you might be resting your head.

HOTELS

The hotel association in Switzerland, which supervises the hotels and hotel rates throughout the country, uses the familiar star system – five stars is the highest. Within this rate system, of course, you can expect considerable variety, particularly in establishments graded three stars and below.

You can reserve a hotel room through a travel agent or by contacting the hotel directly. The municipal tourist offices have desks at the Swiss airports and in the train stations in large cities, where, for a small fee or free of charge, you can get help reserving a room. Some train stations have a special phone for calling hotels in the area, according to a displayed list; the call is free of charge. You can, of course, just call and reserve a room. For your convenience, lists of recommended hotels in various cities are provided further on this guide.

In the mountain areas you can

Fondue, Switzerland's national food, is as delicious as it is fun

also stay at an inn. The price per person in a double room is about 60 francs on average, for bed and breakfast.

In some of the villages in Switzerland you can rent a room for one night or more from local residents. Simply look for the sign *Zimmer*, which means "room," and go in and ask. The average price is 50 francs per night. The regional tourist offices can provide you with addresses of people who rent such rooms.

If you want to have "your own home" in Switzerland, you can rent a mobile one. For details, contact the companies in the following cities: Zürich, Tel. 984.07.48, fax 984.19.89; in Bern, Tel. 371.04.62, fax 371.53.61.

The main office of the Swiss Hotel association (SHA) is 130 Monbijoustrasse, Post-fach, 3001, Bern. Tel. (031) 370.41.11, fax (031) 370.44.44.

Food and Drink

You don't really know a country until you have seen its cuisine, smelled the aroma of its specialities, sat down at a table, and of course, eaten its food. Getting to know the national menu is an important experience of discovering any new place.

Switzerland's cuisine is distinguished, like its people, languages, and scenery – by its amazing variety. First of all, in each region, the traditional influence of either French, German or Italian cooking is felt. Each canton also has its own specialities. Many Swiss are not proud of their cuisine. The country has a reputation for "heavy" food, the kind suited hard physical labor, or low temperatures – rich foods that "warm their insides." Many restaurants and several hotels offer an "international" menu; those who seek local cuisine must choose restaurants that specify this on their menu.

A restaurant menu is called *karte*

in German, and *carte* in French. If you ask the waiter for the *menu*, it is likely that you will be brought the special dish of the day, called *tagesplatte* in German, and *plat du jour* in French.

Meals generally begin with soup, and every region has its own typical soup: in Ticino it is an Italian-style soup similar to minestrone; in Bern it is a white pea soup with pig's ear; in the Schwyz canton it is a Swiss soup based on butter, cream and flour. Soup plays an important part in Swiss cooking; it is considered good for warming the body and enhancing the traditional family custom of gathering around the soup pot. There are some soups that constitute a full meal in themselves.

After the soup comes the first course. Here there is a wide variety of possibilities: dried or smoked meats, different types of sausages (most popular in the German regions), river and lake fish, hard cheeses, eggs cooked in many ways, hot savory pies, fresh or dried mushrooms, and more. Many of these dishes would make an adequate light meal or snack on their own.

The main course, usually meat and a side dish, is representative of rich Swiss cuisine, both in quantities and in cooking style, with plenty of local butter, excellent cream and sauces. A good example of such a dish, which has become known outside of Switzerland as well, is ground veal in the style of the canton of Zürich, *geschnetzeltes kalbsfleisch*, made with butter, cream, white wine, mushrooms and other delicacies.

The meal on the menu does not usually include dessert, which must be ordered separately. Most desserts are based on chocolate, of course, and milk. Cakes, rich in butter or whipped cream, are a central part of the selection. Of the wide variety available, worthy of special mention are Geneva-style pear pastry, St. Gallen-style chocolate cake and Luzern's honey cake.

That is the basic, traditional Swiss meal. However, when you talk about Swiss food, the first thought that often comes to mind is *fondue*. Fondue is the best known of the Swiss specialities. According to many Swiss, especially those from the French cantons, fondue is the "national food," and for good reason. The main component of fondue is *Emmental* and *Gruyère* cheese, a prized product of Switzerland.

Every French canton – be it Neuchâtel, Vaud, Valais or Fribourg – has its own local type of fondue, accompanied by special side dishes and its own secret regarding the proportions of the various ingredients. In principle, fondue is made of Emmental, Gruyère or *Vacherin*, melted (*fond* means "melt") in dry white wine boiled in a ceramic pot whose sides have been rubbed with garlic. When the cheese mixture becomes smooth and silky, spices and a little alcohol are added. The pot is transferred to the table and placed on a small burner which keeps it gently boiling throughout the meal.

Fondue is eaten with special long forks, with a piece of bread stuck on the tongs. You dip your bread in the pot, stir it a bit in the mixture, remove it and... wait a moment, as many a newcomer to fondue has burned their tongue.

By the way, every fondue fork has a mark, usually a color so you know which fork is yours. If your bread falls into the pot you are punished: if the meal is at home, you wash the dishes; if you are eating out, you pay for the white wine drunk with the meal. Between the wine in the cheese mixture and the wine accompanying the meal, there is no such thing as a fondue meal that fails to make the diners festive and joyful.

Another well-known Swiss culinary innovation, second only to fondue, and actually its relative, is *raclette*. Originated in Valais, raclette is made almost solely from a special Valais cheese. The original, traditional method of preparation is simple: half a block of cheese is placed with its cut end up near a fire (traditionally a fireplace, but there is a special electric device for modernists). The part that softens in the heat is grated onto the plate, and eaten on potatoes cooked in their jackets, with pickles on the side.

Switzerland has its own meat specialities as well. There is the famous dried meat of the Graubingen canton – *bunderfleisch*. It is prepared by a very special process: half-cooked beef is smoked and dried, and then cut into paper-thin slices. The resulting taste and aroma are a real delicacy.

The traditional fast food of Switzerland is the veal sausage, *kalbsbratwurst*, which evidently originated in Zürich. It is pale in color, melts in the mouth, and has a unique taste, so special that you have to try it in order to know if you like it. It is sold in restaurants, snack bars, and of course, at food stands on the street.

There are also other worthy competitors for high positions on the list of national dishes. The "Bern Plate" (*Berner Platte*) is an excellent collection of smoked cold cuts, sausage and boiled meat, served with cabbage and pea pods. *Rôsti* is a dish of potatoes cooked in water and then puréed and fried with butter, pieces of smoked meat and spices. The preparation of rôsti varies from canton to canton. Some add *Emmental* cheese, some spread apple sauce on top, and some include eggs in the mixture.

The high quality of the Swiss milk, cream and chocolate ensure an excellent standard of desserts and baked goods. Remember to taste Kirsch cakc (made with cherry liqueur) from Zug; *Tourte de Covent* from St. Gallen, made with almonds and wild berries; the carrot cake of Aargau (*tourte aux carottes*); Basel-style cherry cake (*gâteau aux cerises*); pear turnovers (*beignets aux poires*) from Unterwald. And, of course, acquaint yourself with the "tongues of Schaffhausen" (*Schaffhauserzungen*), baked and decorated with butter cream, nougat, cocoa and other good things, truly an unforgettable experience!

What to Buy

Anyone who comes to Switzerland intending to find bargains is misinformed. On the other hand, it is possible to return home with a varied selection of souvenirs which capture the memory of Switzerland.

If money is no problem, you can of course purchase a Swiss-made clock. The most recommended places are Geneva and Zürich.

In Geneva's art and souvenir shops, you can buy another special local product – enamel crafts.

The famous multi-purpose Swiss Army knives (the red ones decorated with the national white cross) are of course worth buying in Switzerland, even though they are sold all over the world. The recommended places for purchasing them are the cities of Delémont and Schwyz.

Lovers of embroidery, fine muslin and delicate lace have come to the right place. Switzerland is central to the development of this industry. St. Gallen, Chur, Appenzell, Saas-Fee and Lauterbrunnen are good places to make your purchases.

The famous *Gruyère* and *Emmental* cheeses can be found throughout the country, but why not get them from the source: the cantons of Neuchâtel, Vaud and Fribourg. The best wines are found in the canton of Valais.

Traditional handicrafts, ceramics and small, painted wooden figures should be purchased where they are produced: Bern, Brienz, Stein and Zürich. Minerals and crystals are found in Andermatt.

Chocolate is last, but not least. You can find it anywhere – in

every shop, store, delicatessen, department store or food stand. The price is fixed, the quality heavenly. The most highly recommended brands are Frigor, Lindt and Suchard.

General Information

Working Hours

SHOPS

Shops, stores and shopping centers are generally open 9am-6:30pm weekdays, and 9am-4pm on Saturdays. On Sundays shops are closed, except for those in railway stations and highway rest stops. This is, of course, only a general guideline; hours may vary from place to place.

It should be noted that in the tourist season most souvenir stores at tourist sites are open on Sundays and holidays as well.

BANKS

Most banks are open Mon.-Fri, from 8:30am-4:30pm. Large branches remain open all day, without an afternoon break. Agencies for currency exchange in the airport and central train stations in the large cities are open from 6:30am-9:30pm, seven days a week.

Postal and Telephone Services

Postage sent to Switzerland must carry the CH prefix and the area mailing code. For instance, a letter to Bern must be addressed CH-3000 BERN.

The telephone booths in Switzerland can be recognized by their gray color and the picture of a black telephone receiver inside a circle. The telephone takes 10, 20, and 50-centime coins, and 1 and 2-franc coins. All operating instructions and important phone numbers are listed inside the phone booth.

For the international operator dial 114. All post offices and major rail stations have booths and operators for international calls. The cheapest time to call is 5pm-7pm during the week, and after 9pm on weekends.

When making a telephone call from your hotel, inquire in advance about charges for longer calls or calls to another country. The hotel may add a surcharge to the official Swiss rate to cover overhead costs.

Tipping

Throughout Switzerland, by law, a set service charge of 15% is col-

lected in all hotels, restaurants, cafés, pubs and the like. You are not obligated to add any more than a small extra sum, only if you really want to express your appreciation of the service.

Taxi drivers expect a tip of 10-15% of the fare. In hotels, you should tip the porter about 2 francs for every suitcase.

Members of the hotel staff who provide you with special services, such as room service, should be tipped about 3 francs each time.

Electricity and Time

Throughout Switzerland, the electricity in the outlets is 220v. You will need a two-pin adaptor for electrical goods from the U.S., Canada and the U.K.

The Swiss clocks, world-famous for their accuracy, are precisely one hour ahead of Greenwich Mean Time.

A Suggested Tour of Switzerland

We start our tour in Geneva. Next, it is most natural to visit Lausanne, with the enchanting shores of Lake Léman (Geneva) on the way. From Lausanne you can choose one of three possibilities: go north via Neuchâtel and the Jura region to Basel; travel toward Bern via Fribourg; or go south to the eastern tip of Lake Léman and through the Rhone Valley.

The route recommended here is north to Basel and then south to Bern. Continue to the area of Interlaken, where you'll find some of Switzerland's most breathtaking mountain scenery and lovely resort towns.

From there, travel in the direction of Luzern and the Lake of the Four Cantons. The route goes on to Zürich, the economic center of Switzerland. Not far north are the Rhine waterfalls and St. Gallen, where we head for Lake Constance and then south toward Liechtenstein.

Continue south toward Chur, the Graubünden region, St. Moritz and southwest to the Italian canton of Ticino, Bellinzona, Lugano and Locarno, with their towering mountains and blue lakes.

Later, turn back north, to Andermatt, and from there, on to the marvelous route through the Rhône Valley, via Brig and Sion, back to Lake Léman. The circle usually closes with a flight back home from Geneva.

A Language Guide to Names of Places

The many languages spoken in Switzerland can make it quite difficult to identify place-names, so we have included a short list of place-names in German and French to help you get around.

GERMAN	FRENCH
Aarau	Argovie
Basel	Bâle
Bern	Berne
Burgdorf	Berthoud
Biel (Beiler See)	Bienne (Lac de Bienne)
Brig	Brigue
Chur	Coire
Konstanz	Constance
Bodensee	Constance (Lac de)
Genf	Genève
Glarus	Glaris
Leuk	Loèche
Luzern	Lucerne
Murten	Morat
Pilatus	Pilate
Vierwaldstättersee	Quatre-Cantons (Lac des)
Rhine	Rhin
St. Gallen	St. Gall
Schaffhausen	Schaffhouse
Schwyz	Schwyz
Solothurn	Soleure
Thun	Thoune
Thurgau	Thurgovie
Unterwalden	Unterwald

SWITZERLAND

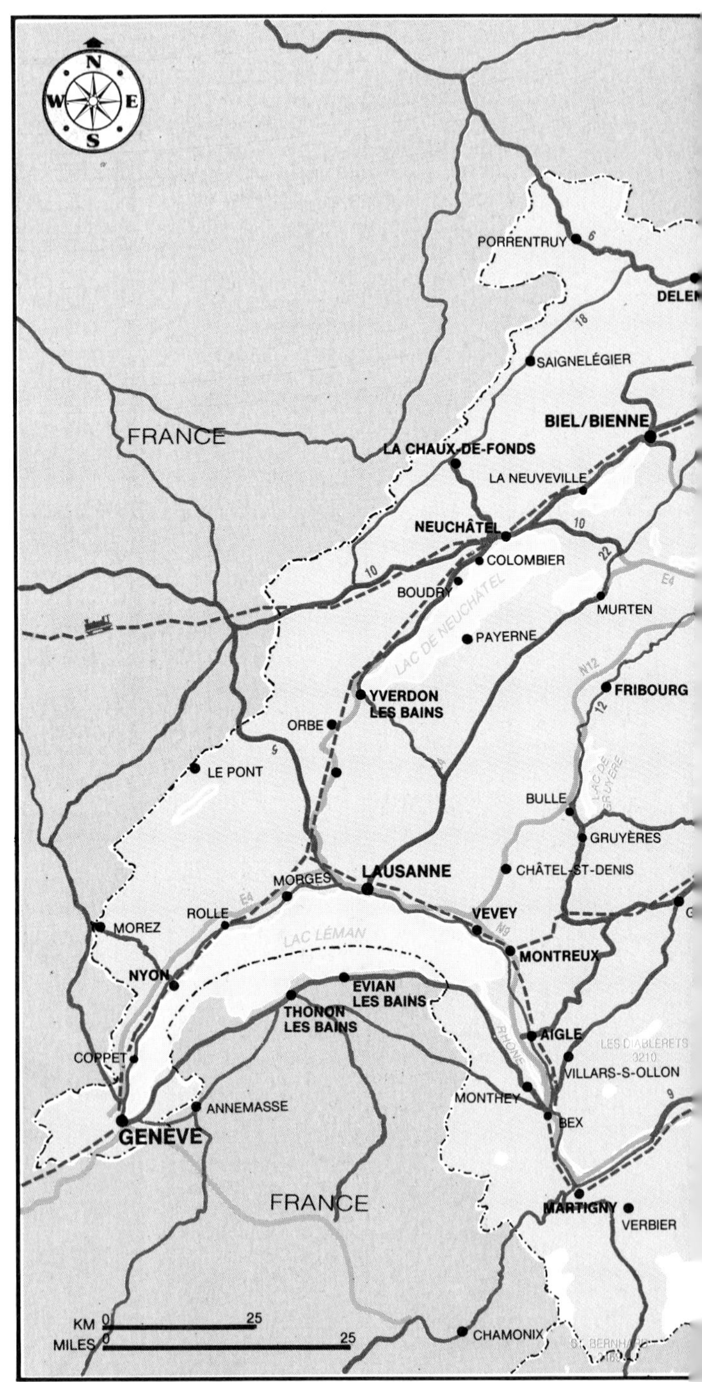

WESTERN SWITZERLAND

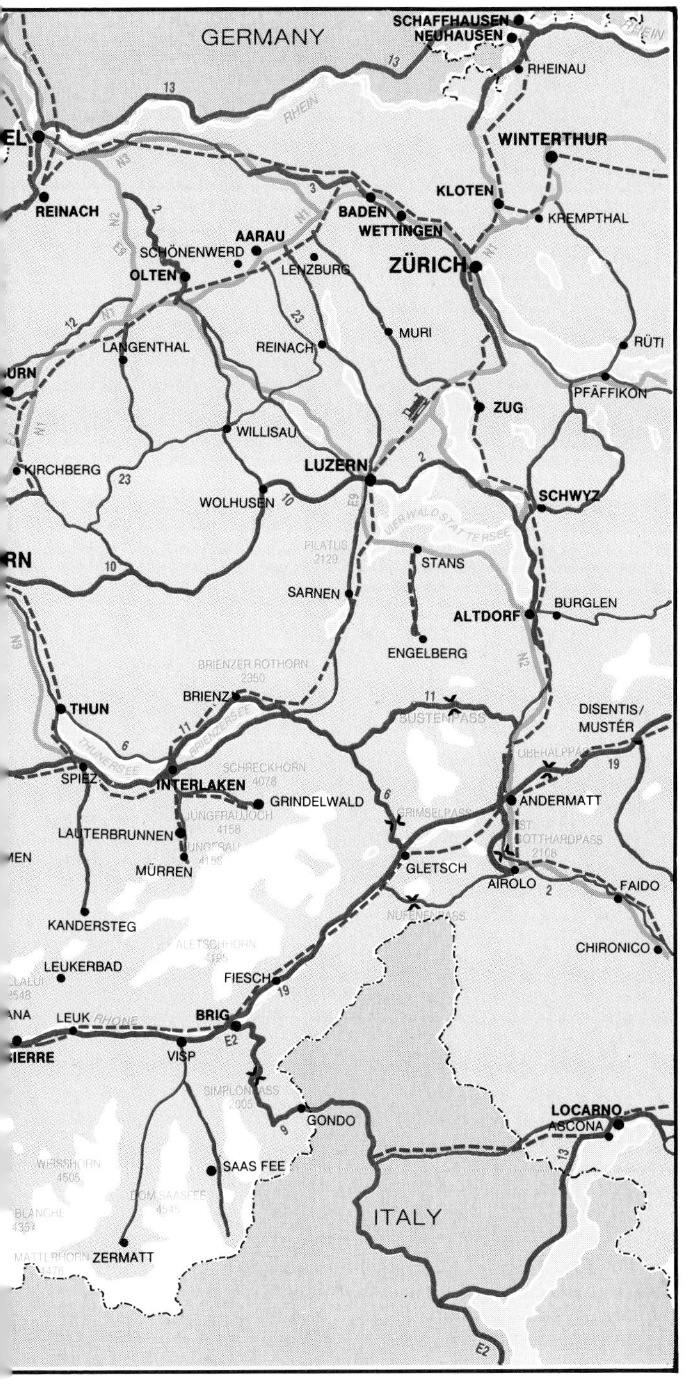
GERMANY
SCHAFFHAUSEN
NEUHAUSEN
RHEINAU
RHEIN
WINTERTHUR
KLOTEN
KREMPTHAL
REINACH
BADEN
WETTINGEN
AARAU
SCHÖNENWERD
OLTEN
LENZBURG
ZÜRICH
LANGENTHAL
REINACH
MURI
RÜTI
PFÄFFIKON
ZUG
WILLISAU
KIRCHBERG
LUZERN
WOLHUSEN
SCHWYZ
VIERWALDSTÄTTERSEE
PILATUS
2129
STANS
SARNEN
BURGLEN
ALTDORF
ENGELBERG
BRIENZER ROTHORN
2350
BRIENZ
THUN
SUSTENPASS
DISENTIS/
MUSTÉR
THUNERSEE
BRIENZERSEE
SCHRECKHORN
4078
OBERALPPASS
SPIEZ
INTERLAKEN
GRINDELWALD
ANDERMATT
JUNGFRAUJOCH
4158
GRIMSELPASS
LAUTERBRUNNEN
JUNGFRAU
4158
ST. GOTTHARDPASS
2108
MÜRREN
GLETSCH
AIROLO
FAIDO
NUFENENPASS
KANDERSTEG
CHIRONICO
ALETSCHHORN
4195
LEUKERBAD
FIESCH
LEUK
RHONE
BRIG
VISP
SIMPLONPASS
2005
GONDO
LOCARNO
ASCONA
WEISSHORN
4505
SAAS FEE
DOM SAASFEE
4545
ITALY
ZERMATT
MATTERHORN
4478

GENEVA – A LITTLE BIG CITY

Geneva has been called the smallest large city in the world. The implication is clear: Geneva's population is only about 160,000, but its international importance is truly great. Geneva is called the capital of diplomacy; it hosts many international organizations, United Nations institutions, summit talks and East-West meetings.

The city, Genève to French-speakers and Genf to German-speakers, is a central European crossroads, one of the important gates to Switzerland, among the established symbols of the country and a place with a rich historical past. Because of its beauty, its sights and its surroundings, it is an absolute must on any visit to Switzerland.

History

Geneva began as a primitive village on stilts, located on the shores of Lake Léman, adjacent to the source of the Rhône River. Just as the ancient settlers recognized the strategic importance of the location, so did Julius Caesar, who conquered the region and built an important Roman city here, the capital of the entire region. The ancient quarter of Geneva, known as **Bourg-du-Four**, was the location of the Roman forum in those days.

Some time later, with the rise of Christianity, the city became the home of the bishop. When the Franks conquered it in 532, Geneva's development was halted until it was annexed to the kingdom of Burgundy and made its capital. In the Middle Ages, Geneva became an important city of commerce. Earlier, its inhabitants had already exploited the struggles between the princes of the church of the Holy Roman Empire and the noblemen of Savoy, and had obtained partial autonomy for themselves within their city. This independent status greatly contributed to the city's development as an important crossroads for economics and trade, as a center for fairs and markets, and as a bridge between Italy and northern Europe.

In the late 15th century, the most important process in the history of the city began. As a result of the fight between the prince of the church and the noblemen of the dukedom of Savoy (over the rule of Geneva), a patriotic party emerged which tried to make an alliance with the free cantons of Switzerland. This confrontation, which was essentially political, also led to a religious crisis – the inhabitants of the city moved away from Catholicism and closer to Protestantism. In 1534, the inhabitants of Geneva signed an alliance with Protestant Bern; they expelled the Catholic bishop, and from 1536 on, the city was ruled by a Calvinist. Calvin made Geneva the most important Protestant center of that period, establishing a college of theological studies based on the teachings of the Reformation. Geneva was dubbed "The Protestant Rome."

In 1584, fearing that these developments might arouse the anger of the

Catholics, and particularly those of Savoy, the people of Geneva made a "common citizenship alliance" with Zürich (in addition to that with Bern). Their fears were indeed justified. On the night between December 11 and 12, 1602, the Duke of Savoy attacked the city and tried to capture it. His men placed tall ladders at the city's walls and tried to climb over them, but they failed and were pushed back. Since then, every year, on this date, the citizens of Geneva celebrate their victory in the streets of the ancient city.

In the 17th century, the city began to prosper economically, because among other reasons, many Huguenots had arrived, fleeing the religious wars in France. The Huguenots, tradesmen and skilled craftsmen, developed Geneva's economy and laid the base for its famous clock making industry.

In the 18th century, Geneva reached the peak of its cultural wealth. The opposing philosophers Voltaire and Jean Jacques Rousseau, and others, all made Geneva a highly important and influential intellectual center. In 1798, the city was conquered by the French army. On May 9, 1800, Napoleon stayed one night in an inn, in the old city, and this event has been engraved in its history. The years that followed were stormy. In 1815, after the Vienna Congress, Geneva and its environs joined the Swiss Confederation, as its 22nd canton.

Since the end of the 19th century, Geneva has become an important center of international activity. The Red Cross established its center in Geneva, and it was from here that its Geneva Treaty was published. The League of Nations was also set up in Geneva, as were the UN organizations, WHO, the International Labor Office and the European Center for Nuclear Research (CERN).

Geneva – a general view

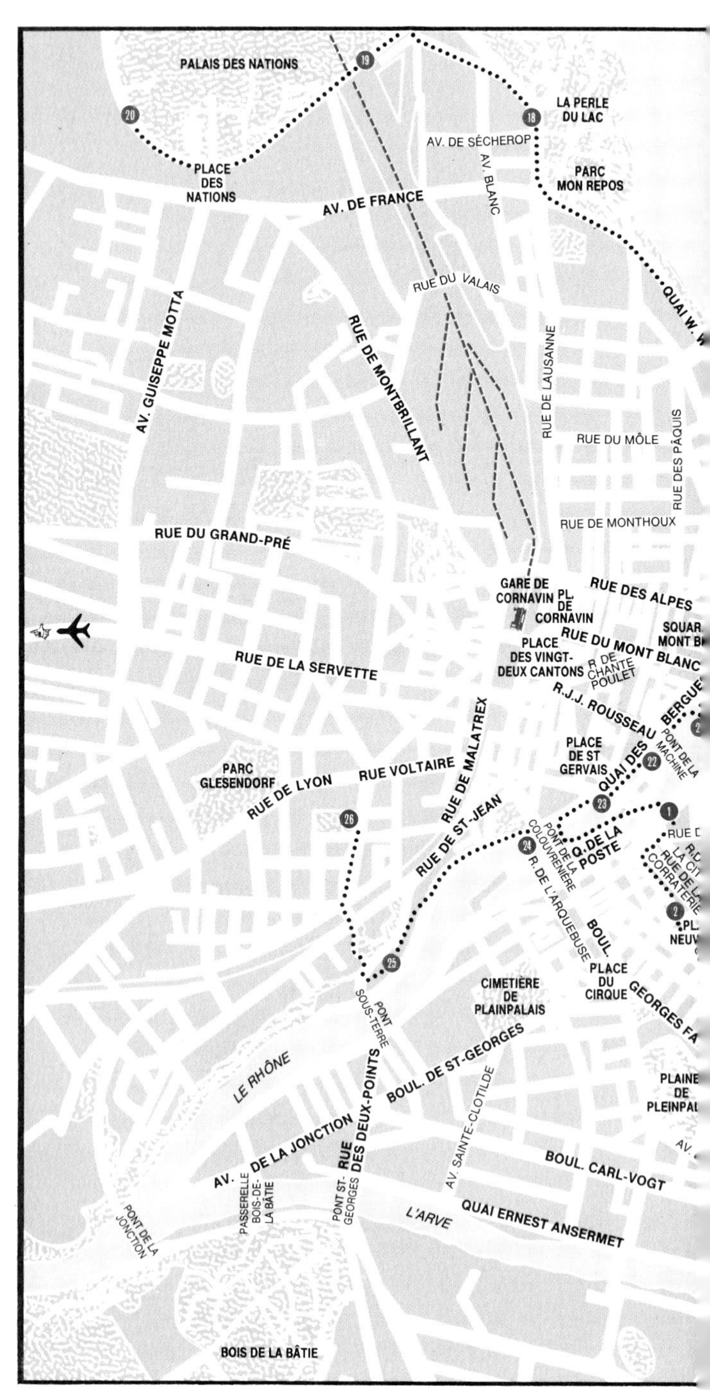
PALAIS DES NATIONS
LA PERLE DU LAC
AV. DE SÉCHEROP
AV. BLANC
PARC MON REPOS
PLACE DES NATIONS
AV. DE FRANCE
RUE DU VALAIS
AV. GUISEPPE MOTTA
RUE DE MONTBRILLANT
RUE DE LAUSANNE
RUE DU MÔLE
RUE DES PÂQUIS
RUE DE MONTHOUX
RUE DU GRAND-PRÉ
GARE DE CORNAVIN
PL. DE CORNAVIN
RUE DES ALPES
RUE DU MONT BLANC
PLACE DES VINGT-DEUX CANTONS
R. DE CHANTE POULET
RUE DE LA SERVETTE
R.J.J. ROUSSEAU
BERGUE
PONT DE LA MACHINE
PLACE DE ST GERVAIS
QUAI DES
PARC GLESENDORF
RUE DE LYON
RUE VOLTAIRE
RUE DE MALATREX
RUE DE ST-JEAN
PONT DE LA COLOUVRENIÈRE
Q. DE LA POSTE
R. DE L'ARQUEBUSE
BOUL.
PLACE DU CIRQUE
CIMETIÈRE DE PLAINPALAIS
PONT SOUS-TERRE
LE RHÔNE
BOUL. DE ST-GEORGES
AV. SAINTE-CLOTILDE
RUE DES DEUX-POINTS
AV. DE LA JONCTION
BOUL. CARL-VOGT
PASSERELLE BOIS-DE-LA BÂTIE
PONT ST-GEORGES
L'ARVE
QUAI ERNEST ANSERMET
PONT DE LA JONCTION
BOIS DE LA BÂTIE
18
19
20
22
23
24
25
26
1
2

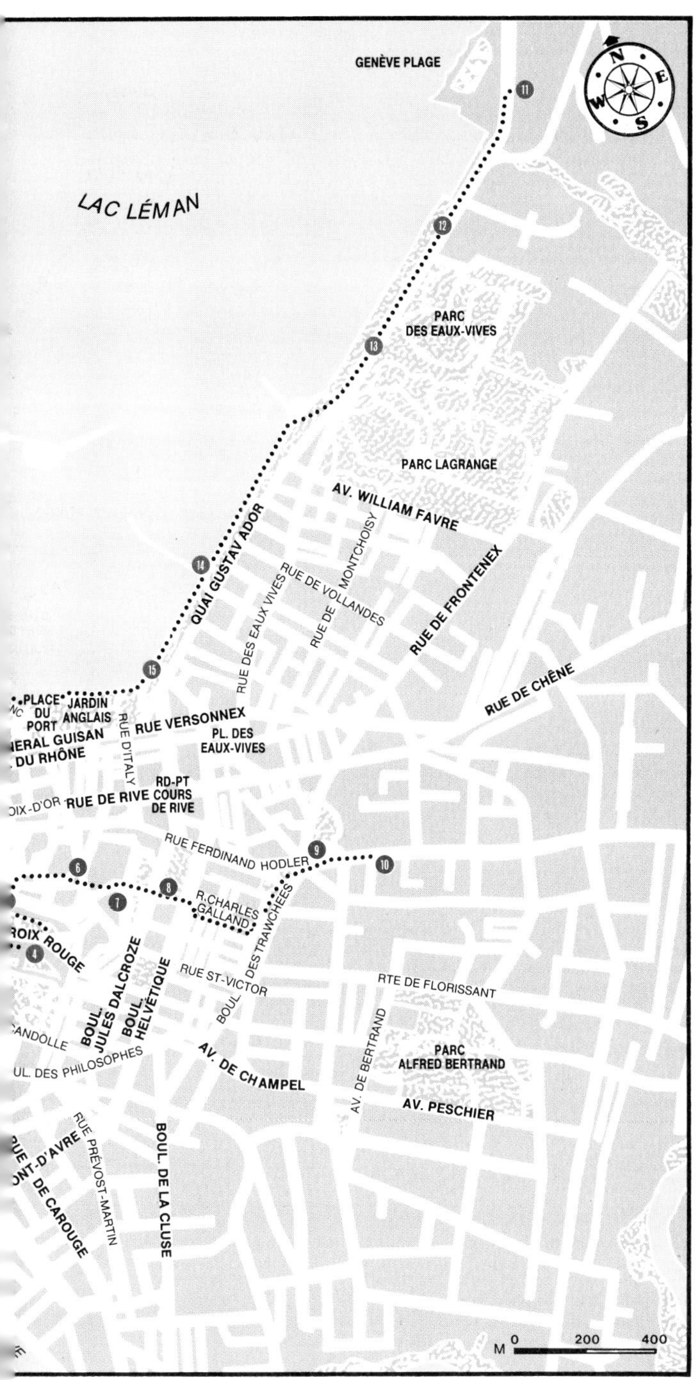
GENÈVE PLAGE
LAC LÉMAN
PARC DES EAUX-VIVES
PARC LAGRANGE
AV. WILLIAM FAVRE
QUAI GUSTAV ADOR
RUE DE MONTCHOISY
RUE DE VOLLANDES
RUE DES EAUX VIVES
RUE DE FRONTENEX
RUE DE CHÊNE
PLACE DU PORT
JARDIN ANGLAIS
RUE D'ITALY
RUE VERSONNEX
PL. DES EAUX-VIVES
DU RHÔNE
RUE DE RIVE
RD-PT COURS DE RIVE
RUE FERDINAND HODLER
R.CHARLES GALLAND
BOUL. DES TRANCHÉES
RUE ST-VICTOR
RTE DE FLORISSANT
BOUL. JULES DALCROZE
BOUL. HELVÉTIQUE
AV. DE CHAMPEL
AV. DE BERTRAND
PARC ALFRED BERTRAND
AV. PESCHIER
UL. DES PHILOSOPHES
RUE PRÉVOST-MARTIN
BOUL. DE LA CLUSE
RUE DE CAROUGE
M 0 200 400

A General View

Geneva is situated between the Alps and the Jura Mountains, in the southwest corner of Switzerland, near the French border. To its north lies Lake Léman, also known as Lake Geneva, to the south is the Arve River, and if you come to it from the Alps, you meet the Rhône River, cutting the city from northeast to southwest.

Lake Léman, which "invades" the city at its nearly triangular southern end, is the largest lake in Switzerland and in western Europe. It measures 227 sq. miles, lies 1,250 ft. above sea level, and runs 45 miles long, with a maximum breadth of 9 miles and maximum depth of 1,000 ft. Most of its eastern shore is in French territory; the rest belongs to Switzerland.

The Rhône River runs into Lake Léman at its northeastern end and runs out of it at the outskirts of the city of Geneva. Immediately past the source is a tiny island – Rousseau – and further on another island, known simply as "the Island," where you will find, among other things, Geneva's tourist office.

To the left of the Rhône (with your back to the lake) is the ancient city, as well as the banking and commerce district. To the right is the train station, the new residential neighborhoods, the parks, and the international district where the Palace of Nations, built in 1937, the center of the Red Cross, and other international organizations are located.

The Arve River runs through the southeastern part of the city; it marks the boundary of Geneva, and on the opposite side lies Carouge (once part of Savoy, and later of Sardinia) and other suburbs. Of some 360,000 residents of the canton of Geneva, 160,000 live in the city of Geneva, about one-third of them foreigners. The large majority of these, of course, are employees of the international organizations and their families, which explains the cosmopolitan character of the city.

Climate

Geneva is located at an altitude of 1,260 ft. above sea level, its

GENEVA *(see previous page)*

1. *Bel-Air Square*
2. *Rath Museum*
3. *Promenade des Bastions*
4. *Monument of the Reformers*
5. *Old City*
6. *St. Pierre Cathedral*
7. *Bourg de Four*
8. *The Museum of Art and History*
9. *The Museum of Natural History*
10. *Watch and Clock Museum*
11. *The beach*
12. *Black Port*
13. *The parks*
14. *The Water Pillar*
15. *Niton's Stone*
16. *Brunswick Monument*
17. *Päquis Jetty*
18. *Villa Bartholoni*
19. *The Botanical Garden*
20. *The Palace of Nations*
21. *Rousseau Island*
22. *Pont de la Machine*
23. *The Island Tower*
24. *Art and Culture Center*
25. *St. Jean Promenade*
26. *Voltaire Museum and Institute*

climate is a mixture of the climates of eastern and western Europe. Westerly winds bring it warmth and humidity, while winds from the north bring the cold (including the famous *Bise*), and the *Fôhr* from the south brings an oppressive heat.

Frequent changes in the weather are a permanent feature of Geneva. On the very same day, cloudy skies might turn crystal clear and then cloudy again. The average temperature in the winter is approximately 4ºC; in summer, about 20ºC. The average precipitation in the winter is four inches; in the summer, 3.5 inches. According to local residents, September is the most pleasant month in the year, weather-wise, though, of course, there is no guarantee against rain.

Getting There

Geneva's international airport, **Cointrin**, lies northwest of the city, about three miles from its center. It is one of the oldest in Europe, opened in 1920, and its new terminal, built in 1968, now serves some 41 airlines and 70 charter flight companies. Direct flights leave from Cointrin for 99 cities in 70 countries.

The airport is within walking distance from the city center. But there is no need to go on foot, especially with your suitcases. The public transportation from the airport to the city is very convenient. For instance, Bus No. 10, which leaves from the exit, reaches the center of Geneva and also passes near the city's train station. This bus line operates from 6am-midnight, every 7 to 15 minutes on average.

You can also go by train, from the station in the airport to the city's Cornavin train station. This is the quickest way to get to the city, as it is not affected by traffic, and it takes just six minutes. Many trains leave the station every hour.

Taxis are also available. The taxis stand at an organized collection point next to the exit.

City Transportation

TPG – these are the initials of Geneva's public transportation company, which takes you relatively comfortably and at varying speeds (depending on the hour of the day) around the city, from 6am-midnight, every day of the week. On Sat., Sun. and holidays, buses are less frequent, particularly on routes to the area of the UN offices – whose employees don't work on these days.

The city has an extensive network of buses, with one electric track and electric buses (sort of trolleys on tires, without tracks), called "trolley buses." Incidentally, there is a plan to build a subway in Geneva, which is, in the meantime, only on paper. Twenty bus routes appear on the easy-to-use map that is distributed free of charge in any tourist office in the city, at the airport, and in major bus stations.

You must purchase your ticket before boarding any public transportation vehicle. You don't have to show it unless an inspector asks you to. There are automatic ticket machines in the stations: press the button indicating the price you need (set according to the length of the ride and the number of lines used), put in the coins, and the ticket comes out. The machines do not give change.

You should be sure to stamp the trip on the ticket card as indicated on the ticket machine in the station. If you have a day pass, you need only stamp your first trip in the machine.

All types of tickets and passes can be purchased in the major bus stations, in tobacco shops that carry the TPG sticker, and at the CFF (Swiss railroad) information counter at the airport.

Bus information is available at Tel. 308.34.34.

TAXIS

During the day, there is usually no problem finding a taxi in the city. They wait at special stations, or the hotel clerk can call one for you.

A 24 hour, 7 days a week taxi service can be reached by Tel. 331.41.33.

CAR RENTAL
In the Geneva airport you will find counters for most of the leading European car rental firms. These companies have offices in the city; the following is a list of the largest:

Avis: 44 Rue de Lausanne, Tel. 731.90.00, fax 242.88.31.

Eurorent: 80 Rue de Lausanne, Tel. 731.24.00, fax 731.23.44.

Budget: 37 Rue de Lausanne, Tel. 732.52.52, fax 731.86.50.

Europcar: 65 Rue de Lausanne, Tel. 731.51.50, fax 738.46.50.

If your pocketbook, or expense account allows, you can rent a limousine and a driver from the following companies:

Prestige Rent-a-Car: 20 Route de Pré-Bois, Tel. 791.09.21, fax 798.78.84.

Executive Car Service: 59 Rue de Pâquis, Tel. 732.79.77, fax 731.42.71.

MOTORBIKE, SCOOTER AND BICYCLE RENTALS
To counterbalance the listing of limousines, we suggest a motorbike or bicycle – wonderful vehicles for touring the city, with no traffic delays, or parking problems. You can hire them at:

Elite: 51 Rue de Pâquis, Tel. 732.94.94, fax 731.90.87.

Horizon Motos: 22 Rue de Pâquis, Tel. 731.23.39, fax 738.02.82.

D. Ludi: 2 Rue de la Puiserande, Tel. 329.04.20.

HITCHHIKING
Switzerland is an orderly country. One sign of this is that there is a special organization to help you get a ride wherever you are headed. For details, call Service Tel-Stop, Tel. 731.46.47; (021) 964.16.64.

Accommodation

As befitting a city with such a reputation as a center of commerce and tourism, Geneva offers a wide selection of accommodation, from the most luxurious to the relatively inexpensive. The hotels that appear here were taken from a selection recommended by the local tourist authority. All are within a walking distance of maximum 20 minutes from the center of the city.

FIVE-STAR HOTELS
Le Richemond: Jardin Brunswick, near the lake, Tel. 731.14.00, fax 731.67.09.

Noga Hilton: 19 Quai du Mt-Blanc, Tel. 731.98.11, fax 738.64.32 (near the lake).

Bristol: 6 Rue du Mt-Blanc, Tel. 732.38.00, fax 738.90.39 (near the lake).

Des Bergues: 33 Quai des Bergues, Tel. 731.50.50, fax 732.19.89 (near the point where the lake meets the river).

Du Rhône: Quai Turrettini, Tel. 731.98.31, fax 732.45.58 (near the river, opposite the Island).

Hotels and restaurants along the Rhône River front

FOUR-STAR HOTELS

Ambassador: 21 Quai des Bergues, Tel. 731.72.00, fax 738.90.80 (near the lake).

Carlton: 22 Rue. Amat, Tel. 731.68.50, fax 732.82.47.

Royal: 427 de Lausanne, Tel. 731.36.00, fax 738.85.57.

THREE-STAR HOTELS

Suisse: 10 Place Cornavin, Tel. 732.66.30 (near the train station).

Savoy: 8 Place Cornavin, Tel. 731.12.55, fax 731.65.01(near the train station).

Moderne: 1 Rue de Berne, Tel.732.81.00, fax 738.26.58 (near the train station).

Rivoli: 6 Rue des Pâquis, Tel. 731.85.50, fax 738.41.17 (near the train station).

Touring Balance: 13 Pl. Longemalle, Tel. 310.40.45, fax 310.40.39 (in the city center).

TWO-STAR HOTELS

Central: 2 Rue de la Rôtisserie, Tel. 311.45.94, fax 310.78.25 (in the city center).

Lido: 8 Rue Chantepoulet, Tel. 731.55.30, fax 731.6501 (near the train station).

Pâquis Fleuri: 23 Rue des Pâquis, Tel. 731.34.53 (near the lake).

Tiffany: 18 Rue l'Arquebuse, Tel. 29.33.11 (near the old city).

Des Tourelles: 2 Bd. James-Fazy, Tel. 732.44.23, fax 732.76.20 (near the lake).

Rio: 1 Place Isaac-Mercier, Tel. 732.32.64, fax 732.82.64 (near the river).

ONE-STAR HOTEL

De lâ Cloche: 6 Rue de la Cloche,Tel. 732.94.81 (near the lake).

YOUTH HOSTELS

Geneva also offers a selection of

inexpensive accommodation.
In the youth hostels, general hostels and hotels for youth, the conditions are generally very comfortable, the cleanliness is definitely adequate and the atmosphere depends on the composition of the group of guests at any given time. It's a matter of luck.

Auberge de Jeunesse: 28 Rue Rothschild, Tel. 732.62.60, fax 738.39.87. A new youth hostel, opened Spring 1987; located next to the western bank of the lake. Open Jan. 23-Dec. 19, card-holding members only.

Centre Masaryk: 11 Av. de la Paix, Tel. 733.07.72. A hostel located about a half-hour walk from the center, near Ariana Park.

Hôtel Luserna: 12 Av. Luserna, Tel. 344.16.00 fax 344.49.36. A hotel for young people and families, open all year round, located next to Glesendorf Park, about a half-hour walk from the center.

Information on accommodation for the young, and general information, is available at the following address, or by phone, all days of the week, 13 Rue Verdaine, 10am-6pm, Tel. 311.44.22.

CAMPING

There are, of course, no camping grounds in the city itself, but there are several in the surrounding area. The most well-known and popular are:

Sylvabelle: 10 Ch. de Conches, 1231, Conches, Tel. 347.06.03.

Pointe-à-la-Bise: Vesenaz, Tel. 752.12.96.

L'Abarc: Vernier, 151 Route de Vernier, Tel. 796.21.01.

Restaurants

Geneva is, without a doubt, one of the most important cities on the world's gastronomic map. It has numerous restaurants (more than in any other city relative to the number of inhabitants), which appear in the prestigious international food guides. The local cuisine tends to be French style but it has a special Swiss taste.

We have divided Geneva's restaurants into three categories according to price range:

EXPENSIVE

Le Gentilhomme: Le Richemond Hotel, Jardin Brunswick. Tel. 731.14.00, fax 731.67.09. A rich culinary combination of French, Italian and Swiss gourmet. Considered by many to be the most excellent establishment in Geneva.

York: 22 Rue du Cendrier, Tel. 732.33.30. French and Italian cuisine. Open for lunch (11:30am-2:30pm) and dinner (6:30pm-11:00pm), closed on Sat. and Sun. Buses 6, 5, 8.

Edouard 1er: 3 Place Montbrillant, Tel. 733.88.65. International and

Having a lunch break

Anyone for a pint?

local Swiss cuisine, specializing in seafood. Open evenings only (7 pm-midnight), closed on Sun. All buses that go to the Cornavin railroad station.

Red Ox: 8 Bd. des Tranchées, Tel. 347.33.47. American-style steaks, an American menu. Open seven days a week, 11:30am-midnight. Buses Nos. 1, 3.

MODERATE

Les Armures: 1 Rue du Puits-Saint-Pierre, Tel. 310.34.42. French, Italian and Swiss cuisine, fondue and raclette. Open seven days a week, 11:30am-3pm and 6pm-midnight. A short walk from the Old City.

La Berline: 4 Rue du Vieux-Collège, Tel. 310.17.43. French, Swiss and local dishes, meat and fish. Open 11:30am-2:30pm and 6:30pm-10pm. Buses 2, 12.

Cave Valaisanne et Chalet Suisse: Place du Cirque, Tel. 328.12.36. International and Swiss dishes, fondue and raclette, as well as a vegetarian menu. Open daily 9am-3pm and 5pm-1am. Buses 1, 15.

INEXPENSIVE

Café Bon-Vin: 17 Rue Versonnex, Tel 736.87.90. Swiss and local dishes, fondue. Open continuously 11am-11pm, closed Sun. Buses 2, 5.

Café Papon: 1 Rue Henri-Fazy, Tel. 311.54.28. Family-style local dishes crêpes and ice cream. Open 11:30am-2pm and 6pm-10pm; closed Sun. Take a bus to the Old City and walk from there.

Relais de la Poste: 27 Rue de Lausanne, Tel. 732.84.83. Swiss local dishes, fondue and raclette, fish and seafood. Open 11am-2pm and 5pm-11:30pm. Bus 444.

Entertainment

The entertainment in Geneva depends on your budget and your taste. Some 30 movie houses are available for film-lovers. The films are generally shown with the original sound track and dubbed in French. This is indicated in the daily newspaper by the letters V.O. (Version Originale); you can also ask at the ticket office. Hit movies open in Geneva at the same time as in other major world cities.

THEATER, OPERA AND DANCE

Comédie de Genève: 6 Bd. des Philosophes, Tel. 320.50.01. Classical and modern theater.

Grand Théâtre: Place Neuve, Tel. 311.31.28. Ballet and opera.

Nouveau Théâtre de Poche: 7 Rue du Cheval Blanc, Tel. 310.37.59. Classic and modern theater.

Grand Casino: 19 Quai du Mont Blanc, Tel. 732.00.00. Entertainment shows, artistic performances, concerts and games of chance.

Les Marionnettes de Genève: 3 Rue Rodo, Tel. 329.67.27. The city's well-known puppet theater.

NIGHT CLUBS
New Milord: 19 Neuve-du-Molard. Tel. 328.45.26.

Le Velvet Night Club: 7 Rue du Jeu de L'Arc. Tel. 735.00.00

Moulin Rouge: 1 Av. du Mail. Tel. 329.35.66.

Maxim's: 2 Rue Thalberg. Tel. 732.99.00.

Festivals

July – Independence day.

August – Fêtes de Genève: flower parade and fireworks.

September – La Bâtie Festival de Genève: a pop and rock music celebration.

October – Salon l'Automobile (Motor Show).

December – Escalade: historic procession throughout the city; sports events.

Organized Tours

On a nice day, there is no greater pleasure than a boat ride on the lake. You might, for instance, ride by the castles on the southern shores of Lake Léman. *Mouettes Genevoises* offers a two hour ride twice a day, at 10:15am and 3pm, from 8 Quai du Mont-Blanc, opposite the large casino. Price: about 20 francs per person. For further details, Tel. 732.29.44, fax 738.79.88.

You can also sail down the Rhône River, to the Verbois Dam, a trip of about two and a half hours. The boat leaves from the same place at 10am and 2:30pm daily. Price: about 20 francs per person.

For serious boat-lovers we recommend the 11-hour trip around the entire lake. For details about the schedule of daily trips Tel. 311.25.21, or inquire at the sailing dock opposite the English Garden (Jardin Anglais). Call CGN (the Lake Geneva Navigation Company). The company issues a daily card which allows you to cruise on any scheduled line during the day.

You can also take a bus tour to get acquainted with the city; especially recommended is the tour leaving the Gare Routière bus station at Place Dorcière. The tour takes two hours, and costs 25 francs per person. There are several buses a day.

From the same station you can also take bus tours outside the city, like the tour of "rural Geneva," which lasts four hours and includes a trip to the Compesières Castle.

For more details contact *Key Tours*, 7 Rue des Alpes, Tel. 731.41.40, fax 732.27.07, or the Geneva Tourist office, Tel. 310.50.31, fax 311.89.65.

Important Phone Numbers

Area code: Tel. 022.
Tourist office: Rue de la Tour de l'Ile, Tel. 310.50.31, fax 311.89.65.
Train station: Tel. 731.64.50.
Airport: Tel. 799.31.11.
Central Bus Station: Tel. 304.84.72.
Police: Tel. 117.
24-hour Medical assistance: Tel. 731.21.20.
Dental assistance: Tel. 733.98.00.
Information for youth: Tel. 27.64.61.
Municipal Information: Place du Molard, Tel. 311.99.70.
Road information: Tel. 163.

Walking Tours

A Trip into the Past: the Old City and the Museums

From the island on the Rhône River, go to **Bel-Air Square**, and turn south on de la Corraterie St., to the wide square called **Place Neuve**. The Square is a key location in the city, a central point of departure with many possibilities. To the right, in the square, stands the **Rath Museum** (Tel. 310.52.70), which hosts varying exhibits, next to the "Great Theater" building. Behind it, on the edge of the square is the **Conservatory for Music**. In the center of the square is a statue of General Dufour of Geneva, erected in 1886, who led the Federal army in the Civil War of 1847, Switzerland's last war. Not far from there, in the northern corner of the Square, facing Tertasse St., is a bust of Henri Dunant, the founder of the Red Cross organization. As fate would have it, this symbol of honor for a man who did so much in the name of humanitarianism stands precisely on the former location of Geneva's guillotine, where criminals were beheaded in public.

The Rath Museum

At the southeastern side of the square is the main entrance to the park, **Promenade des Bastions** (the Promenade of the Fortresses), which was built in the 18th century immediately outside the walls of the **Old City**.

On a nice day you can stop for a moment to the left of the entrance and watch the ground-chess players, moving huge men on a large, checked board. There is also a very nice café-restaurant-ice cream parlor here. In the southern part of the park is the Old University of Geneva and the university library.

The Rhône River and the Old City

But the real attraction of the park, that which has made it famous, is the **Monument of the Reformers** (Monument de la Réformation). This huge wall, some 330 ft. long, was built adjacent to part of a 16th-century fortress wall; sculpted into the stone are the figures of the four leaders of the Reformation: John Knox, Théodore de Béze, Jean Calvin and Guillaume Farrel. The wall, erected in 1909-1917, is covered with inscriptions and images depicting the history of the Reformation and the persecution of its early supporters in Europe. Among the symbols inscribed in the stone is the symbol of Geneva, the royal eagle and the Episcopalian key, as well as the bear of Bern, its ally, and the lion of Scotland, Geneva's sister in religion and in the historic struggle.

From the central gate of the park, to the right,

go up to the southern entrance of the old city, **via Treille St.** On the route straight ahead we find two amusing stops: a bench which the local residents proudly claim is the longest bench in the world. At the end of the boulevard is an ancient chestnut tree; the appearance of its first leaf at the end of the winter, according to tradition, officially announces the coming of spring to Geneva.

The Monument of the Reformers, with the statues of the four leaders of the Reformation

Before that, turn left, onto Henri-Fazy St. At the left turn lies **St. Germain Church** (Église St. Germain), whose ancient foundations date from the fourth century. In 1959, the building underwent major renovations including the addition of stained glass windows.

On the right is a crowded collection of buildings which belongs to the Geneva municipality. Most of these were built in the 16th and 17th centuries, and the oldest part is a lone tower, from the mid-15th century.

In the inner courtyard is the "elevation ramp." The original purpose of such ramps is irrelevant: they were made to enable the litter carriers to take their important masters to their rooms, without having to walk up any stairs themselves.

On the ground floor you can visit Alabama Hall, an historical site. It was here, in 1864, that the first Geneva Treaty, founding the Red Cross, was signed. At the intersection in front, turn left to

Grand Rue (the Big street), a very ancient, charming and picturesque street, where the ground floors of the well-preserved houses have been converted into art galleries, antique stores, book shops and other stores of the like. At No. 40, the philosopher Jean-Jacques Rousseau was born.

To the right of the intersection is the ancient arms warehouse of Geneva; today it is part of the municipality complex. Under the arched hall, facing the street, you will find a few heavy bronze cannons which once belonged to the Helvetian Republican army, which was established after the French Revolution.

Opposite the armory, at 6 Puits St. Pierre Street with a tower adjacent to its front, stands **Tavel House** (La Maison Tavel), one of the oldest buildings in Geneva, and now a museum. It is open 10am-5pm, closed on Mon. Free admission.

On the various floors of the house are exhibits of historical collections related to the city. There are household implements, furniture, weapons, art objects and other items, from various periods. A special part of the museum is devoted to the memory of General Dufour.

Further down the street is **Perron Plaza** (Place du Perron), a lovely spot with a beautiful fountain and a staircase going down to Perron St. To the right of the little street there is a delightful shop, with antiques from the world of science: old medical instruments, various measuring devices from past generations and medicine bottles of long ago. To the right of the Square itself is a path leading to **St. Pierre Cathedral** (Cathédrale St. Pierre), the major stop on our tour of the Old City.

St. Pierre Cathedral has been the religious heart of the city since the beginning of the Reformation in Geneva. It is open to the public daily from 9am-7pm. The cathedral, built in the 12th and 13th centuries, became a Protestant place of worship in 1536. Inside, in the far left corner of the large hall, stands Calvin's chair. From this spot Calvin directed the spiritual affairs of the community for 25 years. The original building was a Gothic structure. The neo-classical façade was added during renovations in the 18th century.

A statue on Grand Rue, an ancient and charming street

At the marina

The Protestant nobility of various periods, including Emily Mansau, the daughter of William the Silent, Prince of Orange (leader of the Reform movement in France at the time of Henry VIII) and others, are buried here. The large organ of the cathedral is used for special concerts every Sat. at 6pm, from June-Sept. Free admission.

The entrance to the northern tower is at the far left corner of the church hall. Reserve your strength in order to climb the 145 stairs. In return you can enjoy an extraordinary view of the city and the lake, and, on good days a view of the Alps and the Jura Mountains as well.

Outside the building, on the right is the way down to the archeological site under the cathedral. Open daily, 10am-1pm and 2pm-6pm, admission fee). Here excavations have uncovered the remains of a house of prayer from the fourth century, and the city bishop's reception hall which was equipped with a heating system under the floor and decorated with mosaics.

At the exit to the cathedral, to the left, we come to Hôtel de Ville St. Continuing on this street is the square **Bourg de Four** to the left. This is the center of the old city, surrounded by pretty houses and antique shops, art galleries and pleasant cafés. Try the *café crème* (creamed coffee); there is nothing better to refresh you before continuing on the tour. In the center of the square is the traditional fountain. Next to the square are public buildings and educational institutions, such as the Hall of Justice and Calvin College, the main building, which was built in the second half of the 16th century, under the supervision of Calvin himself.

From the square continue eastward, on Rue des Chaudronniers. This street goes by the beautiful promenade of St. Antoine and leads to the **Museum of Art and History** (Musée d'Art et d'Histoire), or as the local residents call it, the Big Museum. Open daily 10am-5pm, closed on Mon., Tel. 311.43.40. Free admission. Buses 1, 3, 5, 8.

The building, erected between 1901 and 1908, opened its doors to the public in October, 1910. Mark Camoletti, an Italian architect, planned its 6,250 sq. yds. over three floors. Some half a million exhibits are displayed in the museum, documenting human activity from prehistoric times to the 20th century.

The rooms on the museum's ground floor are devoted to archeology. There is a particularly impressive collection of artifacts from Egypt, Mesopotamia, Greece and Rome, and of prehistoric findings. There is also a splendid collection of gold and silver coins, from various periods in the history of Switzerland, as well as scales and measures used by traders in the past. On the first floor you will find the museum's collection of paintings. The pride of the museum is *The Miracle of the Fishes*, the masterpiece of the Swiss 15th-century painter, Konrad Witz, with the view of the mountains as seen from Geneva in the background.

The classic-styled building of the Museum of Art and History

Other halls display impressive 12th-19th century collections of weapons and armor, including the William Tell-style crossbow. To complete the picture, you can tour beautiful rooms with furniture and various implements from the 15th-18th centuries, eg., kitchen stoves, beds and cabinets brought from the castles of the nobility.

Slightly to the east of the museum lies a prestigious residential quarter which was built in the late 19th cen-

Taking a break on a street bench

tury. Among the houses in the quarter are two well worth visiting. At 23 Le Fort St. is the **Museum of Antique Musical Instruments** (Musée d'Instruments Anciens de Musique). Open Tues. 3pm-6pm, Thurs. 10am-noon and 3pm-6pm, Fri. 8pm-10pm, admission fee, Tel. 346.95.65. Buses 1, 5, 8 bring you directly there). The museum, which was established as a private institution in 1960 and purchased later by the City of Geneva, houses an exhibit of 350 musical instruments from the 16th-19th centuries, most of which can still be played and are demonstrated as part of the tour. The museum also functions as an international center for lending instruments for concerts of ancient music. The ancient instruments give an authenticity to the performances which could not be staged without them. It is a very interesting museum whether you are a musician or not.

Next to the museum is the **Russian Orthodox Church of Geneva**. You may visit in the afternoon, except on Mon. and during prayer times, admission fee. The golden, onion-shaped domes of the church can be seen glistening from afar. Inside, among other things, you will find Byzantine-style paintings on religious themes. (Tel. 349.94.54).

Tigers on display at the Museum of Natural History

For the last part of this tour, we turn into Charles-Galland St., where the Museum of Art and History is located, heading away from the museum, toward Bd. des Tranchées. We continue on the boulevard, staying to the left toward the point where it meets Route de Malagnou, where we find the Museum of Natural History (Musée d'Histoire Naturelle). 1 Route de Malagnou, open 9:30am-5pm, closed on Mon., Tel. 735.91.30. Free admission. Buses 1, 5, 8.

This museum houses a permanent guest from Ethiopia, who has so far traveled some three million years, and is known by the nickname **Lucy**. According to experts, this is the most complete skeleton that has been uncovered from that prehistoric period.

It is also impressive to see the way in which hundreds of stuffed animals are displayed in what seems to be their natural environment. The aquariums contain sea and lake creatures, and a mineral collection. The cafeteria located in the museum will help you digest the long, exhibition-filled tour.

Behind the Museum of Natural History, slightly up Route de Malagnou, is the **Watch and Clock Museum** (Musée de l'Horlogerie). 15 Route de Malagnou, open 10am-5pm, closed on Tuesday. Tel. 310.70.25. Free admission. Buses 5, 15.

At the Watch and Clock Museum

Geneva has strong historic ties to clocks, and it is only natural that it should have a museum devoted to this subject. Previously, clocks had a special wing in the Museum of Art and Culture, but in 1972 this museum devoted entirely to watches and clocks opened its doors. On its two floors, surrounded by a lovely garden, the history of the measurement of time is displayed. On the ground floor, you can see, among other things, sundials, sand glasses and pendulum clocks from the 15th and 16th centuries, as well as locally produced clocks from the 17th and 18th centuries. Most impressive is the attention given to decoration of clocks and the clock cases made of silver and gold.

On the second floor your cycs and ears will be captivated by musical clocks, which announce the hours with different sounds. Most were made in Geneva and its environs in the 19th and 20th centuries, like the clock jewelry which belonged to the nobility and the wealthy of that generation. The reconstruction of the workshop of the famous expert watchmaker, Louis Cottier, with his delicate tools and precision instruments, is particularly interesting. In addition, the museum also contains a collection of miniatures, made in pastel and colored pencil, on paper and on ivory.

ADDITIONAL SITES

The Baur Collection (Collection Baur), near the intersection of Bd. des Tranchées and Charles-Galland St., at 8 Munier-Romilly St. is open to visitors daily from 2pm-6pm, closed on Mon., Tel. 346.17.29. Admission fee. Buses 1, 5, 8.

At the Petit Palais

Housed in a 19th-century house of the nobility, this museum is devoted to Chinese and Japanese art, mainly from the estate of the great collector in this field, Alfred Baur. In several halls on the ground floor you will find exhibits of exquisite Chinese porcelain and priceless examples that are more than 1,000 years old from the Tàng Dynasty (the seventh to the end of the ninth century), and the Chéing (Manchu) Dynasty (the last Chinese dynasty, from the 17th to the early 20th century). The exhibits on the second floor include Japanese art and implements, decorated Samurai swords, ornate boxes, silk prints, teacups and so on, mainly from the early 17th to early 20th century.

The **Petit Palais** (Little Palace), which is the Museum of Modern Art, is also located close to Bd. de Tranchées, at 2 Terrasse Saint Victor. It is open 10am-noon and 2pm-6pm, Mon. 2pm-6pm only, Tel. 346.14.33, admission fee. Buses 1, 11.

The museum, housed in a Second Empire-style palace of the last century, is occupied mainly by an exhibit of painting and sculpture of impressionist, surrealist and abstract art. Among the best-known names, whose works are displayed here, are Renoir, Monet, Cezanne, Dufy, Chagall, Utrillo, Manne Katz, Soutine and Picasso.

To the east of the Promenade de Bastions Park is a spacious square, closed to vehicles, **Plaine de Plainpalais**. This is the site of the fruit and vegetable market on Tues. and Fri., and the site of the largest flea market in Switzerland, on Wed. mornings and Sat. Here, one can find old books, used furniture and ethnic clothing.

On The Shores of The Lake

Buses 2 and 9 take you to the bathing beach, **Genéve-Plage**, on the southeastern shore of Lake Léman. This is a place for sunbathing and swimming, with lots of tourists. Below the beach, in the direction of the city, is the **Black Port** (Port-Noir), a mooring for sailboats and yachts, located in the place where the Confederation army landed on the shore in 1814. The monument opposite the port is dedicated to this historic event. On the other side of the port are two lovely parks, **Parc des Eaux-Vives** and **Parc la Grange**. These parks are connected (one is a continuation of the other), and they contain rose gardens which many consider the most beautiful in Switzerland; The bushes begin flowering around the month of June. This is also the site, once a year, of the rose growers' international competitions.

The Clock of Flowers at the English Garden

Back to the promenade; At the dock, you get a close-up view of the famous **Water Pillar** (Jet d'eau), one of the best known symbols of Geneva. Huge pumps on the bottom of the lake shoot this artificial geyser into the sky, which in optimal conditions spouts as high as 475 ft. Every second there are seven tons of water in the air! The pillar of water is operated only on balmy days, mainly in the summer. Even then it is constantly watched, and if a wind starts blowing that might spray the water toward the city, it is turned off.

Further down the promenade is the **English Garden** (Jardin Anglais), where you can see the famous clock of flowers, the city's expression of its historic connection to clock making, and a monument to Geneva joining the Swiss Confederation. In the garden there is also a café – try the ice cream, it's delicious.

Opposite the garden, a view of the lake reveals **Niton's Stone** (Pierre du Niton). This stone was set as the basis for measuring all altitudes in Switzerland. Its precise location is 1,225 ft. above the level of the Mediterranean.

Geneva's Water Pillar – one of its most famous symbols

The path from the garden leads to **Mont-Blanc Bridge** (Pont du Mont-Blanc). Under the bridge is a four-story underwater car parking garage. On the left is the tiny island named after Jean-Jacques Rousseau, the philosopher, where there is a statue of him. If you glance back to the peaks of the mountain range in the direction that the bridge goes, on a clear day you can see the white-capped peak of Mont-Blanc. Turn right at the end of the bridge, following the promenade, and you will come to the moorings of the boats that tour the lake.

Further on, to the left of the road, is the **Monument of the Duke of Brunswick** (Monument du duc de Brunswick). This is an extremely fancy copy of the grave of Scaglieri of Verona, built in 1879, to house the body of Duke Charles II of Brunswick (1804-1873). The Duke, a prominent wealthy man, bequeathed all his capital and property to the city of Geneva, on one condition – that this mausoleum be built for him. It was undoubtedly a good deal.

Located on this part of the shore are the city's luxury hotels, the *Angleterre*, the *Hilton*, the *Richmond*, the *Bristol* and others. And of course, where there is money, there is also the "grand" casino of Geneva, where you can get a hint, but no more, of what it feels like to play roulette (Swiss law limits gambling to the sum of about eight francs per turn...), so the really wealthy go to the other side of the French border, where there are no such restrictions.

To the right is the **Pâquis Jetty** (Jetée de Pâquis), where the city's lighthouse and public bathing area are situated. Further on, the Mont-Blanc jetty changes its name to the Wilson Jetty (Quai Wilson). On its left is a row of residences constructed in the 19th century for Geneva's wealthy and official visitors. Beyond this is one of the city's most beautiful areas – the park districts of Mon Repos, Perle du Lac and Barton, which are located next to each other on the shore of the lake and overlook the breathtaking scenery of the sharp edge of Lake Léman, descending toward the city.

This is also the location of **Villa Bartholoni**, an impressive early 19th-century palace, which today houses the **Museum of the History of Science** (Musée d'Histoire des Sciences). 128

Rue de Lausanne, open daily 1-5pm except Mon. Tel. 731.69.85. Free admission. Bus 5.

In the museum is an exhibit of scientific tools, instruments and objects from the 18th and 19th centuries related to great discoveries of the past. There is Goya's electron cannon, a humidity meter used by Horace-Benedict De Saussure, a stethoscope used by Laennec and models of steam engines and medical and dentistry equipment from the 19th century.

On the opposite side of Rue de Lausanne, which runs adjacent to the parks away from the lake, is the **Botanical Garden** (Jardin Botanique de Genève). Open Apr.-Sept. 8am-7:30pm; Oct.-Feb. 9:30am-5pm. The greenhouses are open 9:30am-11am and 2-4:30pm. Free admission. Bus 5.

The Botanical Gardens offer an incredible abundance of things to see and do. Built in 1817, the park features a unique rock garden; hothouses with plants and flowers from all over the world; trees and bushes brought from faraway places; a tremendously large collection of dried plants (some 5 million samples); water pools; an animal corner with deer, roebuck, llamas and aviaries (bird enclosures). The botanical garden library has over 160,000 volumes, some of which are rare antiques, describing the flora of the world.

To the west of the Botanical Garden lies **Parc Ariana**. This marks the beginning of the region of over 200 international organizations whose offices are located in Geneva. **The Palace of Nations** (Palais des Nations) is located in the park itself. You can enter it from 12 Bd. de la Paix, and you can get there on Buses F, O and E from Cornavin station. There are daily guided tours 9am-noon and 2pm-4:30pm.

At the Palace of Nations – the second most important center of the United Nations

The impressive building, almost half a mile long, was built in the early 1930's for the League of Nations, and since 1946 it has been the second most important center of the United Nations, after the UN Building in New York. Here you can tour the various halls, including the

The International Red Cross and Red Crescent Museum

General Assembly hall (which has 2,000 seats) and the council hall, decorated with murals by the Spaniard, Jose Maria Sert, depicting the development of humanity. From the porch of the Palace of Nations you get a view of the lake, the city and the Alps above, and again we discover the white peak of Mont-Blanc.

North of Parc Ariana lies the **International Red Cross and Red Crescent Museum**. 17 Avenue de la Paix, Tel. 734.52.48. The building itself is strikingly modern. By incorporating glass and concrete, the play of light emphasizes the historical documents which are displayed.

The interior, an imposing structure of powerful concrete walls interlaced with high-tech air-handling equipment, forms a perfect setting for the presentation of the Museum's historical documents, such as photographs and films which tell the story of the Red Cross and Red Crescent. Daylight falling through a glass pyramid brings to life the sculpture of of the American George Segal.

Beyond Parc Ariana, further down Av. de la Paix and turn right to 18 Chemin de l'Impératrice, to find **Penthes Castle** (Château de Penthes), which houses the **"Swiss Abroad" Museum** (Musée des Suisses à l'Etranger). 18 Chemin de l'Impératrice, open daily 2pm-6pm. Closed on Mon. Admission fee. Bus O.

This lovely castle and the wonderful garden surrounding it are actually located not far from the city line of Geneva. Its lovely rooms house an interesting exhibition of the relations between Switzerland and the rest of the world, from the Middle Ages to modern times. The display includes original documents, various souvenirs, books, arms, medals, pictures, models, furniture, flags and uniforms.

Parc Ariana is also the location of **Ariana Museum**, 10 Av. de la Paix, open Wed.-Mon. 10am-5pm. Tel. 734.29.50. This is an Italian-style palace, built in the second half of the 19th century to house the art collection of one of the city's wealthy men, Gustave Revilliod (Ariana was his mother's name). The collection of ceramics from the Middle Ages to the current century is considered one of the most beautiful of its type in the world.

As we go down the avenue, we return to the square opposite the Palace of Nations. Next to it are more buildings of international organizations, including that of the International Labor Organization and the World Health Organization.

From the English Garden you can take a shopping trip. Go south, in the direction of the most elegant streets of Geneva; **Rue de Rhône** and **Rue de Rive**. The shops here offer the best of Swiss clocks, jewelry, furs, high fashion, wine, cigars, chocolate and sweets, and to top it all, beautiful antique stores and art galleries.

Playing with ducks and swans at the marina

Following the Rhône River

In the spot where Lake Léman flows into the Rhône River, on the right-hand bank (with your back to the lake) is the tiny **Rousseau Island** (Ile Rousseau). This was once the location of a fortress that protected the entry to the river against foreign invaders. **Bergues Bridge** (Pont des Bergues) leads to the island and to the garden of trees planted on the site of the fortress, where the philosopher and writer Jean-Jacques Rousseau liked to walk, sit and ponder. Now swans, ducks and other birds can be seen doing much the same.

Beyond the island, on the bank, cross the bridge called **Pont de la Machine**, where the plugs to adjust the flow of the lake water are located. Opposite, in the middle of the river, is the **Island**

Tower (Tour de l'Ile). The ancient tower is all that is left of the castle that stood here in the early 13th century, and which, among other things, protected the bridge that led to the city. The tower, with a clock at the top, is now surrounded on both sides by a building where Geneva's tourist office is located. Next to the tower is a statue of Philibert Berthelier, a 16th-century freedom fighter, who was beheaded here.

At the western edge of the island was once the large wholesale market of Geneva. It has been replaced by an **Art and Culture Center**. Here you will find exhibitions, art galleries, and book stores.

We return to the right bank. From here we can continue on a walk to the west, along the river, to the **Saint-Jean Promenade**, and from there up Rue des Délices, where at No. 25 you can visit the **Voltaire Museum and Institute**. You can also get here directly by Bus 6 or 7. Situated at 25 Rue des Délices, open daily 2-6pm, except Mon. Tel. 344.71.33. Free admission. The museum is housed in Voltaire's home from 1755-1765 and its purpose is to study and disseminate his teachings. You can view prints, manuscripts, various documents from Voltaire's life, antique furniture and a 20,000 volume library.

Carouge

Tram number 12, the only one of its kind left in the city, takes its passengers to the little city of **Carouge**, adjacent to Geneva, on the other side of the Arve River. Most of Carouge was built in the 18th century under the command of the King of Sardinia, as the city was a protectorate of his kingdom. The work was done by architects from Torino, who left an architectural "nature reserve" in the Italian style, which is very refreshing.

In the 18th century Carouge served as a base for attacks on its large neighbor. This continued until 1851, when the Vienna Congress decided to transfer rule of Carouge to the canton of Geneva – which then joined Switzerland.

Within a short period cabarets, restaurants and other entertainment spots popped up in Carouge. Its loyal customers were the residents of Puritanical Geneva, stronghold of the strict Reformation, who came here to forget their worries and escape their daily pressures. Another fun-seeking audience that came to Carouge was the mass of gold-seekers who scanned the bed of the Arve River hoping to find the precious yellow metal.

To get to Carouge, get off the tram after Carouge Bridge and from there you can walk through the streets. Walk along St. Joseph Street toward the market square, or tour St. Victor Street, where you can look at the buildings around you, peek into the inner courtyards and stop for a meal, or a glass of wine, in one of the many bistros; a recommended one is *Picadilly*, at 5 Tour-Maîtresse. Tel. 328.17.30.

FROM GENEVA TO LAUSANNE

The road continuing on the banks of Lake Léman, which in official map language is called N1, is definitely worthy of its local name – "the vineyard road." Rows and rows of vines cover the hills down to the lake and the sight is delightful. If you're not in a hurry to get to Lausanne, you can stop at the following places on the way.

COPPET

This is a town whose main street is adorned with arches from the 16th century, reminiscent of the arches of Bern. The street was built after the forces of the Bern canton occupied the area. The 18th-century castle of Coppet, surrounded by a marvelous park, originally belonged to Jacques Necker, Finance Minister in the court of the French King Louis XVI, himself a banker in Geneva. The town earned fame when Necker's daughter, Madame de Stael, the well-known society woman, escaped Napoleon and fled to Coppet, settled here and gathered a group of artists and intellectuals around her. Today, the building houses a museum of Madame de Stael's salon in that period. It is open to visitors from Mar.-Oct. daily 10am-noon and 2pm-5:30pm, closed on Mon.

NYON

This is a small city whose history dates back to Julius Caesar, who established a settlement here called Noviodurum. A statue of Caesar stands above the underground Roman museum in the city, which exhibits archeological findings from the city and the area. Nyon's castle is designed like a medieval fortress. Its foundation was constructed in the 13th century for a castle for the Count of Savoy, which was destroyed, and rebuilt in the 16th century. Today it serves as a combination of various offices, a prison, a history museum and a museum of the famous porcelain produced in Nyon since the 18th century. It is particularly nice to take a walk along the ancient walls of the city, overlooking the river.

ROLLE

A small town with a lovely promenade on the bank of the lake, Rolle has a 13th-century castle, built by one of the princes of Savoy. On an artificial rock in the lake stands a monument in memory of General Frédéric de la Harpe, a native of Rolle, who was the private instructor of Czar Alexander I.

MORGES

A port (yacht mooring) on the lake, Morges serves as a center for the wine growers in the area. The Morges castle was erected in the 13th century by the Duke of Savoy, and now houses the museum of the army of the canton of Vaud. Weapons, armor, and models of battlefields with thousands of lead soldiers are among the displays. The town is also home of the interesting **Alexis-Forel Museum** (Musée Alexis-Forel), which contains a varied collection of antique toys, furniture, engravings, paintings and ceramics.

LAUSANNE – A RESTING SPOT FOR THE ARISTOCRACY

Lausanne has long possessed a special appeal. It attracts many tourists, wealthy vacationers, members of the aristocracy and artists. Victor Hugo, Charles Dickens, Igor Stravinsky, Alexander Dumas, Gustav Dure, Jean Cocteau and George Simenon are only a few of those who have been captivated by the charm of Lausanne. The vineyards, the lake and the Alps give this city its special charm.

History

Lausanne was first made a permanent settlement in the Roman era. It was then that "Lausanna," was built, in what is now known as the Vidy Quarter, on the shores of the lake south of the city, at the end of the *autostrada* from Geneva.

Initially, the city was an important crossroads for tradesmen, merchants and armies traveling on either of the two major European routes: from Italy to France via the San Bernard Pass or from the Mediterranean region to the Rhine Valley via the Rhône Valley Pass. Because of its beauty, it soon became a settlement. Homes and public buildings were constructed in Roman style.

In the period of the Barbarian invasion, the inhabitants of the city abandoned the lake and settled on the hills to the north. They then built the city of Lausanne (today the Old Quarter) and erected a wall around it. In the late sixth century, the first bishop of the city, St. Maire, settled here and the city began to gain regional religious importance and economic power. In the 12th century, an impressive cathedral was built in the city. The cathedral was officially dedicated in 1275 when Pope Gregory X and the Emperor Rudolph of Hapsburg honored the celebrations with their presence.

Among the large homes built by the bishops were the **Bishopry**, which today houses two museums, and **St. Maire Castle**, now the canton's administrative center.

In the first half of the 16th century, the city was conquered twice. Initially, in 1529, the residents embraced the Reformation. The churches became Protestant houses of prayer, and Catholicism was abolished under the leadership of the spiritual mentor, Guillaume Farrel. This reform was concluded and firmly established when the entire Vaud region, including the city of Lausanne, was occupied by the army of the canton of Bern. The military

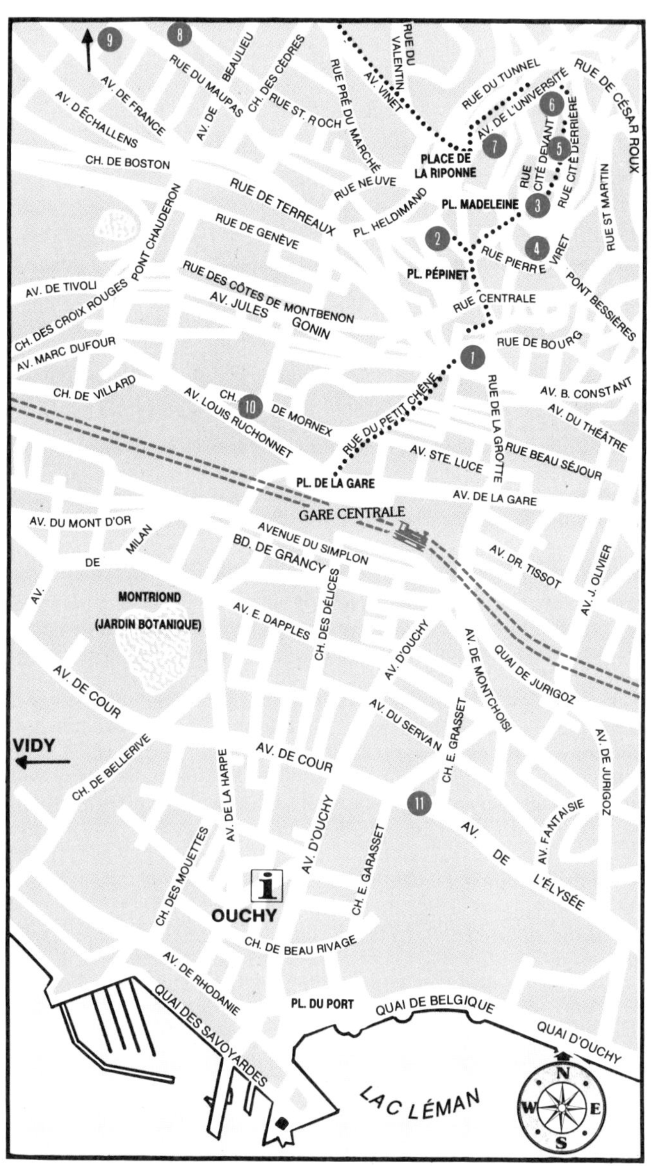

The Bishopry at Lausanne

takeover was followed by several attempts at rebellion, the greatest of which came in 1723. However, the power of Bern was greater and the leader of the rebellion, Major Davel, was executed.

Nevertheless, the city did not stop developing, and in the 18th century it became an important cultural and intellectual center in Europe, attracting many intellectuals, writers and artists.

In 1803, after the fall of the Helvetian Republic, and keeping with Napoleon's decision, the Vaud region was granted autonomy and became a canton of the Confederation. Lausanne was named capital of the region; Many members of the European aristocracy, settled here, thus helping the city prosper. The Federal Court and the Federal Technological Institute were established in Lausanne. Manufacturers and tradesmen from throughout Switzerland gathered here for a large national fair every fall, which further enhanced the city's importance.

Today many international congresses are held in Lausanne. It has been the home of the International Olympics Committee since 1915.

LAUSANNE

1. *Place St. François*
2. *Old City Hall*
3. *Cathedral*
4. *History Museum of the Ancient Bishop's Palace*
5. *The Pipe Museum*
6. *St. Maire Castle*
7. *Romine Palace – The University*
8. *The Museum of Wild Art*
9. *Boulieu Palace*
10. *The Olympic Museum*
11. *The Cantonal Museum of Elysée*
12. *The Roman Museum of Vidy*

A General View

Lausanne lies on the northern shore of Lake Léman, opposite the French coast of Evian, facing the Swiss Alps. The city is the center of the region known as the "Lake Léman District." To the east and west it is surrounded by vineyards and to the north by the forests of the Jura Mountains.

The city lies on a sharp slope, making for a significant difference in altitude between the northern part of the city; Mt. Jura at 3,050ft. above sea level, the city center at 1,620ft. and the Ouchy Quarter, on the shore of the lake, at 1,220 ft.

Lausanne is the capital of the Vaud canton, and the fifth largest city in Switzerland. It has a population of about 130,000, and 250,000 including the outlying suburbs. The language spoken here is French, but in the city you can get a response in almost any language.

Climate

The weather in Lausanne is like that in Geneva. The average temperature in summer (July and Aug.) is 27.5°C. It is decidedly pleasant for swimming and sunbathing. During an average winter, the temperature is around 4°C.

Getting There

Lausanne is 38 miles from Geneva. From Geneva's Cointrin airport, trains leave for Lausanne three times an hour throughout the day; the trip takes 42 minutes. You can also get here by car, on the N1 highway.

Lausanne's railroad station is also connected to the major European cities: the ride takes less than 4 hours from Paris (four times a day on the TGV rapid train), less than 4 hours from Milan, and approximately 5 hours and a half from Frankfurt. Every hour trains make the trip to Bern (approximately 1 hour), to Basel (2 hours and a half) and to Zürich airport (less than 3 hours).

City Transportation

Transportation is important in Lausanne, because of the slope on which it is situated. Buses and trolleys of the TL – the public transportation company of the Lausanne area – will help you cope with the hills.

Inside the city, on lines 1 to 19, two types of tickets are available (according to the length of the ride). The cheapest ticket is valid for up to 5 stops; with the other you can travel any distance for a period of 60 minutes, beginning with the hour stamped on the ticket. The tickets are purchased from the machines in the stations, and are also available in packages of ten.

For more information call Tel. 621.01.11, a 24 hour service.

When using tickets from a package of 10, you must stamp the hour in the machine at the station before boarding the bus. In stations that don't have machines, you can buy tickets from the driver, but then the price is higher. It is best to equip yourself in advance. At the bus company's ticket booths you can also purchase a 24-hour ticket or a 3-day ticket. It all depends on your plans.

There is one metro (subway) line connecting the center of the city with the Ouchy Quarter on the lake shore. The trip is very short, only six minutes. During the day, a train leaves every seven and a half minutes. For this, too, you can buy a package of 10 tickets.

TAXIS

There are more than 40 taxi stands throughout the city. To order a taxi call Tel. 331.41.33.

CAR RENTALS

All major agencies have their branches in Lausanne. Hiring is also possible at the CFF railway station. Tel. 320.80.71.

MOTORBIKE AND BICYCLE RENTALS

Motor Beaulieu: 59 Bergieres, Tel. 646.64.75.

Moto de Chailly: 6 Vallonnette, Tel. 653.07.13.

Bicycles can be rented at the city's train station (you need a particularly strong set of leg muscles for the city's hills, and strong nerves for the sharp descents). Rentals are available Mon.-Fri. 6:30am-8:50pm; Sun. and Sat. 7am-7:50pm.

PARKING FACILITIES

Beaulieu: 10 Av. des Bergières, Tel. 643.24.30.

Bellefontaine: 3 Rue Bellefontaine, Tel. 323.69.50.

Chauderon: 28 Rue de Genève, Tel. 315.11.11. Des Hôpitaux: 25 Av. de Beaumont, Tel. 312.01.06.

Accommodation

Lausanne is the home of a very famous school of hotel management and the city is used to having guests, so the quality of its hotels is well above average. Over 5,000 beds are available here. You should choose your hotel according to the kind of visit planned.

For touring in the city, select a hotel in the upper part. For the sun and water, a hotel on the lake or in the lower city is best.

FIVE-STAR HOTELS

Beau Rivage Palace: Ouchy, Tel. 613.33.33, fax 613.33.34. A luxury hotel with an international reputation, built in neo-classical style in 1861, on the shores of the lake.

Lausanne-Palace: 7 Rue du Grand Chêne, Tel. 331.31.31, fax 323.25.71. Located in the center, close to shopping and commercial centers, not far from the railroad station.

FOUR-STAR HOTELS

Agora: 9 Av. du Rond-Point, Tel. 617.12.11, fax 616.26.05. South of the railroad station, near the metro line to Ouchy.

Continental: 2 Place de la Gare, Tel. 320.15.51, fax 323.76.79. Opposite the city's railroad station.

Hôtel de la Paix: 5 Av. Benjamin Constant, Tel. 320.71.71, fax 323.02.07. A large luxury hotel, in the center of the city, close to the Cathedral.

Carlton: 4 Av. de Cour, Tel. 616.32.35, fax 616.32.35. Halfway between the lake shore and the centre of the city, Ouchy metro station.

THREE-STAR HOTELS

Au lac: Ouchy, Tel. 271451. On the shores of the lake, near the Ouchy metro station.

Alagare: 14 Rue du Simplon, Tel. 617.92.52, fax 617.92.55. Close to the railroad station.

Elite: 1 Av. Sainte Luce, Tel. 320.23.61, fax 320.39.63. A charming hotel in rural style, in the center of the city between the railroad station and the Old City.

Hôtel des Voyageurs: 19 Rue du Grand St. Jean, Tel. 323.19.02. Located in the Old City.

Crystal: 5 Rue Chaucrau, Tel. 320.28.31, fax 320.04.46. Near the Old City.

TWO-STAR HOTELS

Hôtel d'Angleterre: Ouchy, Tel. 617.21.11, fax 616.80.75. On the shores of the lake, to the left of the Ouchy metro station exit.

ONE-STAR HOTELS

Regina: 18 Rue Grand St. Jean, Tel. 320.24.41. In the Old City.

Hôtel du Marché: 42 Pré-du-Marché, Tel. 647.99.00, fax 646.47.23. A simple, pleasant hotel near the Old City.

YOUTH HOSTELS
1 Ch. du Muguet, Tel. 616.57.82. The reception desk is open 9am-5pm. Take trolley No. 1 from the railroad station.

CAMPING
Camping de Vidy: 3 Ch. du Camping, Tel. 624.20.31. Room for some 500 campers, on the shores of the lake; turn right at the end of the Geneva-Lausanne *autostrada.*

Restaurants

Lausanne offers a wide choice of restaurants, from the most elegant and expensive to the simple French bistro style. It also boasts a famous local chef, Fredy Girardet, who attracts zealots of gourmet cooking. Alongside the establishments that specialize in Swiss food and those devoted to the particular dishes of each canton, you can find plenty of fish restaurants, as well as places offering an international menu with every cuisine on the culinary map. All meals are accompanied by wine from the local wineries. Inquire at the tourist office for the "Restaurants and Night Clubs" brochure.

Fredy Girardet: 1 Route d'Yverdon, Crissier, Tel. 634.05.05. The "gastronomic temple" of the famous chef, Fedy Girardet. About four miles west of the city. Take Bus 7 and then 11 to Crissier.

Café Romand: 2 Place St. François, Tel. 312.63.75. In the center of the city; a generous menu, including cheese fondue. Closed on Sun.

Calèche: Hotel Alpha, 34 Rue du

Petit Chêne, Tel. 23.01.31. Near the train station. Swiss dishes, raclette, cheese and meat fondue. Open seven days a week.

Mirabeau: 31 Av. de la Gare, Tel. 320.62.31. In the hotel of the same name, early 20th-century decor. The specialty is grilled fish. Open seven days a week.

Le Shanghai: 6 Place du Tunnel, Tel. 312.62.30. North of the old city, a well-known Chinese restaurant. Open seven days a week.

Restaurant du Port: 5 Place du Port, Ouchy, Tel. 616.49.30. At the port near the Ouchy Metro station. Fish and seafood. Closed on Tues.

White Horse Pub: 66 Av. d'Ouchy, Ouchy, Tel. 616.75.75. In Ouchy near the port. A typical English-style pub-restaurant. Open seven days a week.

Organized Tours

During the tourist season, from May to late Sept., guided bus tours for getting to know the city and the surrounding area set out twice a day. The route goes through the center of the city, the commercial district, the Old City, the historic buildings, the Cathedral and as a final treat, a visit to one of the vineyards and wineries near the city. The buses leave from the tourist office, or from the Lausanne-Palace Hotel (in the center). For further details and reservations, Tel. 617.73.21. Price: about 30 francs per person. Other tours leave the tourist office: Sun. and Thurs., to the Gruyères district, about 40 francs, Sat. to the Alps of Vaud, about 55 francs. From the port of Ouchy you can take a boat trip on the lake. For details on the routes and prices, call the General Navigation Company (Compagnie Génerale de Navigation), Tel. 617.06.66.

Important Phone Numbers

Area code: Tel. 021.
Tourist office: 2 Av. de Rhodanie, Tel. 617.73.21, fax 616.86.47.
Tourist information: Tel. 617.14.27.
Railway station: Tel. 320.80.71.
Lost and found office: 6 Rue St. Laurent, Tel. 319.60.58.
Police: Tel. 117.
Medical first aid: Tel. 144.

Walking Tours

Climbing Through The City

From the city's railroad station we start out on Rue du Petit Chêne, and come to the rectangular plaza that stretches from east to west, **Place St. François**. This is Lausanne's trade and shopping center. In the square and around it you will find numerous shops and department stores, as well as office buildings and banks. The city's central post office is in the plaza.

The square is named for **St. François Church**, which was built on the ruins of a large Franciscan monastery located here in the 13th century. The church has an old bell tower which has been sounding its chimes without a break since the 15th century. To the right of the square is the **Great Bridge** (Grand-Pont), one of the three bridges constructed in the early 20th century to connect the city's three hills; it also crosses over to the **Metropolitan Tower** (Tour Métropole), a modern, office-packed skyscraper.

To reach Bessieres Bridge, another of the three bridges, cross the square to the shop-lined De Bourg Street to St. François Street, which runs north to **Place de la Palud**. The **Old City Hall**; built in the 17th century in Renaissance style is here. The building was extensively renovated in the late 1970's. You can also see the Fountain of Justice, built in the 16th century to refresh tired walkers after the steep climb.

Every first Friday of the month (Mar.-Dec.), from 10am until evening, there is a big arts and crafts fair in the plaza. Twice a week, on Wed. and Sat., the traditional agricultural produce market is held here; farmers from the area bring their goods to the city, as their fathers and forefathers did before them.

Behind the fountain in the plaza is a covered staircase, known as **The Market Stairs** (Escaliers du Marché). Since the Middle Ages these stairs have served those coming to the city's cathedral. The **Cathedral**, which has actually been a Protestant church since the Reformation came to Lausanne in 1536, is considered one of the most impressive structures built in Gothic style, and rightly so. Its construction took from 1175 to 1275 – a century of building. Renovations are continually being carried out in order to preserve the building's ancient beauty.

From inside the church you can get up to the top of the tower overlooking the city, the lake, and the mountains. The view is splendid, but the price

The market street leading up to the Cathedral

The Cathedral at Lausanne has been a Protestant church since 1536

(and we don't mean the few francs you pay to get in) is high – you have to climb 232 worn-down stairs to get there.

Opposite the southern side of the Cathedral is the **History Museum of the Ancient Bishop's Palace** (Musée Historique de l'Ancien-Evêché). This museum possesses a wonderful collection of ancient art and sacred objects, artifacts that tell the story of the city, as well as a large model of the Old Town in the 17th century. Tel. 312.13.68. Open Tues.-Sun. 11am-6pm, Thurs. 11am-8pm. Admission fee.

From the Cathedral, two narrow, ancient streets lead north: Cité Derrière is the eastern one; Cité Devant, the western. Between them is a small street, Rue de l'Académie, where No. 7 is a modest museum offering a unique experience to pipe-smokers. This is the **Pipe Museum**, open Mon.-Sat. 9am-noon and 2pm-6pm, closed Sun. Tel. 323.43.23. Admission fee. On display are hundreds of pipes, from the 16th century to today, from all over the world, and other objects related to the pipe.

The two narrow streets mentioned above lead to **St. Maire Castle**, built in the late 14th century as the home for the bishops of Lausanne. The massive square structure was the palace of the regional ruler during the Bernese occupation until 1798. It now houses the cantonal government of Vaud. The castle veranda, adjacent to the building where the cantonal council convenes, overlooks the scenery to the west of the city. In the front of the castle is a monument to the hero of the struggle for Vaud's independence, Mayor Davel, who was executed in 1723.

From here you can take a short trip north to the **park** and **Museum of the Hermitage Foundation** (Musée de Fondation de l'Hermitage). You can get here on foot via De la Barre St., and then L. Vulliemin Boulevard – or take Bus 16. Here, in a lovely family castle built in the late 19th century, art exhibitions have been held for the last few years (For details call Tel. 320.50.01). But even if you don't catch an interesting exhibit, it is still worth a walk in the marvelous park, with the view of the Cathedral, the city and the lake. There is a very nice cafeteria here, too. Open weekdays 10am-1pm and 2pm-6pm, and Thurs. 10am-10pm, when you can enjoy the park lit up. Closed Mon.

Returning to our route, we walk around St. Maire Castle on the left, via De l'Université St., and come to the huge **Rippone Plaza** (Place de la Riponne). Built on the eastern side of the square are two large houses, one behind the other. The farther one is the old academic building, constructed in the 16th century, from which the university grew. The building closer to the square is neo-Renaissance **Romine Palace** (Palais de Romine), constructed at the beginning of the present century. It is named after the nobleman who bequeathed the money for the project. Inside the thick walls of the building are a large library, the city university and several museums.

First is the **Cantonal Museum for Archeology and History**. It is open daily 10am – noon and 2pm-5pm. Free admission. The museum's most famous exhibit, and unquestionably an impressive one, is the bust of the Roman Emperor, Marcus Aurelius, made from a bar of pure gold, weighing almost 3.5lbs. (7.5 kilos). It was uncovered in 1939 in excavations in Evéché. In addition, many archeological finds that were uncovered in excavations in Vaud are on display, including weapons and pottery from the Neolithic Period and from the Iron and Bronze Ages. There are also vessels from Ancient Greece, as well as objects found in graves of the Burgundy Dynasty dating back to the fifth century AD.

Second is **The Cantonal Museum of Fine Arts** (Musée Cantonal des Beaux-Arts). Open Tues.-Wed. 11am-6pm, Thurs., till 8pm; Fri.-Sun. 11am-5pm. Admission fee. Most of the exhibits in the museum are the work of French Swiss, from the 18th century on. In addition there are also well-known "guests": Renoir, Matisse, Utrillo, Degas and others. The museum is renowned for the International Festival of Artistic Tapestries, held here in the summer, every odd-numbered year.

Third is the **Museum of Natural History**. The museum is open daily 10am-noon and 2pm-5pm. Free admission. The collection, which is not especially interesting, includes geological and zoological exhibits, fossils and more.

At the end of our walk is a very special treat. From Riponne Plaza, climbing the stairs to the right of the Italian church, we come to Vinet Boulevard, which to the west becomes Bergières Boulevard. There, at No. 11, is The **Museum of Wild Art** (Musée de l'Art Brut) in part of the 18th century Beaulieu Castle. You can get here by Bus 2. The museum is open Tues.-Fri. 10am-noon and 2pm-6pm, Sat. and Sun., in the afternoon only. Closed on Mon. Admission fee.

It houses a permanent exhibition of unusual creations, collected in the early 1950's by the Lausanne painter, Jean Dubuffet. There are hundreds of paintings, sculptures and embroidery works, produced by people who lived on the fringes of society: the emotionally ill, mentally retarded prisoners and so on. With no artistic training, these people have created works that express their incredible imagination. This is indeed an extraordinary experience, highly recommended.

On the other side of the boulevard, to the west, is the **Beaulieu Palace**, which currently serves as a large congress and exhibition center. This is the center of the Swiss autumn fair, held every year in September. The *Comptoir Suisse*, as it is called, attracts hundreds of thousands of visitors to see new products and enjoy the folklore and food.

ADDITIONAL SITES

The **Olympic Museum** (Musée Olympique). 18 Av. Ruchonnet, west of the railroad station square. Open Sun. 10am-6pm; Thurs. 10am-9:30pm. Tel. 612.65.11. Admission fee. Here in the shrine of sport at its best, is an exhibit on the history of the International Olympic Movement, the Olympic games, and the individual who revived the Olympic tradition, Count Pierre de Coubertin.

The **Cantonal Museum of Elysée** (Musée Cantonal de l'Elysée). Switzerland's main photography museum, housed in a stately mansion. It exhibits contemporary work as well as the history and science of photography. Situated at 18 Bd. de l'Elysée. Get off at the third stop on the Metro to Ouchy, continue down the street a bit, and the boulevard is on your left. Tel. 617.48.21. Open daily 10am-6pm; Thurs. 10am-9pm; closed Mon. Admission fee.

An exhibit at the Museum of Wild Art

The **Roman Museum of Vidy** (Musée Romain de Vidy). Located in the western suburb of Vidy, on Ch. du Bois de Vaux St., Bus 18. Tel. 625.10.84. Open Tues.-Sun. 11am-6pm; Thurs. 11am-8pm. Admission 4 francs. The museum displays such items as pottery, coins, reliefs and the like that were uncovered at the Roman site of the colony of Lausanne, not far south of here, on the other side of the *autostrada* from Genève.

The **Roman Villa of Pully** (Villa Romaine de Pully). Located in the Pully Quarter, east of the city, near to the lake, next to du Prieure Square and the hotel of the same name. Buses 4 and 8 go to the area, as well as the train. Tel. 728.33.04, 721.33.11. Open 2-5pm (Nov.-March: Sat. and Sun.; April-Oct.: Tues.-Sun.) Free admission. The villa is a reconstructed Roman vacation home from the first century AD, the remains of which were found here in 1921. Findings were uncovered in excavations, and the most important, a huge wall painting some 200 sq. ft. large, depicting a chariot race, are displayed as well. There is also a historical audio-visual program.

For sworn admirers of the detective Sherlock Holmes, there is something special. About 12 miles from Lausanne, on Road E4, you come to the Lucens Castle. In this fortress, built in the Middle Ages, which originally belonged to the bishops of Lausanne, the "Arthur Conan Doyle Foundation" has established a museum devoted to Sherlock Holmes. Here, among other things, is an accurate "reconstruction" of Holmes's work room, where he solved many mysteries along with his friend Dr. Watson. The museum is open to visitors from the beginning of Apr. to the end of Oct., Wed.-Sun., 10am-6pm.

Lausanne's Cathedral, whose construction took a century

FROM LAUSANNE TO BASEL, VIA THE JURA REGION

From Lausanne we travel north (N1), continuing along the northwestern shore of Neuchâtel Lake, and then Biel Lake (N5). From the city of Biel, we go to Delémont (road 6), and from there to Basel (road 18).

DENT DE VAULION

You can get to this mountaintop, one of the highest in the Swiss Jura, from Lausanne via the town of Vallorbe on Road 9 or from Geneva via the E45 and the Joux Valley (this way is prettier).

The climb begins with a one-hour trip on a somewhat bumpy road from the village of Romainmôtier to a cabin-hostel at the foot of the mountain. From the cabin follow the arrows, which take you in a short time to the peak, almost 5,000 ft. high. The view is breathtaking. You can see the entire Jura range, the white peaks of Mont Blanc and Lake Léman.

YVERDON-LES BAINS

This is a city on the southeast side of Neuchâtel Lake. Its famous bathhouses are said to remedy rheumatism and other ailments.

From Yverdon, a narrow ascending road leads north to a pair of pastoral towns, Ste. Croix and Les Rasses, located at the mouth of a wide valley. A beautiful tour leaves Les Rasses for the top of **Mt. Chasseron** (5,362 ft.). A narrow cableway takes you to the top station – from which you can climb (about an hour) to the peak. The fantastic view spread before you includes the Jura and Alps ranges and Neuchâtel Lake. Another narrow path leads from the valley to the Baulmes Mountain (4,283 ft.), another, no less beautiful, observation point.

BOUDRY

This is a small town with a small medieval fortress, begun by the counts of Neuchâtel in the 13th century. It was kept by the courtiers of the family until the mid-18th century when it was transferred to the people of Boudry for use as a police station. It now houses a museum of vineyards and wine. The town is also the birthplace of Mara, one of the heroes of the French Revolution, murdered in 1793.

COLOMBIER

This town adjacent to Neuchâtel (both the city and the lake) has become famous for two things: its white wine and the philosopher Jean-Jacques Rousseau. The fortified castle was built in the 11th and 12th centuries. Once belonging to the local nobility, it was handed over to the counts of Neuchâtel in the 13th century. In the early 18th century, it became Prussian property and among other things, the home of the governor representing the prince George Keith, who offered it to Rousseau. Today the building houses a museum which exhibits weapons from the 14th-19th century. Open for guided tours from Mar. 1 to the end of Oct., Tues.-Fri. afternoons.

NEUCHÂTEL

This city is the capital of Neuchâtel canton and has about 32,000 inhabitants. Its excellent location on the lake shore and the vine-covered mountain slopes, as well as its good air, have always attracted large numbers of tourists and vacationers. It has a French university, which is instrumental in preserving the French-Swiss culture. Neuchâtel has played an important role in the art and study of watch making. It also excels in the field of wine making. If you find yourselves in the area in the last week of September, you will see the grape-picking festival that has been celebrated here for many generations.

A rainy afternoon at Neuchâtel

The city began with a citadel built in the early 11th century. For hundreds of years the citadel belonged to a French family of nobility from Orléans, the Orléans-Longuevilles, and in 1657, a member of the family, King Henri II, made a historic visit here. Legend has it that during the visit, thousands of gallons of red wine were made to flow through the fountain that stands to this day on the street of the castle (Rue du Château).

Colorful paving at Neuchâtel

In the early 18th century, the city became the private property of the King of Prussia; in the early 19th century it became part of the territory belonging to Berthier, one of Napoleon's generals. In 1815, together with the new canton of Neuchâtel, it became a part of the Swiss Confederation. Nevertheless, the city itself retained a strange political tie with Prussia, whose king continued to hold the title, Prince of Neuchâtel, until 1857.

East of the city's port, next to the lake shore, is the **Museum of Art and History** (Musée d'Art et d'Histoire), which is definitely worth a visit. Among the works of art exhibited are 19th and 20th-century paintings by Swiss artists and 15th-16th century religious art. In the history section you will find a large collection of furniture, clothing, everyday items and clocks. Most impressive of all the exhibits, however, are three mechanical creations, the result of the wild engineering of the Jacquet-Droz family of the 18th century. Open Tues.-Sun. 10am-noon and 2-5pm. Tel. 20.79.20. Free admission.

Neuchâtel also boasts a museum of ethnography, at the southern end of the city. The 'Pharaohs of Egypt' exhibit is particularly good.

A unique panoramic view of the lake and the Alps can be seen from the observation point on Osterwald shore, south of the port.

The Office of Tourism for Neuchâtel and the surrounding district is at 7 Rue de la Place d'Armes, Tel. (038) 25.42.42, fax (038) 24.28.52.

For a short trip north from Neuchâtel, ride 16 miles up Road 20 through **Tête de Ran**. The famous 4,500 ft. observation point, to the city La-Chaux-de-Fonds is highly recommended.

LA-CHAUX-DE-FONDS

This is a national and international center of clock making, as well as for the production of stamps for Switzerland and many other countries. It is worth a visit to this city, on a plateau 3,500 ft. high, if only to visit the International Museum of Clock Making located here. The underground museum, established at the beginning of the century, illustrates the history of humanity and time-keeping from prehistory to the present day, with more than 3,000 items. Outside of the museum is the unique carillion by the Italian sculptor, Vignando, a monument to time, weighing 15 tons, which announces the time every quarter of an hour. The museum is open daily in the morning and afternoon; closed on Mon. Admission fee. From here you can continue along the French border to Basel, or return to Neuchâtel, and from there toward Biel (N5).

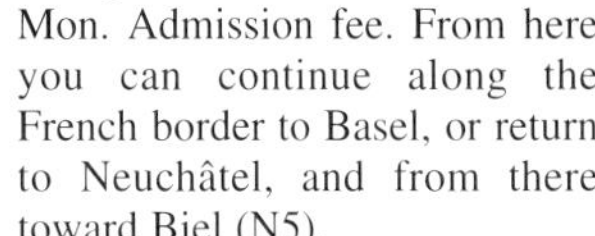

You might also want to take a fascinating trip south (five miles) to **Doubs Waterfall** (Saut du Doubs). Take Road 20 to Le Locle, and turn north there to Les Brenets. Continue by foot along the river about half an hour to the waterfalls, located on the French side (you will need a visa) of the Doubs River.

LA NEUVEVILLE

At the southwestern edge of Biel Lake, is La Neuveville. It is a charming town with a promenade lined with flowers and romantic alleyways, and its main industries are wine, tourism and precision mechanics. La Neuveville is a good departure point for a trip to the famous St. Pierre Island (though today it is actually a peninsula), located in the lake, opposite the town. This was one of the places that Jean-Jacques Rousseau came to during his wanderings. In 1765, the philosopher wrote of the island in his Dreams of a Solitary Stroller: "Of all the places in which I have lived (and there have been many very beautiful ones), none has ever made me so happy." **The Cluni Inn** (L'Auberge Clunisien), located on the island, originally a 12th-century monastery, served for a while as Rousseau's resi-

dence, and here you can visit his simple room, followed by a good meal in the restaurant.

From La Neuveville, a narrow path winds up to the town of St. Imier – a watch making center in its own right. Located on the southern slopes of the Soleil mountain, St. Imier is known for its 11th-century church, as well as for its marvelous location. Three-quarters of a mile south of the city the road turns north toward the **Chasseral**, the highest peak (5,300 ft.) in the Jura mountains. On a clear day, the view from the peak (about a half-hour walk) stretches from Mont Blanc in the south to the Black Forest in the north.

BIEL

Biel (Bienne in French), lies at the northeastern end of Biel Lake, marking the regional border between French Switzerland and German Switzerland. About one-third of its inhabitants are French-speakers; the rest speak German as their native tongue. In the last 100 years the city's population has increased considerably, from 11,000 in 1880 to about 55,000 today, mainly because of a growing clock making industry. It got a boost in 1979, when the first factory of the famous Omega firm opened in Biel.

The history of the city began in the early 13th century, when it was established by the church prince, ruler of Basel. Although it was controlled by Basel, the residents were relatively independent, because of its distance from that city, and were able to make a pact with its neighbor, Bern. In 1792, after the revolution, the city was occupied by the French. During the 1815 Vienna Congress, the small republic of Biel was put under the protection of Bern, whereby it officially became part of the Swiss Confederation.

A walk in the old city of Biel reveals handsome, old buildings, and **Ring Square** (Ring Place), which was the center of the city's activity under the rule of the church prince of Basel. The **Banneret Fountain** (Fontaine du Banneret) in the Square was erected in 1546, and is dedicated to the city's militia. In other parts of the old city, particularly on Rue Haute, you will see buildings with typical Bernese arches.

On the way from the old city to the lake is the **Schwab Museum**, one of the country's major museums of prehistoric archeology. Most of the findings seen here were originally part of the large collection of Switzerland's pioneer archeologist, Colonel Schwab. In addition, objects from the Roman period are also exhibited. The museum is open Tues.-Sun. 10am-noon and 2pm-5pm. Tel. (032) 22.76.03. Free admission.

Some one-and-a-half miles north of Biel on Road 6, is a popular tourist spot, **Taubenloch Cave**. The tour through its labyrinths is the answer to many a child's dream. The road, which continues on a winding climb through typical Jura mountain scenery, takes you to Delémont.

In the Schwab Museum at Biel

DELÉMONT

This little town, inhabited by about 11,000 residents, is the capital of the youngest canton in Switzerland, Jura, which became independent in 1978. Until the late 18th century, Delémont was the spot that the church princes of Basel chose to spend their summers.

The city has numerous lovely buildings, a castle of the church princes, a town hall, St. Marcellus Church, and a relatively small museum of archeology, folklore, ancient religious items and more.

From Delémont, Road 18 takes you to Basel. Approximately half-way there, turn right to get to the village of **Seewen**, where music lovers will enjoy a charming museum of some 400 mechanical music boxes, 250 years old or more. Open afternoons except Sun. and Mon.

BASEL – THE CITY ON THE RHINE

Basel (Bâle to the French-speakers) holds a special place among Switzerland's cities. Situated on the Rhine at the point where it becomes navigable, Basel is the most important of the country's river ports, and its only point of departure to the sea. Basel is located at an important intersection, the border between Germany and France, on the major trade routes of the Old World. It overlooks the landscape of the Jura and Schwarzwald mountains. It is both a city and a canton with a 2,000-year-old history. Basel is a major cultural center, combining the German and the Roman heritage, the location of the first university in Switzerland, and the key city in the country's chemical and pharmaceutical industry.

History

Basel is first mentioned in a written text in 374. Roman historians wrote about the military fortress of Bezilia. Plancus, an officer in the army of Julius Caesar and a good friend of Cicero, established the city of Augusta Raurica not far from here. This occurred in the year 44 BC, the year in which Caesar was assassinated and 14 years after the battle of Bibracte, in which the Roman legions defeated the warriors of the Celtic tribes living in the region, the Raurici and the Helvetians. Somewhat later the city itself is mentioned as the bishopric.

From the sixth century on, the city was included in the territory under the rule of the Franks. In the 10th century, the lords changed, and the Burgundy rulers took control of the city. In the mid-11th century, Basel was annexed to the German Empire, under the direct rule of the Emperor's prince-bishop.

Rathaus – Basel's city-government hall

At the Cathedral in Basel

Between 1160 and 1260, guilds of professionals and merchants were established and slowly gained influence and political power, at the expense of the bishop. In 1356, the city suffered a heavy blow when much of it was destroyed by an earthquake. It recovered at the end of the 14th century and members of the guilds purchased their lands from the church. Basel became a free city of the German Empire and began to prosper, both economically and culturally. In 1460, the University of Basel was founded. The paper and printing plants established in Basel earned it a reputation throughout Europe as a center of book printing. The *Provan Amerbach* print shops of Basel became one of the most famous firms of the continent.

Basel's development was also enhanced by the large fair that it was allowed to organize beginning in 1471, which attracted large crowds of merchants and visitors from all over Europe. The tradition continues to this day, and the fair held every spring draws a million visitors.

As a result of the city's development, many intellectuals and artists came to live in Basel. These included the theologian, Erasmus of Rotterdam, and the painter Hans Holbein. On July 13, 1501, Basel joined the Swiss Confederation, originally in order to defend the city against the Hapsburgs' efforts to take control; afterwards Basel maintained special ties with its neighbors from Alsace and Baden.

In 1529, the Reformation reached Basel. Under pressure from the local farmers and armed citizens in the city, the bishop and his court fled the city, without bloodshed, and the revolution was marked only by the looting and destruction of Catholic statues and religious objects. The city's acceptance of the Protestant religion, under the leadership of Johannes Oekolampadius, drew many Protestants who sought refuge from persecution in France and the Italian Ticino region. These people, mainly skilled professionals, contributed to the prosperity of Basel, especially in the textile and silk industries. They also added to the cosmopolitan nature of the city. Their city prospered, even though the people of Basel did not join the ranks of the mercenaries in foreign armies, unlike the citizens of the other cantons.

In the 17th century, Basel was ruled by several privileged bourgeois families, and increasing tension developed between them and the residents of the surrounding rural areas. The friction reached a climax in 1653 when a farmers' rebellion erupted, ending in failure. In the 18th century, Basel became known for its strong missionary society, which sent members off to Africa and Asia to spread the Protestant religion. In 1798, after the French occupation of Switzerland and the institution of the new constitution, all residents of Basel were temporarily granted equal rights. However, with Napoleon's defeat in 1814, the former social order returned, and the upper-middle-class families again assumed their special privileges.

As a result, farmers' rebellions broke out once again, continuing from 1830 to 1833. In August, 1833, in a crucial confrontation near the settlement of Holftenschantz, the forces of the urban cantonal government were defeated. It became evident that there was no choice but to split the region into two equal autonomous parts: half of the canton became the City of Basel and half, Rural Basel.

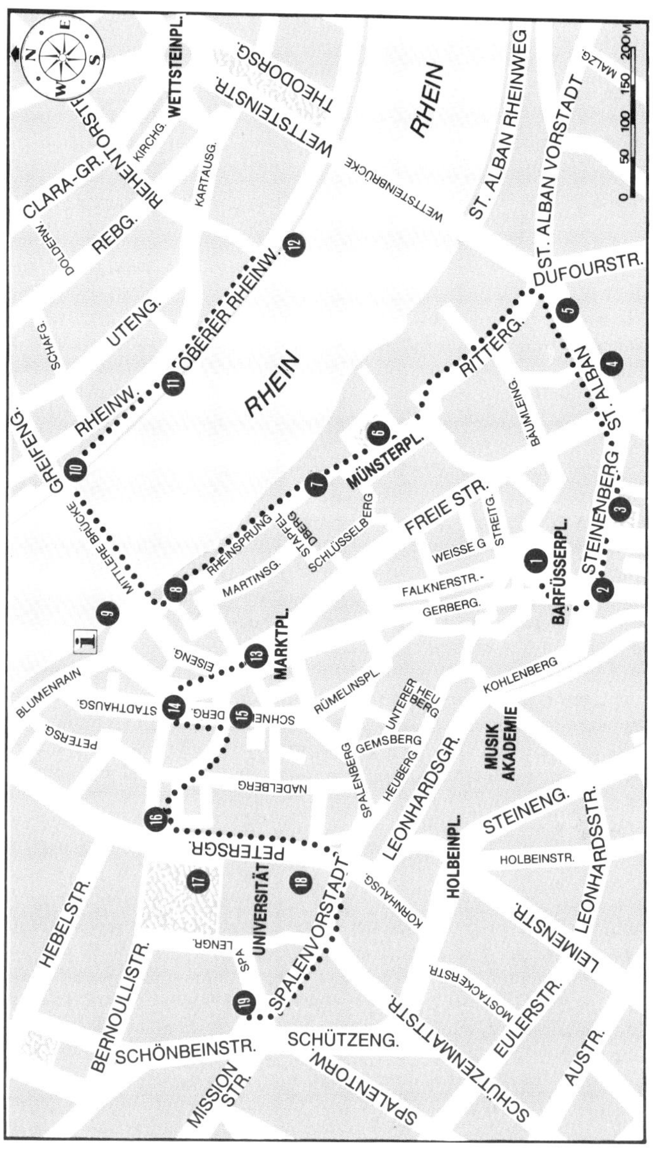

In the Museum of Paper and Printing

Following the division, the city remained under the control of the privileged bourgeoisie. Matters continued this way until 1875, the year of democratic reform in Switzerland. One of the changes instituted under the reform was the decision that the government of the City of Basel would manage the city's affairs instead of the bourgeoisie.

In the late 19th century, Basel witnessed renewed growth in all aspects. It flourished economically, both because of the increased importance of the roads running through it and the success of its industries. Its population more than doubled in number (in 1850 there were only 30,000 inhabitants, while in 1880 there were already about 65,000). Neither did Basel stagnate in the cultural sphere; Friedrich Nietzsche, became a lecturer in classics at the local university (1869-1879); the painter Arnold Bôcklin, and the historian Burckhardt, were also part of the community.

In the 1950's, the two separate parts of Basel requested to reunite into one canton. A committee was set up to formulate a proposal, presented in a referendum to the residents. The residents of the City of Basel accepted the idea, but those of Rural Basel rejected it, and the two Basels remain separate to this day.

BASEL

1. Museum of History
2. Casino
3. Tinguely's Fountain
4. Museum of Ancient Art
5. Museum of Art
6. Cathedral
7. Museums of Ethnography, Folklore, Natural History
8. St. Martin's Church
9. Café Spitz
10. Oberer Rheinweg Promenade
11. Ferry
12. Market square – Rathaus
13. Fish Market Square
14. Museum of Pharmacy
15. Peter's Church
16. Petersplatz
17. Museum of Crafts and Decorative Art
18. Spalentor

A General View

The city of Basel spreads over both banks of the Rhine River. Within the territory of Basel, the river winds and turns from its northern source towards France and Germany. On the southern bank of the river lies "Great Basel" ("Gross-Basel"): the residential center, the Old City, the commercial and administrative district. "Small Basel" ("Klein-Basel"), with most of the chemical industries, pharmaceutical factories, and the new port (built in 1924), is situated on the northern bank. Six bridges over the Rhine (the oldest is a wooden bridge constructed in 1226), and three ferries connect the two parts of the city.

One of Switzerland's lowest cities, 910 ft. above sea level, Basel is separated from the rest of the country by the Jura mountains cutting through the city's south-eastern section. To the north the city reaches right to the German and French borders, and some of Basel's streets are partly in a neighboring country. In the north and in the south, Basel shares a border with the half-canton of Rural Basel.

Two rivers empty into the Rhine in the Basel territory, the **Birs**, which reaches the southern bank through French Alsace, and the **Wiese**, which comes from Schwarzwald (the Black Forest) in Germany. The highest spot in the canton, St. Chrischona (some 1,830 ft. above sea level), is located in the north-east of the half-canton of the City of Basel, on a "finger" of land that goes into German territory.

In terms of population, Basel is the second largest city in Switzerland (after Zürich), its residents number about 180,000. In the half-canton of the City of Basel, there are approximately 200,000 residents, spread over an area of only 14 sq. miles. In this area, the relative population density is the highest in all of Switzerland – about 14,000 inhabitants per sq. mile.

Most of the residents of Basel are German-speakers; only a minority speaks French. About 52% of the residents are Protestant, 40% Catholic, 1% Jewish and the rest belong to other religions or define themselves as atheists. The system of government in the urban half of the canton also differs from that in the rest of Switzerland. The cantonal government institutions – the Greater Council of 130 elected officials and the seven-member Government – also serve as the municipal governing bodies.

Climate

Among the types of climate that are common to Switzerland, the weather in Basel is considered particularly pleasant. The surrounding hills protect it, and at the same time, warmer and more humid winds than those from the continent reach it from the direction of the Atlantic Ocean.

The average temperatures are approximately 0°C in Jan., 15°C in May, up to 20°C in the summer and 14°C in Sept. The annual average is 10°C.

The annual volume of precipitation comes to 32 inches, and on average there are 145 days of rain, some 30 days of snow and 1,700 hours of sunshine a year.

Getting There

It is easy to get to Basel, as it is an important European crossroads. *Autostradas* lead to it within Switzerland from Bern (60 miles), from Zürich (50 miles) and from Luzern (62 miles). From Germany, the *autostradas* come through Karlsruhe and Fribourg; from France, through Strasbourg and Mulhouse, or Besançon and Belfort.

There are three international railway stations in the city: the **German Station** (DB), telephone for information and ticket reservation, Tel. 691.55.11; the **French Station** (SNCF), Tel. 271.50.33 and the **Swiss Station** (SBB), Tel. 157.33.33. This extremely unusual arrangement stems from the unique location of the city on the border of the three countries.

The **Basel-Mulhouse Airport**, serving Basel, is located on the French side of the border, which has, of course, an extra-territorial Swiss area. Daily flights arrive here from many Swiss and European cities, including Amsterdam, Berlin, Brussels, London, Paris, Rome, Vienna, Zürich and Geneva. A special bus service connects the airport and the city. Tel. 325.48.48.

City Transportation

Basel has a good network of public transportation lines, including trolleys and buses. It has special routes serving the suburbs, port and tourist sights in the vicinity of the city. At every stop a clear, detailed map of the various lines is displayed, making it easy to plan your trip alternative stations if necessary.

At every station there is also a ticket machine. Prepare yourself with the correct change and select your destination on the map by pressing the button next to the station on the list; the amount required will then appear. Put the coins into the slot (the green machines require exact change; the orange ones give change). Save the ticket until the end of the ride – you don't need to punch it or show it to anyone unless an inspector asks for it. If you make an error in the process, press the button which says *Irrtum* and your money will be returned. Daily cards for public transport are available at the hotel reception desks. Caution! A fine is charged to anyone caught traveling without a ticket.

It is possible to purchase a daily pass, which relieves you of the trouble of buying a separate ticket for every trip. You can buy this pass from the machine at the ticket

offices of the local public transportation company (BVB), as well as in some kiosks. After you first put the ticket in one of the machines, you don't have to punch it again and can travel on all lines within the city for 24 hours.

Another possibility is to purchase the *Regio* ticket (*Regio Billet*), which lets you travel free for a full day on the buses, trolleys and trains in the city and the surrounding area, a total of 460 miles of transportation lines. Further details are available at the public transportation stations at Barfüsserplatz (6:30am-7pm) either at the main train station, or by calling Tel. 267.89.91, 281.77.41.

TAXI

Taxis can be stopped on the street in the city, or ordered by phone:

Mini Cab: Tel. 271.11.11.
Taxi AG: Tel. 633.33.33
Taxi Zentrale: Tel. 271.22.22.

CAR RENTAL

The following companies offer car rental services:

Europcar: 48 Hochstcasse,
Tel. 155.40.40.
Eurorent: 145 Gartenstrasse,
Tel. 271.22.86.

Accommodation

The hotels in Basel are concentrated more or less in three areas according to the type of guests they cater to. For the sake of those staying in the city in transit, there is a large group of hotels near the train station. For business people visiting fairs and factories, there is another hotel area in the northern part of the city, near the exhibition center. And for tourists, there are many hotels located in the area of the Old Quarter.

The following is a selection of hotels. On the street corners in the city are brown and yellow signs, with the names of the hotels and arrows directing you to them.

FIVE-STAR HOTELS
Basel Hilton: 31 Aeschengraben, Tel. 271.66.22, fax 271.52.20. Located near the Swiss train station.

Drei Könige am Rhein: 8 Blumenrain,Tel. 261.52.52, fax 261.21.53. In the Old City, on the banks of the Rhine.

Le Plaza: 45 Riehenring, Tel. 692.33.33, fax 691.56.33. Located between the convention center and the exhibition center, in the northern part of the city.

FOUR-STAR HOTELS
Basel: 12 Münzgasse, Tel. 261.24.23, fax 261.25.95. In the heart of the Old City, near the market square (Marktplatz).

Europe: 43 Clarastrasse, Tel. 691.80.80, fax 691.82.01. Near the convention center and the exhibition center.

Victoria am Bahnhof: 3 Centralbahnplatz,Tel. 271.55.66, fax 271.55.01. In the square opposite the Swiss train station.

THREE-STAR HOTELS
Spalenbrunnen: 2 Schützenmattstr., Tel. 261.82.33, fax 261.00.37.

Du Commerce: 91 Rieheuring, Tel. 691.96.66, fax 691.96.75.

Admiral: 5 Rosentalstrasse, Tel. 691.77.77, fax 691.77.89. Near the exhibition center, in the northern part of the city.

TWO-STAR HOTELS
Bristol: 15 Centralbahnstrasse, Tel. 271.38.22, fax 271.38.45. Near the Swiss train station.

Rochat: 23 Petersgraben, Tel. 261.81.40, fax 261.64.92. On the northwestern side of the Old City.

ONE-STAR HOTELS
Hecht am Rhein: 8 Rheingasse, Tel. 691.22.20, fax 681.07.88. On the northern bank of the Rhine, near the Mittlere Brücke Bridge.

Steinenschanze: 69 Steinengraben, Tel. 272.53.53, fax 272.45.73.

YOUTH HOSTELS
Jugendherberge: 10 St. Alban Kirchrain, Tel. 272.09.72. West of the Old City, near the southern bank of the Rhine. One of the largest youth hostels in Switzerland. The doors close in the summer at 12:30am, in the winter at 11:30pm. The reception office operates daily 9:30am-4pm. The hostel is closed every year from Dec. 24-Jan. 2. Trolley 3.

CAMPING

Camping Waldhort: Tel. 711.64.29. At Reinach, some six miles south of the city, near the Basel-Delémont Road (18). Open from Mar. 15-Oct. 18.

For more information contact the Camping and Caravan Club: 4 Steinenschanze, Tel. 271.34.76.

Restaurants

Basel is a large city and its many restaurants offer a wide variety of dishes. The following list concentrates on restaurants serving local dishes, but those seeking a familiar menu can even find American-style fast food outlets in the city.

Schützenhaus: 56 Schützenmattstrasse, Tel. 272.67.60. An historic restaurant, with a tradition (at least, so its owners say) going back 400 years. An international and Swiss menu, specializing in local and regional dishes such as *Herrenschnitzel* (veal with smoked ham and goose liver). A real institution in Basel. Open all week to 11pm. Bus 33 or Trolley 18.

St. Wirtshaus Jakob: 377 St. Jakobsstrasse, Tel. 311.72.97. A very old restaurant, close to the football stadium. Specializes in pork dishes such as chops with sauerkraut and fish. Open daily to 10pm. Trolley 14.

Brauner Mutz: 10 Barfüsserplatz, Tel. 261.33.69. A typical Basel restaurant, and a well-known meeting place for beer guzzlers. Soup, pork chops, cheeses, salads, good for snacks as well as meals. Open daily to 11:30pm. Trolleys 1, 3, 15, 16.

Safran Zunft: 11 Gerbergasse, Tel. 261.19.59. This historic meeting place near Marktplatz. serves traditional local Swiss cuisine. The house specialty is Fondue Bacchus. Open daily to 11:30pm, closed Sun. Trolleys 1, 8, 14, 15, 16.

Löwenzorn: 2-4 Gemsberg, Tel. 261.42.13. An inn from the good old days, near Marktplatz, with a marvelous garden for summer days, specializing in roasted meat, including the traditional Rôsti. Open daily to 11:30pm, closed Sun. Trolleys 1, 8, 14, 15, 16.

Gasthof Zum Goldenen Sternen: 70 St. Alban Rheinweg, Tel. 272.16.66. A fish and seafood restaurant, located on the Rhine, in an historic early 16th-century building, which has been renovated from top to bottom, while preserving its ancient charm. This is the place for lovers of snails (escargots). Open daily until late.

St. Alban-Stübli: 74 St. Alban Vorstadt, Tel. 272.54.15. A meeting-place for artists and craftsmen near the art museum, basic food and reasonable prices. Excellent schnitzel and meat patties. Closed Sun. Trolley 2. Open daily till 11pm.

Organized Tours

Bus Tour of the City: An interesting way to get around on your own, a tour leaves daily at 10am sharp, from the square near the main train station, next to the Victoria Hotel. The tour, accompanied by explanations in English, French and German, lasts 1 hour and 45 minutes. Tickets can be purchased from the driver or at the hotels. The tour usually takes you to the observation point at the city port known as the **Corner of the Three Countries**. There, from a large balcony on which a missile-like monument (Dreiländereck) stands, you can see three countries at once: Switzerland, France and Germany.

Tour of the Municipality: This is an opportunity to see the delightful Basel municipality from the inside, and to hear folk stories and a little history about the place. Explanations in English, French and German. May 13-Oct. 7, every Wed. Meet at the entrance to the building at 3pm. The tour lasts an hour and a half.

Trip to the Black Forest: A visit to the famous Schwarzwald, with its beautiful scenery, located on the other side of the German border, leaves every Friday at 1:15pm from the square opposite the main train station, next to the Victoria Hotel. Returns to the same place at about 6:30pm. Trips on the Rhine in a riverboat are also available.

It is best to consult the Municipal Tourist Office for exact departure points and time-tables since changes may occur. Tel. 261.50.50.

Important Phone Numbers

Area code: Tel. 061.
Tourist office: 5 Schifflände, Tel. 261.50.50, fax 261.59.44.
Basel/ Mulhouse Airport: Tel. 325.48.88.
Train station (Swiss): Tel. 272.67.67.
Train station (German): Tel. 690.14.96.
Train station (French): Tel. 271.50.32.
Police: Tel. 117.
Cantonal hospital: Tel. 265.25.25.
First aid: Tel. 251515.
Lost and Found: Tel. 251717.

Walking Tours

The city of Basel is filled with numerous interesting and exciting museums, some of which we have included in our tour. The visitor to Basel can obtain a Museum-pass which admits him free of charge to most museums within 3 days. The Museum-pass can be purchased at the Tourist Office and at the City Information Office at the Railway Station.

From the City to the Cathedral and the Rhine

We begin our tour at **Barfüsserplatz**, a central square in the southeastern part of the Old City, which you can get to on Trolleys 1, 3, 6, 8, 14, 15, 16 or 18. In the eastern plaza of the square there are open-air markets, which change from time to time. These include markets of clothing, jewelry, toys, antiques, sweets and more. Sometimes two markets are combined. Craftsmen and artists bring their wares to the stands, and you can occasionally find a bargain.

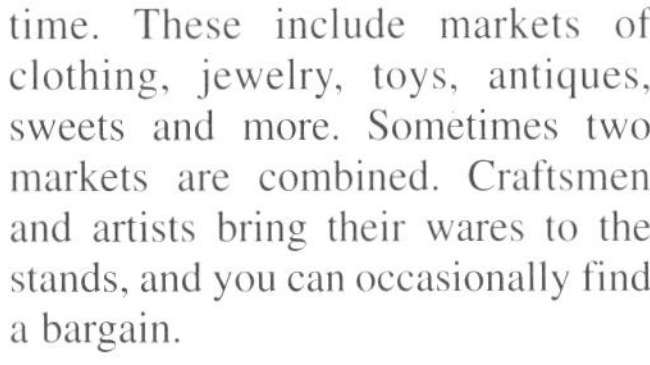

On the other side of the market plaza is the **Museum of History** (Historisches Museum), located in an early 14th-century building that once served as a Franciscan church. Open daily 10am-5pm, closed Tues. Tel. 271.05.05. Admission fee.

This museum presents you with part of the history of Basel and its cultural development. The museum building, a former church, is also an impressive example of the construction of the Franciscan monks. The restrained and economical architecture is based on the order's view of the world.

In the basement is a step-by-step explanation of the history of Basel from the Celtic period, with exhibits and original documents. The exhibits include Roman statues, ceramics from the 5th-7th centuries found in burial sites in the area, and rooms filled with furniture from the 15th-17th centuries.

Next to the entrance, is one of the museum's basement treasures, "King Lally", the famous "tongue king". This is a small, mid-17th century statue, one foot high, that moves its eyes and tongue. Legend has it that it was designed to make fun of the residents of the City of Basel.

In what was once the central hall of the church are furniture and objects brought from the city's cathedral, as well as sculptures and fountain pillars from the Middle Ages. In the "treasury hall" you can view precious objects from the 17th-century Ammerbach Collection, the first museum in the world to be open to the public. In the southern part of the hall there are colorful tapestries, for which the textile industry of Basel was famous.

The upper gallery contains exhibits from the cathedral. Among the most impressive is a gold figurine of King David, made in 1320, and a silver and gold bust of St. Ursula, which the city commissioned in 1300 to encase her holy remains.

At the exit from the museum to the square, in the left-hand corner, is Basel's **Casino**. This is where the First Zionist Congress was held; a plaque, in German and Hebrew, notes the event. The building, with a pleasant open café facing the square, serves as a concert and performance hall, with 1,500 seats.

A picturesque alley in Basel

Turn left from the square to Steinenberg St., which leads to the new theater square of Basel, built on the location of the city's old theater. The theater has some 1,200 seats. Plays, operas and other performances are held here. In front of the theater is the famous **fountain by Jean Tinguely**. Since its installation in 1977, it has become one of the new symbols of Basel.

Down Steinenberg St., at No. 7, is the **City Gallery of Art** (Kuntshalle), where changing local and international exhibitions are shown. Open Tues.-Sun. 11am-5pm, Wed. till 8:30pm. Tel. 272.48.33. Further on the road leads left to a wide promenade, **Freie Strasse**, a large prestigious shopping area where there are many wonderful stores. North of the square is St. Alban Graben St. where there are two important museums. At No. 5 is the **Museum of Ancient Art** (Antikenmuseum), which was recently renovated and reopened to the public in late 1987. You can visit Tues.-Sun. 10am-5pm, closed Mon. Tel. 271.22.02. Admission fee.

This is the only museum in Switzerland devoted entirely to classical ancient art: Etruscan, Greek and Roman works, mainly from the year 1000 BC to 300 AD. There are also earlier works, from the civilizations of the Aegean Sea from 2700 to 1500 BC.

One of the museum's best known works is the head of the Goddess Athena, crowned with a helmet, made of marble from circa. 430 BC. You can also see painted plates and vessels, some of which are preserved extraordinarily well, with mythological images (such as the story of Theseus and Ariadne, on a huge pitcher) and daily scenes of ancient Greece, as well as part of a stone relief, from about 480 BC, known as *The Doctor of Basel*, showing a bearded physician sitting on a chair with cupping glasses next to him.

Basel's Cathedral – built from pink sandstone

At 16 St. Alban-Graben St. is the **Museum of Fine Art** (Kunstmuseum), a "must" for every visitor. Open Tues.-Sun. 10am-5pm, closed Mon. Tel. 271.08.28. Admission fee.

Under the impressive arches of the building, which was constructed from 1932 to 1936, the entrance leads into a square courtyard, in the center of which stands the work of the French sculptor, Auguste Rodin, *The Bourghers of Calais*.

Halls 1 to 15 are devoted to a comprehensive exhibit, unmatched in scope, of the group of artists known as the Upper Rhine painters, from 1400-1600. The most outstanding of these are the senior Hölbein and his two sons, Ambrose Hölbein and Hans Hölbein the younger. The masterpiece of the latter, *The Artist's Wife and Two Children* (1528) is a beautiful, joyous work. Many other artists are represented in this wing: Konrad Witz, a resident of Basel in the first half of the 15th century, Martin Schongauer, Niklaus Manuel Deutsch of Bern and others.

"The Bourghers of Calais" – a sculpture by Auguste Rodin on exhibit at the Museum of Fine Art

Halls 16 to 21 contain exhibits of the 17th-century Dutch and Flemish artists. Topping the list, of course, is Rembrandt, and here you can see his work, *David with Goliath's Head, Facing Saul*, which was one of the artist's firsts, created in 1627 when he was 21 years old.

Halls 22 to 25 focus on the work of Swiss and German artists, mainly from the 18th and 19th centuries, including Hodler and Arnold Böcklin. The museum has 60 of Böcklin's paintings and 115 of his drawings, sculptures and sketches. It is the most comprehensive collection of this artist's work (one of his most famous is *Ulysses and Calypso*, created in 1883).

In halls 27 to 33 hang the work of many well-known artists from the Romantic to the impressionist period: Delacroix, du Maurier, Manet, Courbet, Monet, Sisley, Pissaro, Renoir, Cezanne (including 150 drawings from 5 of his notebooks), Van Gogh and Gauguin.

The second floor of the museum is devoted entirely to 20th-century art. Visitors are given the pleasure of viewing works of Pablo Picasso and Georges Braque. Also presented here are Soutine, Chagall, Dali, Miro, Klee, Max Ernst and Kandinsky.

Upon leaving the museum, go to the square on the right and take Rittergasse, the street that runs to the left, to a long rectangular plaza surrounded by houses, the **Cathedral Square** of the city of Basel, **Münsterplatz**.

Over the years several churches have stood at this location, but in the 11th century, when the bishop (the church prince) gained power over the city, planning began for a cathedral that would reflect the city's importance. Construction began only at the end of the 12th century. It was built in pink sandstone in the Romanesque style. In the late 13th century, two Gothic towers, as well as the main entrance, were added. The massive earthquake of 1356 brought ruin and destruction to the entire area and the cathedral suffered serious damage. Restoration work continued until about 1500 and the cathedral became a Protestant house of worship when the Reformation came to Basel in 1529. It has since been renovated twice, in the 19th century and in 1975.

The Cathedral is open to visitors in the summer Mon.-Fri. 10am-6pm; it closes on Sat. at noon-2pm; open Sun. from 11:30am. In the winter it is open weekdays 10am-noon and 2pm-4pm. You can climb up into the tower where there is a view of the landscape (admission fee).

Inside the cathedral you should take a look at the segments of a 13th-century fresco, uncovered in its northern corner, close to the entrance to what was once a basement and burial area. Close by is the magnificent tomb of Queen Anna of Hapsburg and her infant son Karl.

Leave the cathedral, and turn around to the right, to the balcony garden called **Pfalz** (as the bishop's palace was once called), located in the shade of the roof of the cathedral which is decorated like a snake skin, in diamond shapes. From the balcony is a view of the Rhine, beyond it the northern part of Basel and on the horizon the

Youngsters admiring some interesting artifacts at the Museum of Ethnology

Schwarzwald Mountains. It is definitely a good spot for a short rest.

After your rest, go back to the Cathedral Square. On the northern side of the square (at No. 8) is the city's puppet theater. On the other side of the square is **Zum Issak**, a theater café. The exit from the square to the west leads to a lovely street, **Augustinergasse**. No. 2 houses three museums under one roof: the **Swiss Museum of Folklore**, the **Museum of Natural History**, and best of all, the **Museum of Ethnography** (Museum für Vülkerkunde). Open Tues.-Sun. 10am-5pm. Closed Mon. Tel. 266.55.00. Admission fee.

Exhibits at the Museum of Natural History

The ethnographic collection began in the 14th century when merchants, missionaries and travelers from Basel returned home with souvenirs, which they used to illustrate the tales of their travels. The souvenirs were usually folk art, precious items, household implements and ritual objects from various primitive cultures. These are now exhibited in the Museum of Ethnography, and are unique since their places of origin have long since disappeared.

The impressive building housing all this was built in 1849 by the Basel architect of widespread reputation in his time, Melchior Berri.

Some 150,000 items fill the museum. Approximately 30,000 of them come from Oceania, and it is one of the major collections in the world on this subject. It includes wooden statues and paintings on palm leaves from Papua, New Guinea, pictures on cloth and masks from Bali, Java, the Indonesian islands, Malaysia and more. In other halls there are exhibits of mummies and coffins from ancient Egypt, as well as weapons, totems, ceramics from South America, trinkets from India, ritual objects from Africa, and more.

In the rooms devoted to nature, visitors can see stuffed animals (contemporary animals and reconstructions of extinct prehistoric creatures), insects, sea and lake creatures, minerals and fossils. If you have been to a natural history museum in any other large city, you will not find anything particularly different here, but if you are an enthusiast of this subject, the more you see, the better.

The part of the building that serves as the Swiss Museum of Folklore and Folk Art contains a delightful exhibit of scenes of the day-to-day life of farmers, residents of the mountain areas and others, created through paintings and various objects. Most of the exhibits are from Switzerland, but there are some from elsewhere in Europe, and some that have been influenced by the Swiss culture. There is an impressive collection of ploughs, household implements, ceramics (most outstanding are those from Switzerland and Romania), decorated Easter eggs, folk masks, toys, jewelry, fabric and embroidery and weaving tools. Exhibitions devoted to different themes are held every season.

When you leave the museum, turn left on Augustinergasse, which becomes Rheinsprung, a charming narrow street, most of whose houses are from the 15th and 16th centuries. To the right the street overlooks the Rhine. No. 11 was formerly the first faculty of the University of Basel, founded in 1460. Turn left to **St. Martin's Church** (Martinskirche), which is apparently the oldest community church in the city. It is mentioned in documents from as early as 1288, and it was renovated in the second half of the 14th century, after the earthquake of 1356. The church is generally closed to visitors.

In the narrow plaza in front of the church is a fountain with a statue of a warrior designed by Hans Tobell in the mid-16th century.

Go back to Rheinsprung St., and turn right to Shifflände, the ancient mooring point of the city. Here, in the corner building on the bank of the Rhine, is the city's tourist office. This is also the location of the **Middle Bridge** (Mittelere Brücke), which was first built as a wooden bridge in 1225, and was rebuilt from stone at the beginning of this century, while preserving the small capella from 1478 in its center. At the northern end of the bridge, in the right-hand corner, is a well-known local institution, the charming **Café Spitz**, established in 1383 and splendidly renovated in the late 1960's. In front of the café are steps leading down to the bank of the Rhine. Here is the **Oberer Rheinweg**, a **promenade** on the riverbank with a marvelous view overlooking

A statue on Middle Bridge

the old city on the other side and the towers of the cathedral. On the promenade itself, outside the 19th-century buildings, are benches, shady trees and the ferry.

The **ferry** here is unique and, at first encounter, very amusing. The boat, tied to a cable pulled across the river, makes its way to the other side and back again, pulled by the current of the river. You can take it to the spot under the balcony garden of the cathedral (afternoon break from noon-1:30pm, does not operate on Fri.). Further down the promenade, on the left, is the **Waisenhaus**, an orphanage with a 13th-century wall surrounding the garden and a tower in the corner. Return to the city via Wettsteinbrücke, the large bridge constructed 1877-1879.

SITES NEAR THE ROUTE

To the right of the square next to the Museum of Art is a street that leads to the St. Alban Quarter (you can get there directly on Trolley No. 3). This is St. Alban Vorstadt, which takes you to St. Alban's Monastery. In 1083 the monks of Cluni built a monastery here, outside the walls of the city of the time. In 1480 the building was enlarged and the church was added, but after the Reformation it was abandoned. Religious activity was renewed here in 1845; it is closed to visitors most of the time.

The road ends at **St. Alban's Gate**, originally built as part of the city walls at the end of the 13th century. In 1871 most of the fortifications and cannon posts around the gate were destroyed, and replaced by a park.

St. Alban-Tal St. leads from the park to the river. There, at No. 37, is the **Museum of Paper and Printing** (Papiermuseum). Tel. 272.96.52. Open Tues.-Sun. 2pm-5pm, closed Mon. Admission fee.

The location of this museum in the city of Basel, historically a center of printing and publishing, is only natural. The water mill and wheel for producing paper, run by the river current, were constructed in the Middle Ages and recently renovated. The exhibit here includes tools and equipment used in different periods for paper pro-

At the Museum of Paper and Printing

duction, printing and bookbinding. In the museum the work of the typesetter, the printer and the press operator are demonstrated.

Further down the St. Alban Rheinweg Promenade in the direction of the city, at house No. 60, is the **Museum of Contemporary Art** (Museum für Gegenwartskunst). Tel. 272.81.83. Open Tues.-Sun. 11am-5pm. Admission fee.

The museum buildings, originally a 19th-century industrial plant, now house works of art from the 1960's on, representing the modern schools – minimalism, conceptualism and others. There are works by some outstanding contemporary artists such as Frank Stella, Bruce Nauman, Carl André and Donald Judd.

The point where Mittelere Brücke Bridge meets the northern bank is the beginning of Greifengasse St., leading to **Claraplatz**, the central square in the northern section of Basel. This is the district of nightclubs, bars and burlesque shows. During the day it is a lively shopping area.

Return to the end of the bridge, turn west and continue with the Unterer Rheinweg Promenade to No. 26, home of the City **Museum** and the **Cathedral**. Tel. 267.66.42. Open Tues.-Sat. from 2pm-5pm, Sun. 10am-5pm. Admission fee.

In what remains of the 13th-century Dominican monastery, you will find an exhibit of statues and reliefs, in wood and stone, from the city's cathedral. There are also halls here devoted to the history of the city and its development, as well as rotating exhibits on these subjects.

From St. Alban-Graben St., go south on Elisabethenstrasse. Here, at No. 27, is the 18th-century **Kirschgarten Palace**, which houses part of the Museum of History. Open Nov.-Apr., Tues.-Sun. 10am-noon and 2pm-5pm; May-Oct., Tues.-Sun. 10am-5pm. Tel. 271.13.33. Admission fee, free on Sun.

This palace was built in 1775 for the wealthy silk manufacturer, Johan Rudolph Burckhardt-De Barg. Since 1951 the building has contained the 18th and 19th-century exhibits of the Museum of History. Here you can wander through dozens of rooms furnished and decorated in baroque, Louis XVI and other styles. On the ground floor is an exhibit of clocks, some dating back to the 16th century. There is an impressive collection of porcelain dishes and figurines as well. In the palace basement one can see carved wine barrels from the 18th century, the largest of which can hold 2,500 gallons. The museum also contains a collection of ancient scientific instruments that were used by researchers in the 18th and 19th centuries.

Elected Public Officials and Market Merchants

This walk begins at the **Market Square** (Marktplatz), the very heart of the Old City. You can get to the square by public transportation on lines 1, 6, 8, 14 and 15. The square is the site of the fruit, vegetable, spices and flower market, held daily from 7am-noon. Twice a month, on the second and fourth Wed. of every month, a flea market is held here. On the first and third Wed. of every month there is an open-air clothes market (both are in the afternoon).

In general, shopping is done in the square and around it. In the local cafés you can rest and have a drink, and in the many restaurants and inns in the area you can eat to your heart's content. The lovely houses, some of which were built in Art Nouveau style, provide a special context for the lively activity in the square. The best of them all is the ancient building of the City-Government Hall of Basel, the **Rathaus**.

The main part of the structure, with three arches in the front, is the oldest, built between 1508 and 1514 by the city architect of the time, Jerg Rouber. In the early 17th century the building was renovated, and in the last two years of the 19th century the part on the left and the tower on the right side of the building were added. In the gust of renovations, wall paintings by Hans Holbein were unfortunately lost. On the other hand, the 17th-century murals on the wall of the inner courtyard, and even a statue from the 16th century of the ancient founder of the city, Munatius Plancus, were preserved.

The guided tour held here (see Introduction on Basel) provides the opportunity to peek into some of the halls and rooms of the building, including the meeting room of the cantonal council, with its splendid decor, including wood carvings, stained glass with the symbols of the various cantons and antique furniture. Each object has a story behind it. Here's one: An Italian carpenter came to Basel in the 17th century, married the widow of a local carpenter and asked to join the guild of his fellow craftsmen. As an "entrance fee" he was required to make a carved wooden table; this is the beautifully decorated table that stands in the entrance hall, in the southeast corner of the second floor.

Marktgasse, on the northwestern corner of the square, takes you to its sister square, **Fish Market Square** (Fischmarktplatz). The fountain here is adorned by a statue of Holy Mary and the saints Peter and Paul. The original statue, made in 1390, is now in the Museum of History; the one on the street is an exact replica.

The entrance to the Museum of Applied Arts

Turn south from the square on Stadthausgasse. The street forks and continues to Schneidergasse and Spalenberg Sts., which house a wide selection of shops selling antique books, ornaments and trinkets, new and old alike. But before you get there, turn right, to *Totengässlein* (the Lane of the Dead). Here, at house No. 3, stands the **Museum of the History of Pharmacy** (Pharmazie-Historisches Museum).

The Market Square at the very heart of the Old City

Open Mon.-Fri. 9am-noon and 2pm-5pm. Free admission.

Basel is an international center of the pharmaceutical industry and maintains this lovely corner as a salute to the history of pharmacy. The museum exhibits various tools for preparing medicines and cures from the Middle Ages on, a large collection of bottles used by pharmacists, various documents, prescriptions and an 18th-century laboratory reconstructed with all its equipment. It is a real treat for hypochondriacs! Also amusing is the mobile pharmacy, which the pharmacist would take on trips to the mountains and villages to distribute medicines.

At the other end of the narrow lane with the cheerful name you come to Nadelberg St., and **Peter's Church** (Peterskirche). There was already a prayer house here as early as the ninth century, according to ancient texts. However, the oldest parts that we find today were constructed in the 13th century out of pink sandstone. The main hall was completed near the end of the 14th century. The present church tower was built in 1430. Inside the church are well-preserved wall paintings from the 14th century, depicting events in the life and death of Jesus. The church is usually open to visitors Sun.-Thur. 10am-4pm. West of the church, from the other side of Petersgraben st., is the Green Square, **Petersplatz**, a very old spot in Basel designed for mass celebrations, which was given its present design in the late 18th century. On Saturdays the best flea market in the city is held here. On your visit to the market take care – you need a keen eye to distinguish between real and fake "antiques".

Turn south from the square on Petersgraben and continue until it meets Spalenvorstadt St. At this corner is the **Museum of Applied Arts** (Gewerbemuseum). Tel. 261.30.06. Open Tues.-Fri. noon-7pm, Sat.-Sun. noon-5pm. Admission fee. The museum contains collections representing the work of various artisans (bookbinding, leather crafts, carpentry, silk work and more), showing the development of techniques and industries as well as graphic art, design and decoration. There is also a major library here, with more than 100,000 books on these subjects.

Continue on Spalenvorstadt St. east to the square where the St. meets Schützenmattstrasse on the left. Here is the **Holbein Fountain** (Holbeinbrunnen), erected in the 16th century. The figure of the *bagpiper* was inspired by Duhrer's etching and the farmer's dance by Holbein's painting.

Continuing, we come to one of the symbols of Basel – the **Spalentor**, a fantastic, impressive gate in the wall, built along with the other fortifications of the city in the 14th century. The gate stands on the road leading to Basel from Alsace. The two jagged towers and the pointed turret covered with tiles in the center were renovated in the 19th century.

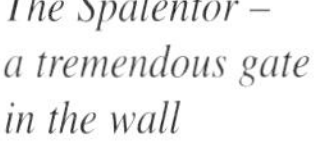

The Spalentor – a tremendous gate in the wall

SITES NEAR THE ROUTE

At the intersection of Petersgraben and Spalenvorstadt Sts., near the end of the walk, is Kornhausgasse, where at No. 8 stands the **Jewish Museum of Switzerland** (Jüdisches Museum der Schweiz); Tel. 261.95.14. Open Mon. and Wed., 2-5pm, Sun. 10-noon and 2-5pm. Free admission. This is a relatively small museum, but the only one of its kind in Switzerland. In the museum contains documents, certificates and religious objects, as well as some ancient Judaica. Special emphasis is placed on the history of the Jewish community in Basel, and on the Hebrew book, retelling the special role of the city in printing and publishing.

A Torah Scroll at the Jewish Museum of Switzerland

Near the Jewish Museum, at No. 18 on the same street, is the **Swiss Fire Brigade Museum** (Feuerwehrmuseum). Tel. 272.22.00 Every Sun., from 2pm-5pm, fire fighters and other curious individuals come here to examine an exhibit of documents and equipment, from the first water pumps to closed circuit fire-fighting apparatus. Free admission.

From the other side of the Spalentor, Missionsstrasse runs west. No. 28 houses the **Swiss Museum of Sports** (Schweizerishes Sportmuseum). Tel. 261.12.21. Open Mon.-Fri., Sun. 10-noon and 2-5pm.; Sat. only in the afternoons. Free admission.

This is the home of the history of all types of sports. The building is handsome, but too small to hold the entire collection, therefore the public is presented with only a small part of the tens of thousands of objects it possesses. The rest of the collection is presented in rotating exhibitions, next to the permanent exhibit. There is a special collection of bicycles, from 1820 on, as well as an impressive collection of equipment for different ball games, and accessories of the national sport of the German cantons – *Hornuss* – a game in which the teams lift their defenders on high poles to stop the ball in flight. There is also a large library related to the history of sport open to visitors.

The Zoo: Anyone who comes to Basel should visit the city's zoo, known throughout Europe as one of the most beautiful and best of its kind. You can get to the zoo, located half a mile west of the main train station, on Trolley 7 or Bus 36, 37.

The zoo is open all week 8am-6pm, continuously. Tel. 295.53.53. Admission fee. Inside the zoo, to the right of the entrance, is a self-service café-restaurant for snacks, drinks and a rest.

At the Zoo in Basel

Founded in 1874 by the Basel Society for the Study of Birds, it now has almost 6,000 animals from all over the world.

This zoo is known for its success in cultivating and protecting rare animals, such as the spectacled bear and the shelled rhino from Asia, monkeys from Java, different types of gorillas and dwarf hippopotamuses.

A Journey To the Roman Past

Augusta Raurica is the first stop in the history of Basel. This was the first Roman colony established on the Rhine by Montius Plancus, friend of Julius Caesar, in the year 44 BC. By the second century BC, the colony had already become an important trading city, with some 20,000 residents. Public buildings, cultural institutions and luxurious palaces were built here, and it was a lively place, until it was conquered and destroyed in 260 by Allmannic tribes. The ruins left from that period make a visit to this site well worthwhile.

There are several ways to get here from Basel: by train – from the main train station to Kaiseraugst, and from there by foot, about ten minutes to the center of the site; by bus – on line 70 from Aeschenplatze, almost half a mile northeast of the main train station; by boat – from the Shiffland dock, near Mittlere Brücke, on boats leaving several times a day, June-Sept. (May- Oct., Sun.,

Tues., Wed. and Thurs. only); or by car – along the *autostrada* going east; get off at the exit marked "Augst," and continue about 10 km, to the sign of "Augusta Raurica."

WHAT TO SEE AT THE SITE

The theater, in the center of the ancient city, contained 8,000 seats in its prime. It has been accurately restored, and is used for concerts and performances.

The Schônbühl Temple (Schônbühltempel), situated opposite the theater, was built in the second century BC, on the site of the temple of the first Roman colony.

The forum was the public center of the city, the location of the temple to Jupiter, and later of a basilica. There is a huge, restored building here, with a basement full of mosaics. You can go down into the basement daily from 7:30am-5pm (Mar.-Nov.).

The tavern (taverne) was uncovered in the 1960's near the theater and restored, including its large impressive stove.

The **Roman Museum** and the **Roman Building** are also next to the theater, in the center of the site. Tel. 811.11.87. Open Tues.-Sun. 10-noon, 13:30-6pm; Mon. 13:30-6pm; Nov.-Feb. until 5pm. Admission fee. The museum contains an exhibit of the most lovely and interesting of the

500,000 objects found in the excavations of the Roman city. The highlight of the tour is a visit to the Roman Building, a faithful reconstruction of a residential and commercial building, including its contents: kitchen, bedroom, dining room, bathroom, work room and shop. Some of the items spread about the "house" are original and others are accurate reproductions.

In the treasury room (Silberschatz) of the museum is a display of the entire treasure discovered in the area in 1961, evidently a "safe" of one of the wealthy residents of Kaiseraugst, situated north of Augusta Raurica in the fourth century. Among other things, the treasure contained 68 luxurious pieces of tableware, including decorated plates, goblets and cutlery, as well as bars of metal, a figurine of the goddess Venus and 186 coins and medals.

KAISERAUGST

At the site of the fourth-century fortress are ruins of walls, some of which have been reconstructed. Nearby are the ruins of a baptism room; also from the fourth century. These are the oldest Christian remains in Switzerland. To the west is a bathhouse from the third century AD, with warm and cold baths, and a system for heating water.

The theater at Augusta Raurica – the first Roman colony established on the Rhine in the year 44

FROM LAUSANNE TO BERN

The route continues along the lake (N9); from the town of Vevey it turns northeast (N12) toward Fribourg. It is highly recommended that you pass up the turn to Bern for a while, and continue about six miles to Montreux and the Chillon Castle, before turning back.

VEVEY

This is Switzerland's historic city of chocolate. It is here that the sweet industry began to develop and here that the **Nestlé** concern has its headquarters. There is a museum set up by the firm to demonstrate the process of production, preservation, storage and so forth of foodstuffs. Another unusual museum in Vevey is devoted to an exhibit of photography equipment, cameras and all accessories from the late 19th century on.

MONTREUX

This town owes its reputation to Jean-Jacques Rousseau, who fell in love with the beautiful scenery, the bay and the special charm of the area. All these have also delighted the many tourists who come here to vacation and to enjoy the festivals held here, such as the international meeting of choral groups, held around April, and the jazz festival in the summer.

From Montreux there are several tours to the peaks of the mountains overlooking the large lake: **Naye Cliffs** (Rochers de Naye) – an exciting cable-car route (approx. 3 hours) climbs the cliffs, which reach a height of 6,500 ft. On the way, you pass two popular tourist sights – Gilion and Caux. The view from the cliffs is breathtaking and includes the Jura mountains to the west, the Bern mountains to the northeast, and Lake Léman and the Savoy Alps to the south.

LES PLÉIADES

This is a long trip (some 30 miles) to the north, to which the Les Avants mountain roads and observation points along the range may also be added (an additional 12 miles). A detailed map showing these routes is available at the tourist office.

CHILLON CASTLE (CHÂTEAU DE CHILLON)

Slightly south of Montreux (buses leave the city for the castle frequently), on a small rocky island near the bank of the lake stands one of the largest and most beautiful castles in Switzerland. This is

The ancient castle of Count Gruyères

a unique feudal fortress, the foundations of which were laid in the 10th century. The present fortress was built by Pierre II of Savoy, and was captured by the army of the canton of Bern in 1536. The soldiers freed the famous prisoner confined in the fortress, François Bonivard, whose attempt to introduce the Reformation had angered the Catholic Duke of Savoy. For four years, Bonivard was chained in the basement, and visitors are invited to see his footprints in the stone. The prisoner's story became famous after the 1816 visit of the English poet Lord Byron, who put his strong impressions into poetry. A tour through the castle is fascinating. Among the things you will see are underground tunnels that the Bernese army used for storing weapons, expansive halls, original furniture and more. For details about opening hours call Tel. (04) 963.39.11/12. Admission fee.

GRUYÈRES

Arguably, the most picturesque village in Europe, which gave its name to the famous cheese, Gruyères has become a tourist sight in its entirety, which somewhat detracts from its natural charm. Nevertheless, it is worth taking the lovely trip to the village, and visiting its central square and castle. This is the ancient castle of Count Gruyères, the feudal lord of the region in the 12th century. There is also a small wax museum here, with exhibits depicting scenes from Swiss history.

BULLE

A small town located not far from the *autostrada* to Bern, in the heart of the Gruyères region, Bulle is definitely worth a stop. On its main street you'll find stores selling the area's famous cheese, and this is generally a place where you should do some shopping: it is a completely different experience than in the big cities. There is also a museum in Bulle that attracts many curious visitors, and rightfully so. This is Musée Gruèrien, situated entirely underground, and devoted to an extraordinary review of the history of this special region told via archeological finds, antique furniture, household objects, work implements, weapons, costumes, folk art and more. The castle of Bulle was built in the 13th century by the bishop of Lausanne, and despite many renovations, it still retains its ancient beauty.

FRIBOURG

Capital of the canton of Fribourg, the city of the same name has 34,000 residents. It began in 1157 as a fortress built by Berchtold IV of Zähringen at a bend in the Sarine River. Due to its strategic location, the fortress changed hands again and again – from the Kyburgs to the Hapsburgs, followed by its conquest by Bern, and later by the Savoys. In 1481, the canton joined the confederation. It has remained a bastion of Roman Catholicism throughout, and in the late 19th century its status was further raised when the Catholic University of Switzerland was opened here.

Fribourg marks the border between French and German languages and cultures. The boundary is the Sarine River: on the left bank, the names are written in French; on the right, in German.

If you stop in Fribourg, walk through its Old City, which runs from St. Nicholas Cathedral to the bend in the river. The houses, the lanes and the small squares all bear the mark of the Middle Ages, and crossing the Zähringen Bridge (Pont de Zähringen) reveals the great steep banks that the river has cut into the stone.

BERN – THE SWISS HEART

The city of Bern lies in the heart of Switzerland. It is the capital of the Swiss Confederation and the location of the government offices, the Parliament, the National Bank and over 70 foreign embassies.

One of the neighborhoods across the Aare River

The most outstanding feature of the city is its arches. There are four miles of arches in the old center, which were once used as balconies and today are part of the street.

Another typical feature is the basements. There are usually two or three basement levels under the ground, once used as wine and food cellars, and now house shops, workshops, art galleries and cabarets. The record is held by a building north of the casino, which has seven basement levels. There are also many amazing street fountains from the 16th century.

In Bern's modern center is the ancient Bern, surrounded on three sides by the bend in the Aare River. The streets of this quarter are bustling; street artists, musicians, clowns, magicians and so forth. The cafés and restaurants are always crowded.

History

Even before the Roman rule there was a settlement. It was not large, and it was destroyed leaving no real trace. The city of Bern was established because of the need of the ruler of the area, the Duke Berchtold V of

Zähringen, to protect the western border of his territory. The year 1191 is generally noted as the date on which the duke commanded one of his high-ranking knights, Kuno von Bubenberg, to carry out this mission.

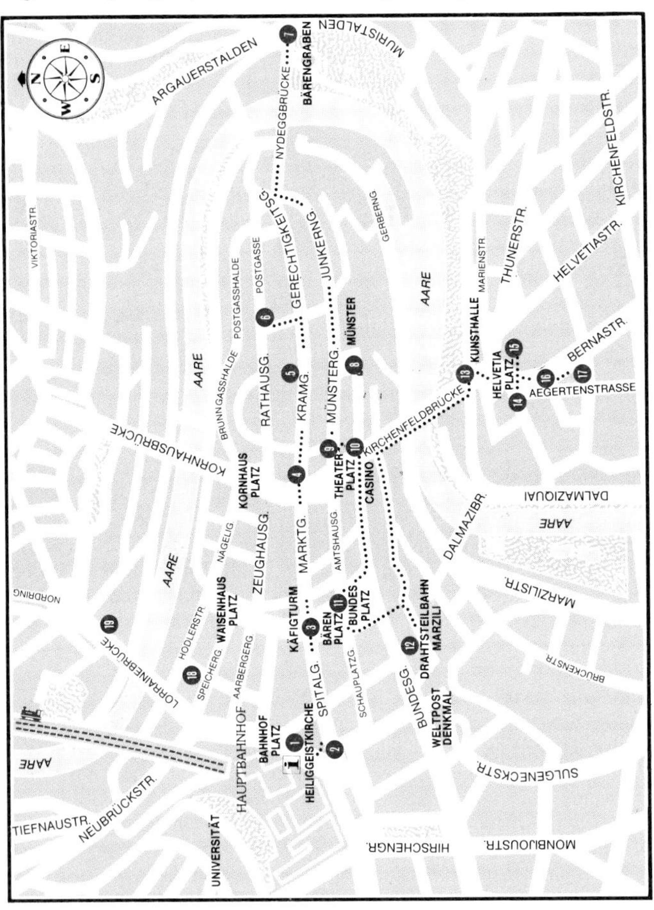

BERN

1. Train Station
2. Church of the Holy Spirit
3. Prison Tower
4. Clock Tower
5. Albert Einstein's House
6. Rathaus – Town Hall
7. Bear Pits
8. Cathedral Square
9. Theater
10. Casinoplatz
11. Federal Palace
12. Marzili Drahtseilbahn (cable car)
13. Gallery of Art
14. Alpine and Postal Museums
15. Museum of the History of Bern
16. Museum of Marksmen
17. Natural History Museum
18. Museum of Art
19. Botanical Gardens

The sharp turn in the Aare River provided a spot with good protection from three sides. At the time, the peninsula was dense with chestnut trees; these were cut down and used to build the first houses.

The first wall built to protect the "open" side of the city stood where today we find the clock tower, then the location of the central turret of the entrance gate. An old legend tells us that on the day that the new city was dedicated, the duke held a hunting party for his important guests. Spirits heightened with wine, he proclaimed to them all that the city would be named for the first animal to fall, whose image would also adorn the flag. And so it was: the first animal to be hit was a bear (Bär in German), so the city was named *Bärn* (Bern).

In the 13th century, under the rule of Count Pierre of Savoy, the city expanded westward. It was declared a royal city and its power and influence over the neighboring villages and settlements grew. Many merchants and craftsmen chose to settle here, and it assumed a crucial economic position in the region. The residents were then forced to break down the old wall and erect a new one at the line on which the prison tower now stands. But the new wall didn't give the city enough room either. Before long, the city had attracted so many new residents that in the 14th century the wall was moved again – this time to the present line of the railroad station. The city chronicles proudly recall that the construction of this third wall was completed in only a year and a half, a noteworthy engineering feat at the time.

The first major battle in which Bern was forced to defend its independence took place in 1339. The united knights of the Burgundy kingdom threatened the city, 900 fighters were called in from neighboring cantons to join the Bernese soldiers at the last minute and tipped the scales in favor of the city's army. This assistance, it seems, planted the seeds for cooperation between Bern and its neighbors. In 1353 Bern joined the Swiss federal union, although it continued to protect its independent interests.

In 1405, a terrible tragedy occurred in the city. A great fire broke out, destroying the great majority of the wooden houses which stood close together. When the residents began to restore and rebuild, they chose sand-

stone from the nearby quarries. The new houses were built exactly on the foundations of the houses that had burned, and were renovated or rebuilt again in the 16th and 17th centuries. These are actually the houses of today's Old City. The recovery after the fire was rapid and the building boom also gave birth to a wide project of conquests. In the 15th and 16th centuries, the Bernese army annexed the regions of Gruyères and Vaud, thus establishing Bern as the leading canton in the Swiss Federation.

In 1528, religious reform reached Bern. Its leaders, who had been chosen on behalf of the strong aristocratic families of the city, expropriated the property of the church and turned the city's cathedral into a Protestant house of worship. The civil government also took on the role of the church in taking care of the ill and the needy.

The city was twice shaken by uprisings against the ruling families. The first time was in the mid-17th century, when a rebellion erupted among the farmers of the area, and the second was in the mid-18th century, when the urban lower classes tried to gain greater rights and more influence over city matters. Both attempts at rebellion failed.

When Napoleon's armies conquered Switzerland in 1798, the city was also taken, and democratic law was introduced. This lasted until 1815, when the new Switzerland was born. Then, for some 15 years, the city returned to the rule of the aristocratic families. But times change, and after tasting democracy, the people were not willing to let the new-old situation continue. In 1831, a democratic constitution was again adopted in Bern. In that period, the power of the city declined, also because large sections of the territory of the canton Bern had been taken and had become the cantons of Vaud and Aargau.

In 1834 Bern joined the "educated cities." The Bernese University was established, and it quickly earned a respected reputation and attracted learned scholars and students from Switzerland and abroad. The university became known for a unique feature: a person who had not completed high school studies could nevertheless be admitted to doctorate studies. This attracted many students from Eastern Europe, at the turn of the present century. In 1848, with the centralization of the Swiss Federation, Bern was declared its capital, the seat of the government and a cultural and political crossroads – located at the center, between the German and French parts.

In the course of World War I, Bern attracted attention as a refuge for political exiles from Russia. Among the revolutionary leaders who found refuge there was Lenin, the father of the communist revolution in Russia, who lived there from 1914 to 1916.

In the last 50 years the city has gained strength and expanded, among other things because of the modern bridges built over the Aare, which make it possible to cross the river easily to the new neighborhoods established in the vicinity. Its industries – machinery, chocolate, metal, printing, textiles have all grown, as has tourism.

A General View

Bern, the capital of the Confederation, is also the capital of the canton of Bern, the second largest canton in the country. It is located in the middle-lands of the Aare River, which is the largest all-Swiss river, 190 miles long. Its location makes it an important crossroads between the Alps and the Jura, and Switzerland's railroad lines run through it.

The center of the city is spread over a plateau at an average height of over 1,500 ft.; hence the high bridges connecting the old city and the neighborhoods across the river. In terms of population, Bern is the fourth largest city in Switzerland, with approximately 138,000 residents, and some 300,000 counting the suburbs. With the exception of a small minority, most of the residents are Protestants and German-speakers. The city spreads over 20 sq. miles, a third of which is parks, groves and public gardens.

Climate

The climate in Bern is the "temperate" Swiss climate typical of the middle-lands. Some 40 inches of precipitation fall annually, and

A view of some of Bern's grand buildings, with the green domes of the Federal Palace to the left

there are about 1,700 hours of sunshine a year. The average annual temperatures are between 7°C and 9°C, and the differences between seasons are not generally very great: Mar. 4.1°C, May 12.7°C, July. 17.6°C, Sept. 13.6°C and Oct. 8.3°C.

Getting There

There are *autostradas* to Bern from Geneva, via Lausanne and Fribourg (100 miles); from Basel, via Olten and Solothurn (60 miles), and from Zurich, via Baden, Aarau and Olten (75 miles).

Rapid trains leave all the major cities for Bern frequently. From Zürich, for instance, there are about 25 trains a day; from 4:45am to 12am. From Geneva there are about 29 trains a day, the first at 4:50am, the last at 11pm. The **train station** in Bern is located right on the border of the Old City, a few minutes walk from the center, the shopping district and the hotels.

City Transportation

Bern has a great advantage for the visitor – most of its special places and treasures are located in the center, which is the size of a medieval city. In other words, it can be covered on foot. Nevertheless, there is a SVB network of buses and trolleys, serving the city and the neighboring vicinity.

The city's modern trolleys are very comfortable and very fast. All you have to do is keep coins in your pocket for the ticket machines in the stations. A clear and easy-to-use map is displayed next to the machine, showing you where you are now, where the lines go to and how much to pay according to a color code. It is most convenient to get on a trolley at the square outside the city's train station. Five different lines pass through here. Any place that the trolley doesn't get to, the buses do, and the system for finding your way around and for paying is the same. The tourist is also offered a convenient package deal, the Tourist Card,

for unlimited travel on all lines. Tickets may be purchased at the local tourist office in the city's train station.

TAXIS

You can call a taxi by phone (Tel. 311.18.18, 301.53.53), or hail one at the main stops, Casinoplatz and Waisenhausplatz .

PARKING FACILITIES

Covered parking with a charge (for an unlimited time):

Bellevue-Garage: Kochergasse, Tel. 311.77.76.
Metroparking: Waisenhausplatz, Tel. 311.44.11.
City West: Belpstrasse, Tel. 381.93.04.
Rathaus: Schüttestrasse, Tel. 311.13.66.

Free parking (for a limited time) can be found in Bundesplatz, Kochergasse, Casinoplatz, Bärengraben and Hodlerstrasse.

Accommodation

Visitors to Bern have a choice of over 40 hotels of different grades. In order to help you find the hotel of your choice, there are brown signs at intersections throughout the city, showing the names of the hotels and arrows directing you there. The following is a selection from the list of hotels, that are members of the local tourist office that are located in the center of the city, an important advantage. If no bus or trolley number is indicated next to the name of the hotel, it is within walking distance from the train station. The approximate prices

which include breakfast, service and taxes are: Five-star hotels – 220-320 francs for a single; 330-480 – francs for a double. Four stars – 140-220 francs for a single; 200-300 francs for a double. Three stars – 120-200 francs for a single; 150-250 francs for a double. Two stars – 80-170 francs for a single; 120-220 francs for a double. One star – 70-100 francs for a single; 90-150 francs for a double.

FIVE-STAR HOTELS

Bellevue-Palace: 3 Kochergasse, Tel. 320.45.45, fax 311.47.43.

Schweizerhof: 11 Bahnhofplatz, Tel. 311.45.01, fax 312.21.79.

FOUR-STAR HOTELS

Bären: 4 Schauplatzgasse, Tel. 311.33.67, fax 311.69.83.

Bristol: 10 Schauplatzgasse, Tel. 311.01.01, fax 311.9479.

THREE-STAR HOTELS

Krebs: 8 Genfergasse, Tel. 311.49.42, fax 311.1035.

Kreuz: 41 Zeughausgasse, Tel. 311.11.62, fax 311.3747.

Metropole: 28 Zeughausgasse, Tel. 311.50.21, fax 312.1153.

TWO-STAR HOTELS
Blocke: 75 Rathausgasse, Tel. 311.37.71, fax 311.10.08. Trolley 9.

Goldener Schlüssel: 72 Rathausgasse, Tel. 311.02.16, fax 311.56.88. Trolley 9.

Hospiz Zur Heimat: 50 Gerechtigkeitsgasse, Tel. 311.04.36, fax 311.33.86. Bus 12.

ONE-STAR HOTELS
Marthahaus: 22A Wyttenbachstrasse, Tel. 332.41.35. Located north of the city, across the river. Bus 20.

YOUTH HOSTELS
4 Weihergasse, Tel. 311.63.16. Bern's youth hostel is open all year round (with the exception of a short period at the end of Feb./beginning of Mar.). It is located behind the Federal Palace. The office is open Mon.- Sat. 7am-9:30am and 5pm-midnight, Sun. from 5:30pm.

CAMPING
Eichholz: Tel. 961.26.02. 2 miles southeast of the center of Bern, on the road to Belp. Open May-Sept.

Eymatt: Tel. 901.10.07. 3 miles northwest of the center, on the road to Wohlen. Open all year round.

Restaurants

When you are in Bern choose restaurants that serve typical local dishes. To suffice with a hamburger or a pizza is to miss out on one of Bern's greatest attractions.

The restaurants listed below, all specializing in local cuisine, are recommended.

Della Casa: 16 Schauplatzgasse, Tel. 311.21.42. Swiss cuisine as well as international and Spanish food. Closed Sun., open daily until 11:30pm.

Federal: 31 Bärenplatz, Tel. 311.16.24. Located opposite the Federal Palace; Swiss and local cuisine. Open daily to 11:30pm.

Kornhauskeller: 18 Kornhausplatz, Tel. 311.11.33. Classic Bernese and Swiss cuisine, known for its *Berner Platte*. Closed Mon. Open daily until 11:30pm.

Ratskeller: 81 Gerechtigkeitsgasse, Tel. 311.17.71. A historic restaurant in a huge ancient cellar; traditional Swiss cuisine, local delicacies and wines. Open daily to 11:30pm, closed Mon.

Schmiedstube: 5 Zeughausgasse, Tel. 311.34.61. Swiss and local cuisine, sea food. Open daily to 11:30pm.

MARKETS
Bern has numerous markets to delight its visitors, most famous of which is the Onion Market (Zibelemärit).

Onion Market: throughout the city on the 4th Mon. of November.

Geranium Market: On Münsterplatz in Mid-May, morning only.

Flea Market: On Mühleplatz on the 3rd Sunday of each month, May-October.

General Market: On Waisenhausplatz each Tues. and Sat.

Organized Tours

Around the City: A guided bus tour that will familiarize you with ancient Bern and some of the new quarters operates May-Oct., daily at 10am and 2pm; in Apr. daily except Sun. at 2pm; Nov.-Mar., Sat. only, at 2pm. Leaves from the platform opposite the train station; tour lasts two hours.

Visits to the Clock Tower: May-Oct., daily at 4:30pm. Participants go to the tower and observe the medieval clockworks, as well as enjoy a view of the city rooftops from the top of the tower. The tour meets next to the Tower Church (on eastern side) and lasts about one hour.

Trip to the Gurten: This is a highly recommended short trip, about one-and-a-half miles out of Bern. Trolley 9 and then the cablecar (the fastest in all of Europe) will take you to a charming park overlooking the city from a height of 2,600 ft. There is a playground for children. Tickets available at the tourist office and in most hotels.

Important Phone Numbers

Area code: Tel. 031.
Tourist office (main railway station): Tel. 311.66.11, fax 312.12.33.
Main railway station: Tel. 157.33.33.
Bern-Belp Airport: Tel. 961.34.11.
Police: Tel. 117.
Medical first aid: Tel. 311.22.11.
Night pharmacy service: Tel. 311.22.11.
Lost property office: 18 Zeughaus-gasse, Tel. 321.50.50.

Walking Tours

The Old City

The train station of Bern, which is also the first stop on the route, marks the border of the Old City. It was at this line of latitude that the third and last wall was built, and today you can see its remains, which were left as a memento, in the underground passage to the trains, among the shops selling food, film for your camera and other essential items.

North of the train station stands the University of Bern. Since its establishment in 1834, many modern buildings have been added to the university complex. The residents of Bern will remind you that

Albert Einstein received a chair at their city's university, and that this is where he sat and pondered his theory of relativity.

Walking south from the train station, you pass the **Church of the Holy Spirit** (Heiliggeist-Kirche). Completed in 1729, this is an example of true baroque style. In the late 1950's and early 1960's the church underwent extensive renovations.

Turn left at the church to the wide street, Spitalgasse, in the center of the street, you make your first encounter with Bern's marvelous fountains. Here is the Fountain of the Bagpiper. The original statue was erected on a post in 1546 and the pool around it was added in 1899.

There are 11 historical fountains standing in the streets of ancient Bern. They were erected around the 16th century as testimony to the prosperity of the city. A few of the original statues have been removed in recent years, transferred for preservation to the historical museum and replaced by accurate copies. Others are preserved in their original locations and are painted every few years in their original color.

Further on, the street meets a long square, Bärenplatz, the site of fairs and cafés, situated under the **Prison Tower** (Käfigturm). The tower was built in the mid-17th century to replace the guard tower of the gate of the second wall, which enclosed the city from 1256 to 1350. It received its name when it was used to host the female criminals of the city. In 1897, part of the general archive of the canton of Bern was stored in the tower. In 1980, after an extensive renovation, the tower was reopened as a cantonal information center and a place for rotating exhibitions on various themes. Free admission.

Go through the gate of the tower to **Marktgasse**, a street which, like the previous one, runs between two rows of arches, with doors to the basements between them. This was the main street of the Old City, and today it is the heart of the bustling commercial district of the city. The many stores face the street, or are hidden in the passageways facing left and right in between the crowded houses, which were built in the 17th and 18th centuries. There is a mixture of shops here, which offer a great selection of luxury items, food, flowers and, of course, the famous sweet shops specializing in beautiful creations in amusing shapes.

There are two more fountains on this street. The first is of Anna Seiler, the woman who initiated the establishment of the first hospital in Bern, in the mid-14th century. The original statue was erected in 1549, and today it is located in the Historical Museum. The second fountain is the Fountain of the Musketeer, created in 1543. On it stands a statue of the commander of the infantry, wearing his armor and waving a flag, with a bear cub at his feet.

From here the street continues to another large square, **Kornhausplatz**, which takes its name from a large wheat silo that was located at No. 18 of the square, at the beginning of the 18th century. Here you can see yet another fountain, the Fountain of the Ogre, which depicts a giant eating a child. It was erected in 1544 and according to local legend was meant to reflect the warning of the Bernese mothers, who told their children not to go beyond the walls because of an evil child-eating giant awaiting them there.

The Clock Tower standing at Kornhausplatz

The square leads to the most famous tower of the city, the **Clock Tower** (Zeitglockenturm). You can visit the tower only with an organized tour (see the "Organized Tours" section). Originally, the tower was a guard point on the gate of the first wall, which was built in 1191, when the city was founded. When the wall moved west, the tower became a popular meeting place for residents and they even etched fixed length measurements into the walls of the inner arch, for the town's merchants to "take sizes." Markings are found to this day etched into the inner arch of the tower.

In 1405, the tower burnt down with much of the rest of the city. In the overall restoration project, it was rebuilt in stone and in 1530, the famous clock, the masterpiece of Kasper Brunner, was set in it.

Four minutes before every full hour the golden rooster breaks out in song and flaps his wings energetically, as though giving a warning of the hour about to come. A guard of small bears comes out for a walk around the feet of Chronus, the God of time in Greek mythology. Only after another call of the rooster and the ringing of the quarter-hour bell does a knight dressed in golden armor, standing at the head of the tower, awaken and ring the bell according to the hour of the day.

Next to this clock is an astrological clock, also set into the tower, and also the work of Brunner. It shows the hours of the day, the days of the week, the months of the year and the seasons, and is operated by the mechanism of the tower clock.

Touring inside the tower, you can see this mechanism yourself. It is operated by 800 lb. weights, which are lifted once a day (guided tours: daily between May-October, 4:30pm.). The clock is said to lose three minutes a year.

39 steps lead to the top floor of the tower. They are not particularly comfortable ones, but the effort is well worth it. From the windows you can look east and west, at the city and beyond. It offers a much better view than you might expect when looking at the tower from the outside.

Inside the Albert Einstein's House

From the Clock Tower, continue westward, along Kramgasse St., where No. 49 was once **Albert Einstein's House**. Tel. 312.00.91. The house is open Mon.-Thurs. 10am-5pm, Fri. 10am-4pm. Admission fee. Bus No. 12.

The house contains an exhibition of documents and photos from the life of the famous scientist, Albert Einstein. It was here he worked on the theory of relativity in 1905, got married, and had his first son, Hans Albert. Einstein came to Bern in 1902 and was accepted as a third-rate technical expert at the city's patent office.

On this street, too, there are fountains. The first is the Fountain of Zähringen, named after the duke who founded the city. It was erected in 1535 and the citizens of Bern decided that under the duke's head-armor, he would have the face of a bear, the animal that through his inspiration became a symbol of the city. The pool was added in 1889. The second fountain is the Fountain of Samson, the biblical hero, placed here as a symbol of the strength of the city. The statue was erected in 1545 and was replaced by a copy in 1973. The original statue was moved to the Historical Museum.

Bern's Town Hall

Further down the street, take a peek to the left through Kreuzgasse at the fountain bearing the flag (from 1542) and opposite it the **Town Hall** (Rathaus). The lovely building with its triangular front was constructed in 1406-1417, by the well-known architectural team of the time, Gengenbach and Hans Hetzel aus Rottweil. It was extensively renovated from 1932 to 1942. Today both the municipal council of Bern and the cantonal council serve here.

We return to the part of the street that becomes Gerechtigkeitsgasse. In the center is a lone post, on which stands the statue of the Fountain of Justice, erected in 1543.

You are now approaching the Old City via the bridge over the Aare River, the Nydeggbrücke, with the **Bear Pits** on the other side. This is one-of Bern's most famous tourist sites. Open daily from 8am-6pm (Oct.-Mar. 8:30am-4pm) the bears are brought out to be seen in their sunken yard. Bus No. 18, stops at "Tierpark". Free admission.

The residents of Bern are very proud of their bears. The Swiss tell many jokes about this relationship between the city and the animal. For instance, there is one joke about the great similarity between the Bernese and bears: it is said that both are lazy, slow and clumsy. There are some 80 brown bears living in the pits, and their forefathers were also presented here as part of the local tradition that began in the 15th century. Their present home was built in 1857 and since then crowds have been coming to watch them

Peering into the Bear Pits, one of Bern's most famous tourist sites

play, growl and dance, (not all at once; only small groups are let out at any one time) in return for bits of carrot.

From this point, those with strong legs can cross the intersection next to the pits and climb up the stairs, northward, to the Rose Garden (Rosengarten). This is a pleasant, pretty place to stroll or rest, and from its balcony you have a breathtaking view of the city lying to the west.

You can also return in the direction of the city, over the bridge and left to the street parallel to the one we came on, **Junkerngasse**. The beauty of the exteriors of the old buildings makes a beautiful mosaic. Worth an extra look is No. 47, known as **Erlacherhof**, which was built in the mid-18th century as the home of the Mayor Hieronymus Erlach. For 10 years in the mid-19th century this was the seat of the federal council, and since 1832 it has been the location of the city administration.

The bear – the animal which lent its name to the city

At No. 59 of the same street is the **Beatrice V. Wattenwyl House**, built in 1446 as the home of an aristocratic family. Its top floor was added in 1560, and in the many years that followed it passed hands several times, until 1934, when it was purchased by the federal government.

Now you come to **Cathedral Square** (Münsterplatz). On the southern side of the square is an 18th-century castle, which now serves as the cantonal tax office. In the northwest corner of the square is the fountain of Moses, holding the Ten Commandments in his hand. The statue was built in 1791, to replace its 1544 predecessor which had been worn down by time. The northern side of the square is dominated by the city's **Cathedral**.

You can tour the cathedral; Summer: Tues.-Sun. 10am-5pm; Winter: Tues.-Fri. 10-noon and 2-3pm, Sun. 10-noon and 1-5pm. You are permitted to climb to the cathedral tower till 30 minutes before closing time.

High above the roofs of the city stands the tower of the cathedral, the highest of all church towers in Switzerland, reaching 330 ft. This cathedral is actually the last that was built in true Gothic style, and it is called a cathedral, a Catholic concept, even though it has actually served as a Protestant house of worship since the Reformation reached the city.

In the same spot there was once a small church which existed in the first years of the city, mentioned in texts as early as 1224. As the city grew, its leaders reached the inevitable conclusion that they should destroy the church and replace it with a much larger one. The work began on Mar. 11, 1421, under the direction of Matthaus Ensinger, son of a family of architects, who also built the cathedral of Strasbourg.

The project took a long time, and was continued by other architects, Erhart Küng and Daniel Heintz, until it was officially dedicated in 1573. The cathedral tower reached its final height only in 1893, and its builder, August Beyer, made sure that the Gothic style was maintained here, as well.

The residents of Bern joke that the work actually is still not complete. Few remember ever seeing the cathedral without scaffolding or construction materials around it. For 17 years, between 1964-1991, the cathedral underwent complete renovation, and it is still in need of constant preservation work.

The main entrance to the cathedral is adorned with hundreds of statues, some depicting the Day of Judgement. Most of the original statues are now kept in the Historical Museum. Inside the cathedral you will see exquisite stained glass windows, the most impressive of these being the very old ones, located at the eastern end, around the dais. They portray important events from the Old Testament, and were created between 1441 and 1450. The local artists responsible for the work kept the components of their colors a strict secret – and they took this secret with them to their graves. There are noticeable differences

The fountain of Moses, holding the Ten Commandments in his hand

between these and the later stained glass windows in the cathedral.

The huge organ was built in 1726, and it contains 5404 pipes, the smallest 4 inches long, and the longest 30ft. It weighs 1,650 lbs. Concerts are held weekly.

The cathedral has nine bells, three of which belonged to the ancient church that stood here. One of the later bells, dated 1611, is the largest in Switzerland, and weighs 1,650 stone. To the left of the main entrance is a door leading up to the tower. There are 254 stone steps leading to the first balcony, 30ft. above the ground, 90 more steps lead to the second balcony. The marvelous panoramic view, overlooking the Bernese Alps is worth the climb. However, you can also get a beautiful view of the Aare River with much less effort from the high balcony, called the platform, located on the southern side of the cathedral.

SITES NEAR THE ROUTE

From the prisoner's tower, a detour to the left of the tour route leads to the end of the square, where the police headquarters are located in a building which was formerly the city orphanage. To the left, at 8-12 Hodlerstrasse, is the **Museum of Fine Arts** (Kunstmuseum). Open Mon. 10am-9pm, Tues.-Sat. 10am-5pm. Admission fee.

The museum contains works of art from the 14th

century to the present day, but it is best known for its extremely rich collection of paintings by Paul Klee, a painter who lived from 1879-1940, and spent many years in Bern.

When the museum opened in 1879, it was originally devoted to the work of Swiss artists from different periods, particularly Manuel, Stauffer and Hodler. In the last 50 years, thanks to large acquisitions by funds associated with the museum, many works have been added. These include works by the Italians Duccio and Fra Angelico of the 14th and 15th centuries; works by Delacroix and the Impressionists; Cezanne, Monet, Manet, Bonheur; the Expressionists; Soutine and Modigliani as well as some of Picasso's and Braque's important pieces.

The city's Cathedral, constantly under repair

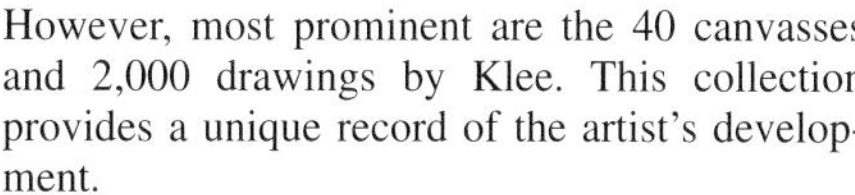

However, most prominent are the 40 canvasses and 2,000 drawings by Klee. This collection provides a unique record of the artist's development.

Further down the street turn right to the Lorraine Bridge with the **Botanical Gardens** on the other side. Open Mon.-Fri. 7am-6pm; Sat. and Sun. 8am-5pm. Free admission. This living, growing museum descends the slopes of the riverbank, with interesting medical plants, Alpine vegetation and exotic hothouses.

From the Federal Palace to the Museums

South of the Clock Tower is **Theater Square** (Theaterplatz). No. 7 on the square is the **Hôtel de Musique**, established in 1770 as a hall for theatrical performances and concerts. At No. 13 you'll find the Great Guard Building (Hauptwache), built in 1766 as the barracks of thc city police. Tel. 634.41.11. From the square, go slightly further south to its sister square, **Casinoplatz**, where you'll also find the casino (Tel. 371.83.78), which despite its name, is not connected to gambling but to performances of music, dance and theater (Tel. 371.83.78). From this square turn west, via Kochergasse, to the **Federal Palace**, the center of power and decision making of the Swiss Confederation.

In the large and impressive building, constructed in Renaissance style in the 19th century, one may join a free 45-minute guided tour. Tours are at 9am, 10am, 11am, 2pm, 3pm and 4pm during the week (Sun. no 4pm tour). These visits are not held when meetings are in session, four times a year, nor during holidays and special events. In addition to offering the visitor a glance at the luxurious interior of the building and the council halls, the visit is also useful for learning more about the complex Swiss form of government (see the section on government in the introductory chapter).

At the exit of the Federal Palace through the northwestern corner of the building, a passage under the stone arches leads you to a garden with a view of hills descending to the Aare. From this vantage point and to the right on the slope is Bern's famous cablecar, the **Marzili-Drahtseilbahn**. Built in 1885, it has been famous ever since as the shortest cablecar in Europe; it only goes 100 yards.

Turning left from the balcony garden of the Federal Palace, you come to the impressive **Kirchenfeld Bridge** (Kirchenfeldbrücke), a bridge of arches built in 1883 by British engineers, at great expense for that time: some one million Swiss francs. It is about 300 ft. high, 700 ft. long, and in addition to transportation lanes it also has electric tracks. Passing over the bridge you get a good view of the landscape on both sides, and end up at **Helvetiaplaz**, the square that serves as the point of departure for touring the museum district of Bern. You can get here directly on Trolley 3.

Immediately upon entering the square on the left is the **Gallery of Art**. Its handsome halls contain rotating exhibits of modern art. Open Wed.-Sun. 10am-5pm, Tues. 10am-9am. On the right-hand side of the square, at No. 4, are two museums, the first of which is the **Swiss Alpine Museum**. Open Tues.-Sun. 10am-noon, 2-5pm; Mon. 2-5pm, in winter it is closed noon-2pm. and Tues. open 2pm-5pm only. Admission fee.

The museum is devoted to the Swiss

The Federal Palace

Alps, and contains a large collection of topographical models and reliefs of the mountains. It illustrates how man has coped with the powers of nature in the Alps, the conquest of the mountains through mapping and researching the region and the life there. A special exhibit reviews the development of equipment for skiing, rescue work in the mountains, shelters and refuges in isolated locations, and the way of life, clothing and folklore of the inhabitants of the Alps. It is definitely a must for mountain lovers.

Next door is the **Swiss Postal Museum**, which has the same visiting hours. Tel. 351.00.31. Free admission. Anyone who has ever collected stamps will enjoy seeing one of the most valuable collections of its type in the world. It includes Swiss, European and other stamps from 1900 on. On the ground floor of the museum is an exhibit of the history of the postal service, from the couriers of the Roman era to private mail, cantonal postal service, the telegraph, telephone and so forth. Among the exhibits is the first mail train of St. Gotthard, from 1832, and the first telephone switchboard in Switzerland.

As you leave the museum, take a moment to look at the large bronze statue in the center of the square, dedicated to the International Telegraph Union, founded in 1865. The statue itself, which

was molded in bronze by the artist Romagnoli in 1915 in Rome, carries on its back a list of all the countries that are members in the union. Behind the statue is the entrance to a turreted castle, built in neo-Gothic style. This is the home of the **Museum of the History of Bern** (Bernisches Historisches Museum). Open Tues.-Sun., 10am-5pm; closed Mon. Admission fee.

This is undoubtedly one of the most outstanding museums of its type in Switzerland and even in the whole of Europe. Its most distinctive feature is the collection of tapestries on the first floor, which includes masterpieces of the Dutch and Flemish school of the 15th century. Of the most famous are *The Judgement of Trajan and Herkanbald*, and those portraying the life of Julius Caesar.

On the ground floor is a marvelous exhibit of furniture, household items, and other daily objects used mainly by the aristocratic families of the 18th century. There is also a unique collection of local objects from the prehistoric age.

A special piece on the second floor, among the arms from different periods, is a huge scale that belonged to the Bernese arsenal. Made in 1752, it had the capacity to weigh cannons and cannon balls weighing up to two tons.

Other noteworthy exhibits shown here are the collection of religious items and sacred implements brought from the Kenigsfelden Monastery, which was founded by the Hapsburgs, the *Dance of Death* paintings by Niklaus Manuel and the statues of Judgement Day, brought from the city cathedral, along with fabulous 15th and 16th-century stained glass and luxurious priests' vests.

At the right turn behind the Historical Museum is the **Swiss Museum of Marksmen** (Schützenmuseum). Tel. 351.01.27. Open Mon.-Fri. 9am-6pm, Wed. till 8pm, Sat. 9am-4pm. The building is owned by the Swiss Association of Marksmen, founded in 1824. In Switzerland, the tradition of marksmanship draws its inspiration from the great archers of its history, especially from the legendary figure of William Tell. The exhibit includes a large collection of documents related to marksmanship and marksmen, medals and trophies awarded to the most famous, and, of course, an impressive collection of weapons, rifles and pistols from the 19th and 20th century. Behind the Museum of Marksmen, further down the same street, is the **Museum of Natural History of Bern** (Naturhistorisches Museum). Tel. 350.71.11. Open Tues.-Sat. 9am-5pm; Sun. 10am-5pm; Mon. 2-5pm. Admission fee.

This is one of the best natural history museums in Europe, with 230 three-dimensional exhibits of mammals and birds from throughout the world, exhibited here in their natural environment. There is also a marvelous collection of fossils, various types of fish, insects and other forms of life. On the third floor you will find an exhibit of minerals, precious stones and geological phenomena accompanied by audio-visual presentations.

FROM BERN TO LUZERN

For those wishing to travel directly to Luzern from Bern, route 10 is recommended. We, however, present the longer route, starting on N6 and turning off from time to time to visit some lovely places. N6 is noted for its breathtaking views of the blue lakes, green slopes and white peaks. If you drive through the Bernese Oberland area, stop every once in a while to observe the view.

Thun

Located at the northwestern edge of Thun Lake (Thunersee), the source of the Aare River, the city is virtually perfect in beauty. Its main road, Hauptgasse, lined with handsome houses with balconies onto the street leads to a staircase up to the city's castle. The castle was built in the late 12th century by the Duke of Zähringen and in time became the property of the Kyburgs. Today it houses the city's Historical Museum, which contains an impressive Hall of Knights, decorated with fantastic tapestries. The balcony of the castle tower overlooks the lake and the mountains.

Near Thun Lake, on the way to Interlaken

Spiez

This is a charming town on the bank of Lake Thun, with a mooring for boats and yachts and a beach for bathing. It gets very busy in the summer. From Spiez you can take the train or Road 11 to **Erlenbach**, a small village from which you can take the cable car up to the **Stock-**

horn Peak (7,300 ft.), where you have an incredible view of the heights of the Oberland from the observation point.

KANDERSTEG

From Spiez the road goes south to the Kander Valley, reaching this small village after 18 miles. The village earned a place on the map in 1913, because of the Lôtsch-berg Tunnel (10 miles) which shortened the way between Bern and the Rhône Valley. The tunnel is designed for trains only, but automobiles can be loaded on the transportation cars.

The way from Spiez to Kandersteg passes by **Niesen Mountain** (1,900 ft. high) on the right. This is one of the most beautiful lookout points in the area, and you can get to it by cable car from the Mülenen station.

From Kandersteg you can get to **Oeschinen Lake**, some 3 miles east of the village, by a combination of walking and cable car. The pastoral lake surrounded by snow-capped mountains is a popular site for hiking.

GSTAAD

This town, lying between the mountains and glaciers, and surrounded by forests and lakes, is located some 30 miles from Spiez on Road 11. It has all the best and most prestigious facilities – golf and tennis courts in the summer and ski resorts in the winter. Those willing to pay get their money's worth. The Palace Hotel in the center of the city says it all.

Interlaken

Interlaken is a town with a total of 5,000 residents. However, it is well known and holds an important position on the tourist map because it is the traditional point of departure for trips in the area, particularly to the **Jungfrau**, the famous peak. The town's name means "between the lakes," as it is indeed situated between Lake Thun and Lake Brienz.

Its long main street, Hôheweg, runs between the city's two train stations.

One side has a lovely park, with breathtaking peaks above, while the other is lined with hotels, restaurants, the casino with the clock of flowers, and numerous souvenir shops. Because tourists have been flooding the city for generations, it is difficult to find anything genuinely Swiss here, but the tourist services are very good.

Area Code: 036

Accommodation

FIVE-STAR HOTELS

Beau-Rivage: Hôheweg, Tel. 21.62.72, fax 23.28.47. A classic hotel on the town's main street.

FOUR-STAR HOTELS

Dulac: 225 Hôheweg, Tel. 22.29.22, fax 22.29.15. A small hotel at the eastern end of the town.

Interlaken: 74 Hôheweg, Tel. 21.22.11, fax 23.31.21. A moderately-sized hotel, on the main street.

Stella: 10 Waldeggstrasse, Tel. 22.88.71, fax 22.66.71. A small hotel at the southern end of the town.

Typical Swiss cottages set in the mountains

THREE-STAR HOTELS

Beou Site: 16 Seestrasse, Tel. 22.81.81, fax 23.29.26. A moderately-sized hotel, on the northeastern side of the river.

Carlton: 92 Höheweg, Tel. 22.38.21, fax 22.03.55. A classic hotel in a beautiful building, near the eastern train station.

Eden Nova: 45 Bahnhofplatz, Tel. 22.88.12. A moderately-sized hotel, near the western train station.

TWO-STAR HOTELS

Rössli: 10 Hauptstrasse, Tel. 22.78.16, fax 22.96.16. A small hotel on the northeastern side of the river.

Bahnhof: 37 Bahnhofstrasse, Tel. 22.70.41. A small hotel near the western train station.

Blume: 30 Jungfraustrasse, Tel. 22.71.31. A small hotel in the town center.

YOUTH HOSTELS

The closest youth hostel to Interlaken is in Bônigen, which you can reach by a 20-minute walk, or by Bus 1 from the town to the Lütschinen-Brücke station, Tel. 22.43.53.

CAMPING
There are numerous camping sites around the town, particularly on the shores of the lakes. The following are a few of them:

Alpenblick: Tel. 22.77.57.
Hobby: Tel. 22.96.52.
Jungfrau: Tel. 22.57.30.
Lazy-Rancho: Tel. 22.87.16.

Restaurants

As an experienced well-travelled tourist spot, Interlaken offers an abundance of restaurants of every possible type. The luxury hotels offer the best food, but here are a few, less expensive suggestions.

Burestube: 57 Höheweg, Tel. 22.65.12. Typical German-Swiss cuisine, grilled meat and of course the well-known *Rôsti*. In keeping with the local atmosphere, the menu also includes international dishes. Closed Mon.

Le Bistro "Chez Pierre": 39 Bahnhofplatz, Tel. 22.94.22. International cuisine, with special emphasis on French-style cooking. Closed Tues.

Pizpaz: 1 Bahnhofstrasse, Tel. 22.25.33. Italian cuisine, pasta, pizza. Closed Sun.

Charolais (Hotel Metropole): 37 Hôheweg, Tel. 21.21.51. International and Swiss cuisine, specializing in high-quality meat and seafood. Open all week.

Tours in the Interlaken Area

The tours from the city can be divided into two types: short tours, lasting a few hours, and longer ones, taking a full day or more.

SCHYNIGE PLATTE
A four-hour tour covers the wonders of the Swiss landscape in a short time. Arrive here by the

The Trümmelbach Falls, south of Interlaken

mountain train that leaves the Wilderswill station and goes almost to the peak (1,000 ft.). In the area of the upper station, you can walk around and enjoy the view of the town, the lakes and the Jungfrau Peak.

GRINDELWALD

The road that climbs up to this charming town (by car or train from Interlaken) is one of the most beautiful in Switzerland. Its fantastic location between the mountains, glaciers and forests, and its picturesque houses are simply stunning. It lies at the foot of the famous Eiger Mountain, whose peak reaches an altitude of 13,230 ft. above sea level. With the clear air and all the climbing possibilities (by foot and by cable car), it is a hard place to leave. Take a train from Grindelwald to the Jungfraujoch (Jungfrau range) to return to Interlaken via the Wengen station.

There is a friendly youth hostel in town where you can obtain information on great walking tours in the area, leading to snow-capped peaks and glaciers. The *Silbernloru Hotel* (4 stars), Tel. 53.28.22, fax 53.48.22, has also a good restaurant.

Make it a point to stop at the spectacular ancient **Glacier**, with its memorable ice statues and subterranean caves. Admission fee.

TRÜMMELBACH FALLS

Off the road going south from Interlaken to Jungfrau are the Trümmelbach Falls. On the site one can view mighty cascades of water plunging through the gorge. A lift that passes through the rock leads to paths through which one can walk and observe these splendid waterfalls.

THE JUNGFRAU

This range is one of the most beautiful mountain spots, and the possibility of reaching it by train makes it also the most popular. On a cloudy day it's not worth going up the mountain, since the view from it is not visible; better to take a trip to Grindelwald, to Lauterbrunnen, and to the tremendous Trümmelbach Waterfalls. On a clear day it is certainly worth going up (by train, the ticket for the tour – Exkursionbillette – makes the trip less expensive) to the Kleine Scheidegg station, from which the train continues to the Jungfraujoch – the highest train station in Europe

The cable car that travels up to the Jungfrau range from Grindelwald

(11,600 ft.). The headache caused by the thin air and the pressure in your ears are part of the experience. Continue in the lift to the top station – to the observation point which gives a view of indescribable beauty. There is also the "ice palace" and ski slopes. Above is the peak of the Jungfrau, 13,560 ft. above sea level.

Brienz

On the other end, the eastern end of the Brienz Lake, lies the town of the same name. Brienz is the boarding point for the Rothorn and a pleasant stop for boats touring the lake. Not far from town (a mile and a half) is the spacious **Ballenberg Museum**. Here you can view characteristic Swiss houses from different generations. There are wooden houses, country houses, mountain shacks and more.

From Brienz you can turn east on Road 11 to the "Route of the Three Passes" (see "From Luzern to Lugano"); but our tour continues on Road 4 toward Luzern.

The Jungfrau

FROM BERN TO ZÜRICH

The *autostrada* from Bern to Zürich (N1) turns first north, and draws a sort of arch, finally turning eastward. It continues following the Aare River, on its way to the Rhine.

KIRCHBERG

To the east of the road lies a settlement on the Emme River, which cuts across the region known as Emmental, home of that famous Swiss cheese with the holes. There is a 16th-century Protestant church here, as well.

At Solothurn

SOLOTHURN

The city of Solothurn, situated on the Aare River, at the foot of the Jura mountains, is the capital of the canton of Solothurn. It is a small city with a large population of 15,000. The ruins of its 17th-century walls give it a special atmosphere and a walk through the streets reveals its charm. In the 16th, 17th and 18th centuries, the city remained Catholic, despite its proximity to Protestant Bern. For this reason the kings of France chose it as the seat of their embassy to the Swiss Confederation. In the course of time, this tradition helped to develop many cultural ties between the city and France.

The Old City of Solothurn, on the northern bank, attracts many visitors, who enjoy the simple pleasure of walking through its streets and viewing the handsome old homes and cafés. The main

Inside the Cathedral of St. Urs, in Solothurn

street, Hauptgasse, leads to the impressive Cathedral of St. Urs, which was constructed in the 18th century in baroque style. On the way, you pass the Jesuit Church, built in the late 17th century, whose inner walls are decorated with beautiful paintings, such as *The Ascension of Jesus*.

Next to the cathedral, on the left, is the ancient arsenal (Altes Zeughaus), which today constitutes one of Switzerland's finest museums of arms. It has a particularly impressive exhibit of soldiers' and knights' armor, on the second floor. The City Museum of Art boasts, among other possessions, the young Holbein's *Madonna of Solothurn*.

Some six miles north of Solothurn you can see the **Weissenstein Ridges**, towering like a wall above the low plains of the city and its environs. Some of the difficulty of climbing the winding mountain road can be eased by using the cableway from the Oberdorf station (located about half way to the mountain). You can take a lovely walk around the peak, winding up at the breath-taking observation point overlooking Neuchâtel, Morat and Biel Lakes and the Bernese Oberland Mountains as well as the Alps from Mont Blanc to Santis.

OLTEN

This city also lies on both sides of the Aare River, in the canton of Solothurn. It is an industrial city, but a Swiss one, which means it is beautiful and clear.

You should take a look at the "old bridge" that connects the two parts of the city, a Luzern-style covered wooden bridge, leading to the Old City on the left bank.

History buffs should go south from Olten, some three miles in the direction of Aarburg, to the **Wartburg-Säli Castle**. Here, on a towering hill, is a small fortress, with a round, jagged turret. The castle was first built in the 13th century by the Baron of Frohburg, and became property of the city of Solothurn in the 16th century, for use as a lookout tower. Until the end of the 19th century, it was always manned by members of the local Säli family – after whom the castle is named today. There is a pleasant café-restaurant here, with a view of the Aare Valley, the city of Olten and the hills around it. It is open daily except Tues., all year round except Feb. Road 5, between the *autostrada* and the Aare, leads from Olten to Aarau; in between them is Schônenwerd.

SCHÖNENWERD

A small, ancient town with a 12th-century monastery, Schönenwerd began to develop rapidly when the major shoe manufacturer, Bali, opened its factories here. The home of the company's founder now houses a special kind of museum – the **Museum of the History of the Shoe**, which surveys the history of people's shoes in different periods and cultures and among different groups – from kings to the masses. Open to visitors the last Friday of every month, 2pm-5pm, except for Jul. and Sept. Tel. 744.35.35. Free admission.

AARAU

The capital of the canton of Aargovia, with about 16,000 residents, Aarau is also situated on the Aare River, from which it gets its name. The city has a beautiful old center, built in a style indicative of the architectural influence exerted by Bern during the years it controlled the area. However, the oldest structure in the city is the medieval castle next to the river. The massive square tower to the left of the church was built in the 11th century. The other part,

A street in Aarau

Bathers enjoying the hot therapeutic water at Baden

with the wooden bridge leading directly to the second floor, was added in the 14th century. Today it houses the city museum in which there is an exhibit of old Aarau, furniture, arms, lead figures and more. Open Sat. afternoon and Sun. morning.

LENZBURG

South of *autostrada* N1, before Baden, on a forested cliff above the city of Lenzburg, towers one of the most outstanding castles in Switzerland. It is the classic fairy-tale castle: jagged walls, pointed towers and all the rest. It was the main residence of the counts of Lenzburg from 1036 to 1173; afterwards it became the property of the Kyburgs, the Hapsburgs and, until 1798, of the canton of Bern. In the 19th and 20th centuries it was occupied by various personalities, such as the German playwright, Frank Wedekind (*Pandora's Box*), the American explorer, Lincoln Ellsworth, who flew to the North Pole, and others. The castle now houses a small history museum. You may visit Apr.-Oct., daily between 9:30am-noon and 1pm-5pm, except for Mon. Tel. (064) 51.66.70.

BADEN

As its German name implies, this is a city of baths. For some 2,000 years, since the Roman era when it was called "Aqua Helvetica," people have enjoyed emersing their bodies to relieve their rheumatic pains in the mineral-rich hot springs (47°C) of Baden. The most common advertisement for the city's bathhouses is one of bathers enjoying the hot waters, with the snow-covered mountains in the background.

But Baden is not only baths and water; it is a lovely city with a long and painful history. It twice suffered heavy blows. In 1415 it was conquered by the army of the Confederation and burned to the ground. In the 17th century, the descendants of its early residents rebuilt it, but their support for Catholicism cost them dearly. The city was destroyed again when it was taken by the cantonal armies of Bern and Zurich in 1712. It has been beautifully rebuilt for the third time.

A walk through the old city of Baden, on the Limmat River, reveals handsome buildings and romantic paths, as well as the **City Tower**. On one side of the tower are the ruins of **Stein Castle**, on the other is the wooden bridge over the river leading to the striking **Governors' Castle** (Landvogteischloss). The building was constructed in late-Gothic style, with a northern wing that was added in the 18th century, and a Renaissance-style entrance. From the early 15th until the late 18th century, it served as the residence of the governors of the city. It is now a history museum, containing a collection of arms, a Roman collection, furnishings from different periods, a relief of Baden from 1670, and more. Tel. 22.75.74. Open Tues.-Sun. 10am-noon and 2pm-5pm. Free admission.

On the way to Zürich

LUZERN – THE JEWEL OF SWITZERLAND

Many writers, painters and musicians have expressed their admiration for the beauty of Luzern and the surrounding area. The Russian author Tolstoy claimed that the beauty of its water, mountains and skies compelled him to write. A visit to Luzern is an absolute must. Its landscapes, its sights and some of its museums simply have to be visited. The city, situated in the heart of Switzerland, has found a place in the heart of every visitor as well. Music-lovers throughout the world come here for the renowned music festival which is held here every year in August.

History

Initially, Luzern was a small fishing village. In the mid-eighth century, Benedictine monks, who left the monastery at Murbach in Alsace, arrived here and chose to set up a "branch" of their monastery. Some 100 years later, in approximately 840, the name of the city appeared for the first time in an official document as "Luciaria."

A view of Luzern

Commercial and agricultural activity began to develop around the monastery. People came from near and far, and in the Middle Ages a real city began to emerge here. In time, a market square, public buildings and a wall were built. In the 13th century, the city was given a crucial boost, when the St. Gotthard Pass was opened, connecting the Netherlands with Italy. Luzern, situated on the crossroads, became a key city.

As the city began to develop, its citizenry needed to be defended, and thus a pact was made with the neighboring cantons of Schwyz and Unterwald in 1332. Extensive commercial ties were maintained with the independent cantons, but it was only in 1386 that it became totally free of the influence of the Hapsburg rule.

When the Protestant Reform came to Switzerland, Luzern served as the flag bearer of the Catholic camp. It stood at the forefront of the counter-Reformation movement in the 16th century. In 1574, the Jesuits opened the first Holy Council of German Switzerland in Luzern.

In the days of the Helvetian Republic which emerged in Switzerland after the French occupation, Luzern was the capital of the state. The republic did not last long, and the city returned to being the capital of the canton of Luzern.

A General View

The city of Luzern is located at the northwestern tip of the Vierwaldstättersee (The Lake of the Four Cantons, sometimes also known as Lake Luzern), which measures 113 sq. km – the fourth largest lake in Switzerland. The lake lies more or less in the center of Switzerland, on the border between the middlelands and the Alps. Luzern is approximately 1,400 ft. above sea level.

The city is cut in two by the Reuss River, which runs from the lake north. It is this navigable river, and the location of the city at the entrance of the valley leading to the St. Gotthard mountain pass that have made Luzern a crossroads.

The eastern and southern sides of Luzern are dominated by mountains. Mount Riga to the east is 6,000 ft. high and the Pilatus to the south is 7,090 ft. Together with the lake they make a very pleasant sight.

Luzern is the capital of the canton of Luzern. Most of its residents are Catholic, German speakers. The population of the city increased greatly in the first half of the century, when the number of residents doubled to 55,000. Today there are about 60,000 people living in Luzern, out of the 300,000 residents of the canton.

Getting There

Autostradas connect Luzern and the major cities of Switzerland. The distance between Luzern and Bern is 60 miles; Zürich, 36

miles; Basel, 62 miles and Geneva, 176 miles.

Since it lies in the center of the country, the city serves as a crossroads for trains. In every important city in Switzerland, at least one train, with Luzern as its destination, leaves every hour.

The closest airport to the city is Zürich Airport, 44 miles away.

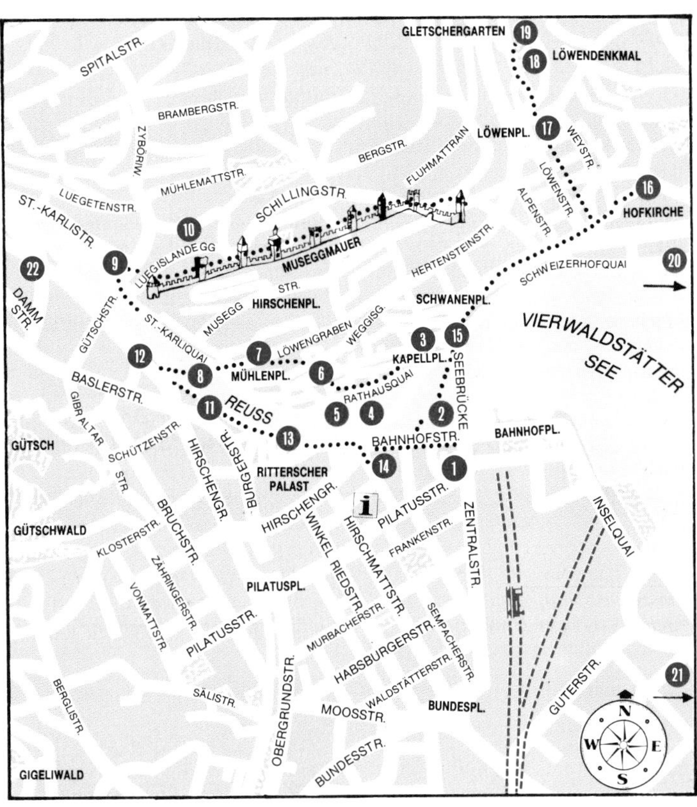

LUZERN

1. *Train Station*
2. *Kappelbrücke*
3. *St. Peter's Church (and the Square)*
4. *Picasso Collection*
5. *Old City Hall and Seed Market Square*
6. *Wine Market*
7. *Mill Square*
8. *Mill Bridge (Spreuerbrücke)*
9. *Road of fortifications*
10. *Towers*
11. *Historical Museum*
12. *Museum of Natural History*
13. *Cantonal Government Palace*
14. *Jesuit Church*
15. *Swan Square*
16. *Cathedral of St. Lager*
17. *Bourbaki Panorama*
18. *Memorial Garden of the Lion*
19. *Glacier Park (museum)*
20. *Museum of Transportation*
21. *Richard Wagner Museum*
22. *Gutsch Castle*

Direct trains go to the airport and back every hour from 5am to after 10pm. The train trip takes about 1 hour and 15 minutes.

City Transportation

Most of the places and sites in the city can be reached on foot. To reach more distant places, located on the outskirts of the city and on the other side of the lake, such as the Museum of Transportation, use the blue and white city buses.

Machines in the stations sell tickets according to the length of the trip. However, it's not worth bothering since at almost every hotel reception desk in the city you can purchase a special Visitor's Pass, which allows you to ride all lines within the city for two days.

In the area of the Old City, Luzern's downtown, which is closed to transportation, there is a special yellow and orange bus, which takes you anywhere in the district, free of charge.

CAR RENTAL

There are offices of all major car-rental companies in Luzern:

Budget: Tel. 36.66.66.
Avis: Tel. 51.32.51.
Europcar: Tel. 41.14.33.
Hertz: Tel. 36.02.77.

PARKING

Most parking spots in Luzern have meters or are in a blue zone. You can obtain the required parking shield for parking in the blue zone without charge at the tourist office.

Accommodation

Over 60 hotels of various categories are available to Luzern's visitors. As befits a true tourist city where tourism is the major source of income, Luzern's hotels are distinguished by their high

Luzern at night

quality service. Those listed here are all graded by the Swiss Hotel Association, and are conveniently located for touring and shopping.

FIVE-STAR HOTELS

Grand Hotel National: 4 Haldenstrasse, Tel. 50.11.11, fax 51.55.39. In the northern part of the city on the lake front, near the docks of the recreation boats.

Palace: 10 Haldenstrasse, Tel. 50.22.22, fax 51.69.76. In the northern part of the city, on the lake front, near the casino.

Schweizerhof: 3 Schweizerhofquai, Tel. 50.22.11, fax 51.29.71. In the northern part of the city, near the Old City.

FOUR-STAR HOTELS

Château Gutsch: Kanonenstrasse, Tel. 22.02.72, fax 22.02.52. A 100-year-old castle-hotel that was a favorite of European aristocracy in the late 19th century, situated on a hill above the southern part of the city.

Des Balances: 7 Metzgerrainle, Tel. 51.18.51, fax 51.64.51. In the northern part of the city in the Old City, on the river front.

Flora: 3 Seidenhofstrasse, Tel. 24.44.44, fax 23.83.60. In the southern part of the city, in the shopping and commercial district, near the train station.

Monopol & Metropole: 1 Pilatusstrasse, Tel. 23.08.66, fax 23.60.01. In the southern part of the city opposite the train station.

THREE-STAR HOTELS

Des Alpes: 5 Rathausquai, Tel. 51.58.25, fax 51.74.51. In the Old City, on the riverbank.

Bellevue au Lac: 79 Seeburgstrasse., Tel. 31.67.31, fax 31.69.55.

Kolping: 8 Friedenstrasse, Tel. 51.23.51, fax 51.11.62. In the northern part of the city near the lion monument.

TWO-STAR HOTELS

Goldener Stern: 35 Burgerstrasse, Tel. 23.08.91. In the southern part of the city, mid-way between the river and Pilatus Square.

Krone: 12 Weinmarkt, Tel. 51.62.51, fax 51.53.15. In the northern part of the city, at the western end of the Old City.

ONE-STAR HOTELS

Linde: 3 Metzgerrainle, Tel. 51.31.93. In the northern part of the city, in the heart of the Old City.

Pickwick: 6 Rathausquai, Tel. 51.59.27, fax 51.51.08. In the northern part of the city in the Old City, on the riverbank.

Touristhotel: 12 St. Karli-Quai, Tel. 51.24.74. On the northern bank of the river, in the western corner of the Old City.

YOUTH HOSTELS

Jugendherberge: 12 Sedelstrasse, Tel. 36.88.00. Located at the northwestern edge of the city. Bus 18 to the area. The hostel is open all year round; closing time 11:30pm every evening. Reception hours 9:30am-4pm.

CAMPING

Lido: Lidostrasse, Tel. 31.21.46. On the shores of the lake, northeast of the city, near the Museum of Transportation. Open every year Mar. 15-Oct. 31. Nearby lake side bathing beach and tennis courts.

Restaurants

A tradition of hosting tourists and visitors with fine taste has developed a high consciousness in Luzern for quality food. Numerous restaurants offer excellent Swiss and international cuisine. In addition to specializing in fondue and *raclette*, there are excellent fish restaurants in the city; after all, Luzern began as a fishing village and is situated on the lake.

Schwanen: 4 Schwanenplatz, Tel. 51.11.77. Up one flight.

Li Tai Pe: 14 Furrengasse, Tel. 51.10.23. Chinese.

Le Manoir: 9 Bundesplatz, Tel. 23.23.48.

Stadtkeller: 3 Sternenplatz, Tel. 51.47.33. Folk restaurant with entertainment.

Romantic: 4 Theilinggasse, Tel. 51.30.45.

Stadt München: 9 Metzgerrainle, Tel. 51.36.31.

Café Urania: Lôwenplatz, Tel. 51.67.08. Light meals.

McCheaper: 12 Weinmarkt, Tel. 51.62.52.

Festivals

February – Mardi Gras: Costumed musicians and a medieval carnival parade.

Luzern's Train Station

August-September – International Music festival.

Organized Tours

The Municipal Tourist Office organizes a guided 2-hour walking tour, leaving daily at 9:30am, Mon.-Sat., March 31-October 31, from the meeting point next to the tourist information office, 1 Frankenstrasse. From Nov. 3-April 13., Tues., Thurs., and Sat. Tel. 51.71.71.

Important Phone Numbers

Area code: Tel. 041.
Tourist office: 1 Frankenstrasse Tel. 51.71.71.
Railway station: Tel. 157.33.33.
Hotel information (in the train station): Tel. 23.52.44.
Hotel Association: Tel. 43.04.04. fax 43.04.06.
Police: Tel. 117.
Lost and Found: 24 Burgerstrasse, Tel. 21.78.08.
Airport: 01.258.34.34.
Medical First Aid: Tel. 111.
Ambulance: Tel. 144.

Walking Tours

To the Old City

This tour begins in the center of the city, near the Luzern **train station**, where many bus lines begin as well. To the southwest lies Pilatusstrasse, the bustling street of commerce with its shops, department stores and banks. North of the train station, between it and the lake, is the **Museum of Fine Arts**, which hosts visiting exhibitions, alongside its modest permanent collection of painting and sculpture, and the **Congress Hall** where the Luzern Music Festival is held, from mid-Aug. to mid-Sept.

A Luzern scene – note the wooden Kapellbrücke

From the Train Station Square (Bahnhofplatz), along the promenade that passes by the meeting point of the lake and river, Bahnhofstrasse runs along the city's central post office to the municipal theater, which was founded in the 1830's. Almost exactly opposite it is one of Luzern's symbols: the covered bridge known as **Kapellbrücke**. This is a wooden pedestrian bridge, which crosses the Reuss River diagonally, at its

Part of the Picasso Collection, which is on exhibit at the Am-Rhyn House

outlet from the lake. Measuring some 650 ft. long, the bridge was originally built in 1333. Walking along the bridge you will discover paintings on wood, the work of Hans Wägmann, a 17th-century artist, and his son Hans Ulrich. The paintings, accompanied by explanations in German, depict the history of the city of Luzern, important events in the history of Switzerland, and events in the religious life of the city. Some of them provide an exact description of houses, streets and clothing of the residents of Luzern in the 17th century – genuine historical evidence. The paintings were restored and reinforced in 1944-1945. In 1993 the bridge was seriously damaged by a fire, but it has been renovated.

Toward the middle of the bridge is the tile-roofed **Water Tower** (Wasserturm), built approximately in 1300, even before the bridge was erected. The tower formerly served as a prison, a torture room, the treasury of the city and an archive; it presently houses the Association of Veteran Artillery Men.

Leave the bridge on the northern bank, opposite **St. Peter's Church**. The church was originally built when the city was founded, in 1178, and was rebuilt in the mid-18th century. The corner building on the right, with the round, pointed tower, is the former residence of the Guilgen noble family of the city, built in the early 16th century.

On the other side of St. Peter's Church is the **Church Square** (Kapellplatz), with a fountain named after Fritschi, a legendary figure of the carnival held in the city since the 15th century. At the left hand corner of the square is Furrengasse, a narrow street lined with houses. At No. 21 is **Am-Rhyn House**, residence of another 17th century aristocratic urban family which became the property of the city and is now home to the **Picasso Collection** (Picasso Sammlung).

The gallery is open Apr.-Oct. 10am-6pm. Nov.-Mar., 11am-1pm, 2-4pm. Admission fee. The collection, which was donated by the Rosengarts, a family of art dealers from Luzern, includes a selection of Picasso's work: paintings, drawings and prints, particularly from the last 20 years of the artist's life. Picasso fans will be pleased to see the artist's well-known adaptation of Manet's *Luncheon on the Grass*, in which Picasso himself appears in the right hand side of the picture.

Nearby is the **Old City Hall** of Luzern (Altes Rathaus). The building was constructed between 1602 and 1606, on top of the ruins of the former City Hall, which had collapsed under the weight of time. The structure is an impressive architectural example of integration of local style with Italian Renaissance style. The statues decorating the building were created by the Italian sculptor, Anton Isenmann. In the northwest corner is a series of weights that were used by the local tradesmen in the Middle Ages.

The square tower of the city halls looks out onto the **Seed Market Square** (Kornmarkt) that lies in front of it. The name of this market (which dealt in wheat and barley) gives us a hint of the commercial activity that once went on here. From the square you can see the beautiful painted façade of the Pepiston Guest House, which stands to the right of the City Hall.

Leave the square, turn left on Kornmarktgasse, and then right. The second square is **Deer Square** (Hirschenplatz). This was once the location for mass gatherings on holidays and special occasions. Today, the decorated exteriors of the houses are its main attraction. Walking via the southwestern corner of the square, you come to a third square, the **Wine Market** (Weinmarkt). Its fountain was originally built in 1481, and the top piece was added in 1738. The fountain that now stands in the center of the square is an exact replica of the first, constructed in 1953. Around the square are pretty bourgeois homes, with decorated and painted fronts.

To the west, via Kramgasse, you get to the fourth square, **Mill Square** (Mühlenplatz). No. 1 is Bell

House, built in 1807 as the home of Vincent Ruttiman, one of the leaders of the Helvetian Republic. The square looks west and south over the river, to the houses on the opposite bank and, of course, to Luzern's second covered bridge, **Mill Bridge** (Spreuerbrücke). The bridge was constructed in the early 15th century, and renovated in the 19th century. In the mid-16th century, a small house of worship was added to it, and from 1626 to 1635 it was decorated with paintings on wood, pictures from Kasper Meglinger's *Dance of Death*.

From here you can choose one of two possibilities for continuing the tour. Those who want to walk a bit (Option 1) can climb up to the fortifications north of the Old City; otherwise (Option 2), cross the bridge to the southern bank of the river, to the Museums of History and Natural History.

OPTION 1

From the river to the northwest, the fortified wall (with nine towers), **Museggmauer**, rises above the Musegg hills. This is one of the most impressive sights in Luzern. The fortifications were first built in the mid-14th century, and they were reinforced and raised in the following years as the cannons of the enemy armies became more effective. The tower closest to the river is **Nülli Tower** (Nülliiturm), 100 ft. high, some 35 ft. wide and with 6ft.-thick walls. After it is **Männli Tower** (Männliturm), with an open observation deck at the top. This is followed by **Luegisland Tower** (Luegislandturm), the first and oldest of the towers, overlooking the surrounding area from a height of 175 ft. A wonderful vantage point with a view of the city, the deck was used to detect fires.

A typical house in Luzern

After this is the **Wacht Tower** (Wachtturm), 30 ft. high. Its first version was destroyed in a tremendous gunpowder explosion in 1701. It is followed by **Zytt Tower** (Zytturm), one of the oldest towers with a clock. The clockworks were made in approximately 1400. On its southern side is a wall painting from 1949. Following it come the **Schirmer** (Schirmerturm), **Pulver** (Pulverturm), **Allenwinden** (Allenwindenturm) and **Dächli** (Dächliturm) **Towers**. The sight of the towers at night, lit up with a special spotlight system, is stunning, and this is indeed one of the favorite photographic shots. From May to Oct., in the tourist season, some of the towers are open to visitors, including Schirmer, Männli and Zytt.

OPTION 2

Go over the Spreuer Bridge, to the southern bank of the river, where there are two museums. The **Historical Museum** (Historisches Museum) at 24 Pfistergasse is open Tues.-Fri. 10am-noon and 2pm-5pm, Sat. and Sun. 10am-5pm; closed Mon. Tel. 24.54.24. Admission fee. The building with the sloping tile roof, in which the historical museum is now housed, was built in 1567-1568, by Roch Helmlin, and was designed to be used as the city's arsenal. Until 1983 it did serve as the arsenal, but much earlier, in the years of the French Occupation, some of the collection that had accumulated was lost, or sold. Of the external decorations, only a painting of the city's emblem remains, on the wall facing the river. The collection of the Historical Museum was moved to the old arsenal building from its former location, in the Old City Hall.

The ground floor is devoted to the political and military history of the canton. Weapons of the soldiers of Luzern, arms taken as booty, armor of noblemen, shields and uniforms of soldiers of different periods all tell the stories of battles in which citizens of the city and the canton took part. There are also stained glass windows, various paintings and exhibits, and the original sculpted Wine Market Fountain, created by Conrad Lux, around 1481.

The first-floor exhibits focus on the economic, commercial and art history of Luzern. The hotel business, production of glassware, ancient measures and scales, silver coins and medals from different periods (there was a mint in Luzern from 1422-1846),

The Jesuit Church on the shore of the Reuss River, with the Kapellbrücke on the left

metalware and clothing are all represented. On the second floor, the museum has rotating exhibitions.

The second museum, in the adjacent square, is the **Museum of Natural History** (Naturmuseum), at 6 Kasernenplatz. A section of the museum is also devoted to archeology, open daily 10am-noon and 2pm-5pm, Sun. 10am-5pm, closed Mon. Tel. 24.54.11. Admission fee. On the first floor of the museum is an exhibit of central Switzerland's geological and mineralogical formations. Rocks, minerals and fossils from the area are shown. In the archeology hall, you can see findings from the prehistoric period in the canton, mainly from the excavation at Elgolzwil. Here, the remains of a neolithic-Age settlement were uncovered, including tools, weapons, pottery and more. On the second floor of the museum is a zoological and botanic collection: stuffed animals, aquariums and so forth.

The road to the riverbank (Reuss-Steg) leads to Bahnhofstrasse. Here, at No. 15, the **Cantonal Government Palace** has been housed since 1804. The palace itself was built in Renaissance style between 1557 and 1564, for the cantonal leader of the time, Lukas Ritter. Nearby is the **Jesuit Church** (Jesuitenkirche), one of the first examples in Switzerland of the special style known as "Jesuit baroque"; it was built in 1666-1677, by the architect Christophe Vogler. The front of the church, which was renovated and decorated in rococo style around 1750, is particularly impressive. The towers of the church were added later, in the late 19th century.

South of the Cantonal Government Palace is the **Franciscan Church** (Franziskanerkirche), the oldest sections of which were built in 1300.

The Sad Lion of Luzern

The new bridge, **Seebrücke**, connects the main train station square, Bahnhofplatz, with **Swan Square** (Schwanenplatz), at the eastern edge of the Old City. This square marks the beginning of the busy, prestigious commercial district, full of shops selling clothing, cosmetics and gifts. To the east, the Schweizerhofquai leads to the luxury hotel area and to the city's casino. Leodegarstrasse street leads to the **Cathedral of St. Leger** (Hofkirche), the city's most important church, dedicated to the guardian saint of Luzern, St. Leodegar (St. Leger).

The original church was built in the first half of the 8th century, and the second one was built on its ruins in the 14th century. However, this was almost completely destroyed in a great fire in 1633. Only the two Gothic-style pointed towers remained. The new construction, which began in 1634, was built in late Renaissance style, according to the plans of the monk architect, Jacob Kurrer.

The interior of the church is especially impressive, particularly the choir in the central hall, with

An exhibit at the Bourbaki Panorama

a metal grate around it. Religious works of art decorate the large space, including paintings, sculptures and wood engravings. The church organ, which was installed here in the late 17th century, is considered one of the finest of its kind, and many come here especially to hear it.

"The saddest and most moving piece of rock in the world" is what Mark Twain said of this sculpture at the Memorial Garden of the Lion

Go back on Leodegarstrasse, and turn right on Lôwenstrasse until you come to the square, **Löwenplatz**. At the square turn right, and there, under a domed roof, is the **Bourbaki Panorama** (Das Bourbaki Panorama), a unique place. Open to visitors daily May-Sept. 9am-6pm; Mar.,-Apr. and Oct.-Nov. 9am-5pm. Other months closed.

A giant work by the Genevan artist, Edouard Castres, is exhibited here. This is a panoramic painting spread round and round, over an area of some 11,000 sq. ft.! Against the background of the snow-covered landscape, the artist depicted a scene from the Franco-German War of 1870-1871, when the French Bourbaki army (which was defeated in the battle of February 1871) retreated to the Swiss border village of Verrières. Castra painted his huge panorama in 1889.

From the panorama building turn north. A small street (Denkmalstrasse) leads from here to the **Memorial Garden of the Lion** (Löwendenkmal), which is undoubtedly the best-known symbol of Luzern. In the small garden, which has a pool, the visitors are met by what the American writer Mark Twain called "the saddest and most moving piece of rock in the world."

This is the monument to the soldiers of the Swiss Guard of the French King Louis XVI who were killed on August, 1792 in the Tuileries Gardens in Paris by revolutionaries. The whole of Switzerland was shaken by the massacre. In 1821, the sculptor Lukas Ahorn expressed this pain in his figure of the dying lion, cut into a piece of sandstone.

Only a few feet away from the lion monument, up the hill, is a unique museum, the **Glacier Park** (Gletschergarten). Open daily, Mar.-Apr. and mid-Oct.-mid-Nov. 9am-5pm; May to mid-Oct.

8am-6pm; mid-Nov. to the end of Feb. 10:30am-4:30pm. Admission fee.

By chance, in 1872 a geological message from millions of years ago – crooked holes, called giants' pots – were discovered here. These are the result of slow chiselling by water of the Russe Glacier, which once covered the entire area. A farmer, Joseph Wilhelm Amrein Troller, had wanted to dig a wine cellar here, but when he hit the rock, he was surprised to see that "someone" bigger than he had dug there before him.

In the rock smoothed by stones (balls of granite that also were found at this location) which the glacier dragged with it, 32 "pots" were eventually found, the deepest of which reaches over 30 ft., with a diameter of some 25 ft. To explain how these holes were created, a simulation was installed in the Glacier Museum in 1896, demonstrating the action of the water and the crooked way it chisels the stone.

At the Swiss Museum of Transportation

The museum of the Glacier Park exhibits a wonderful assortment of different and unusual items: There is the first relief map of Switzerland from 1762, remains of a prehistoric man, fossils, miniature models of typical Swiss houses, rock samples and Alpine minerals, a relief map of Luzern from the late 18th century, furniture and objects from old Luzern. Outside of the museum, you can climb up a path cut into the stone to a mountain cabin, resembling those found in the Alps, and from there get a view of the area. If that's not enough, there is also a labyrinth of mirrors, built in the glacier park some 95 years ago, offering visitors the challenge of trying to find their way out of the misleading and distorted maze.

ADDITIONAL SITES

The Swiss Museum of Transportation (Verkehrshaus der Schweiz) is a must. It provides entertainment and a unique experience for the whole family. You can get here by walking along

the northern bank of the lake eastward, to No. 5 Lidostrasse. This takes about half an hour at a comfortable pace. You can also come by bus No. 2, from the Bahnhofplatz, Tel. 31.44.44. The museum is open daily from the beginning of Mar. to the end of Oct. 9am-6pm; from the beginning of Nov. to the end of Feb. 10am-4pm. Admission fee. It is worth planning at least half a day for the visit (and that's barely enough), in order to get the most out of it. There is a good self-service restaurant on the premises.

This is the largest museum of its kind in Europe, and it was built here in 1959. There are 12 buildings of exhibits chronicling the history of transportation to the present day – on land, sea and rivers, in the air and in space – as well as many aspects of communication and tourism. The museum also has a planetarium and a panoramic movie theater.

The following is just a sampling of the exhibits:

Land transportation: 19th-century carriages, the development of the bicycle since its first appearance, the first motorcycles. Some 40 antique and rare automobiles, including a steam-engine car, the Swiss-made Tori-Nusberg of 1877; the first car to run on gasoline, made by Karl Benz in Germany in 1886; the first Renault AX, produced in 1908 by Louis and Marcel Renault, which succeeded in traveling at the incredible speed of 30 m.p.h.; a 1926 Rolls Royce, the legendary 1934 Mercedes-Benz racing car, called the "Silver Arrow," which reached a speed of 190 m.p.h. with its 3360 cc engine and more.

Railways: Some 60 special engines and railroad cars of different types are exhibited in two large buildings. An historical survey of the development of the railroad train, from the steam engine that blew its first whistle in 1858, to newer steam engines, the largest weighing over 90 tons as well as the first diesel engines, and electric engines. In the same exhibit are the first trolley cars from the turn of the century, the special Swiss mountain trains, the various types of cable cars, including the manual ones for transporting food between mountain villages, and others. In the building devoted to the subject of cable cars, you can witness a very reassuring demonstration of the electromagnetic test applied regularly by law to all cableways.

Train-set lovers will admire the giant models of varied landscapes, covered with a network of tiny tracks and trains, both passenger and freight, speeding over the bridges and into the tunnels, just like in real life.

Maritime Transportation: Old boats, restored from former centuries and originals from the turn of the present century. Many models of boats from distant and recent history, riverboats, ferries and ocean liners. An impressive engine room, copied in precise detail from a steamship, demonstrates how the piston works. An especially interesting model is that of locks for lowering and raising riverboats moving from one depth of water to another. There is also a life-size riverboat command cabin, and much more.

Air transportation: The exhibition begins with a hot air balloon, where you see a real flight basket, one of the largest balloons in the world. You will learn how the pilots sat in it. The exhibition continues with zeppelins, the large airships that were powered by helium. There is a model of the most

The Kapellbrücke, Luzern's most famous bridge

famous zeppelin, the Hindenburg, which exploded and brought about the end of a period in air transportation (some of the remains of this unfortunate zeppelin can be seen here).

The modern era in flight is represented by 35 planes, from the first propeller planes to jets. These include civilian and military planes that were used by *Swissair* and the Swiss army (the largest are parked in the large plaza outside the building), with all their equipment and instruments. The history of civilian air transportation in Switzerland, by means of *Swissair*, is demonstrated in a presentation of amusing curiosities, such as the ticket issued to the Pope when he flew in one of the company's planes.

The conquest of space is also acknowledged with a comprehensive exhibit of models of spaceships, launching missiles, astronauts' cabins, their clothing, instruments and, of course, samples of rocks from the moon that the Americans brought back from the famous landing. The presentation includes a program called Cosmorama, projected on a giant screen, which reviews the stages in the conquest of space to date, and plans for the future.

Postage and Communication: An interesting exhibit of the various stages in the development of the post, including the first mail buggies, antique letterboxes, stamps from different periods and a

demonstration of a working modern mail-sorting machine. In another hall, the development of the telephone, telegraph, radio and television is depicted – from their beginnings to today's state-of-the-art systems, accompanied by demonstrations.

Tourism: An exhibit devoted to the history of tourism in Switzerland, the first country in Europe to transform this industry into an official national source of income. In addition, there is the Swissorama Hall, with a panoramic projection of the beautiful scenery and famous sights of the country.

The **Hans Enri Division**: Devoted to the artistic view of technological development, as seen by the contemporary artist, and resident of Luzern.

The **Museum of Swiss Costumes and Customs** (Trachten und Heimatmuseum): Located on a high hill overlooking the city, in Utenberg. You can get there on foot via Dreilindenstrasse, which runs east next to the main church, or by cable car from Haldenstrasse, near the Museum of Transportation (bus 2 takes you there). Open daily 9am-5pm. Closed in Nov. Admission fee.

This charming rural palace of Autenberg, offers a good view of the city, the lake and the mountains. Situated in a lovely park, this museum exhibits some 100 life-size dolls, clothed in the many national costumes of Switzerland. There are also antique furniture from different periods, household items, stamps and seals, and other objects of daily life. Because the house also serves as the base for the Swiss Association of Yodelers, there is also an exhibit of documents related to this subject and a large collection of accordions.

The **Richard Wagner Museum**: There is a long-standing controversy regarding the personality of Wagner, because of his extreme anti-Semitic sentiments, but few would argue his greatness as a composer and the importance of his contribution to music. At any rate, this museum in his honor is situated in the house where he lived between 1866 and 1872. It is located a short ride away from the center of Luzern. You can get here by bus Nos. 6 or 7, or you can take a boat from the dock opposite the main train station to the shore on which the museum is located. Open daily 10am-noon, 2-5pm. Closed Mon., Wed., and Nov. to Jan.

"No one will get me out of here," is how the composer expressed his feelings on the day he moved into this house, April 15, 1866. The enchanting green surroundings, the ancient trees, the slope descending to the lake, the charming Louis Philippe-style house, all create a unique atmosphere. Here Wagner wrote some of his important works, including *Ziegfried* and the *Fall of the Gods*.

The fountain named after Fritschi at the Church Square

On the ground floor of the house, some of Wagner's personal belongings are exhibited, including souvenirs, music that he wrote and his Erard piano. The first floor contains a collection of ancient instruments, belonging to the city of Luzern.

Gutsch Castle: On the hill overlooking Luzern, some 1,600 ft. above sea level stands an old hotel from the last century, which was once the "in" place among the nobility of old Europe. The British Queen Victoria used to vacation here, and one of her visits is commemorated on a marble plaque hanging in the entrance to the hotel: *Queen Victoria – August-September 1868*. The hotel has declined a little (4 stars we regret to report), but the marvelous view from the café balcony has not changed whatsoever – and this certainly justifies climbing up, or taking the 100-year-old elevator train. The train leaves its station on Baselstrasse every ten minutes, 8:30am-12:45pm and 1:15pm-11:30pm.

Tours in the Luzern Area

Luzern is a good point of departure for touring many sites, peaks and settlements located in the surrounding area. You can leave in the morning by train, by car or by boat on the lake, and come back in the afternoon or evening. Regarding schedules of the regional trains or boats to the different places, the tourist information office in the city will be able to help you.

Near Luzern

PILATUS MOUNTAIN

Approximately 9 miles from Luzern, at an altitude of 7,090 ft., is a stunning view, a real "must" for any visitor to the area.

The mountain train that goes up the mountain travels at some points at a 48% incline (the steepest of its type in the world), and its final destination is the upper station. An easy climb of a few minutes brings you to the peak and the breathtaking view of the Lake of Luzern and the Alps around it.

RIGI MOUNTAIN

Located some 16 miles from Luzern, at an altitude of 6,000 ft., this is a famous point overlooking the Lake of the Four Cantons (Lake of Luzern), and a spot where generations of hikers have spent the night in order to watch the fantastic Alpine sunrise.

The climb up the Rigi begins at **Weggis**, a charming resort town situated on the shores of the Lake of Luzern. The mountain train leaves from the Arth-Goldan station (about a half-hour ride). From the train terminal, continue about ten minutes on foot to the peak, to the wide panoramic view and those romantic sunrises.

ZUG

This is a small town (some 21,000 residents) about 15 miles north east of Luzern. It is the capital of the canton of Zug, one of the smallest of Switzerland's cantons. The town is located at the northern end of Zug Lake, and archeological excavations have shown that this spot was already settled in the Neolithic Period. In the Middle Ages the town belonged to the Hapsburgs; it became independent and joined the Confederation in 1352. Lovely green promenades along the shores of the lake enable a view of the Alpine peaks in the distance. In the Old City you can see ruins of medieval fortifications, the

Capucin Tower, the Gunpowder Tower and a Clock Tower with roof tiles in blue and white, the colors of the cantonal emblem.

In the center of the city is **Kulinplatz**, a square surrounded by old buildings with the Kulin Fountain, named for the city's hero of the 15th century, who fought with the forces of the Confederation in the Battle of Arbedo, against the Duke of Milan.

SURSEE

This is a small ancient city, situated at the northern end of Lake Sempach, about a half-hour ride from Luzern. Large parts of the city were rebuilt after a huge fire in the 17th century. The city hall is particularly beautiful. Built in the 16th century in late Gothic style, it has two towers and an elegant exterior staircase.

ENGELBERG

This is a winter and summer sport resort, some 45 minutes south of Luzern by car.

ALTDORF

A small historic city, with about 8,200 inhabitants, Altdorf is the capital of the Uri canton, one of the cantons that founded the Swiss Confederation in 1291. In the City Square stands the famous statue of the hero William Tell.

Pilatus Street on the waterfront

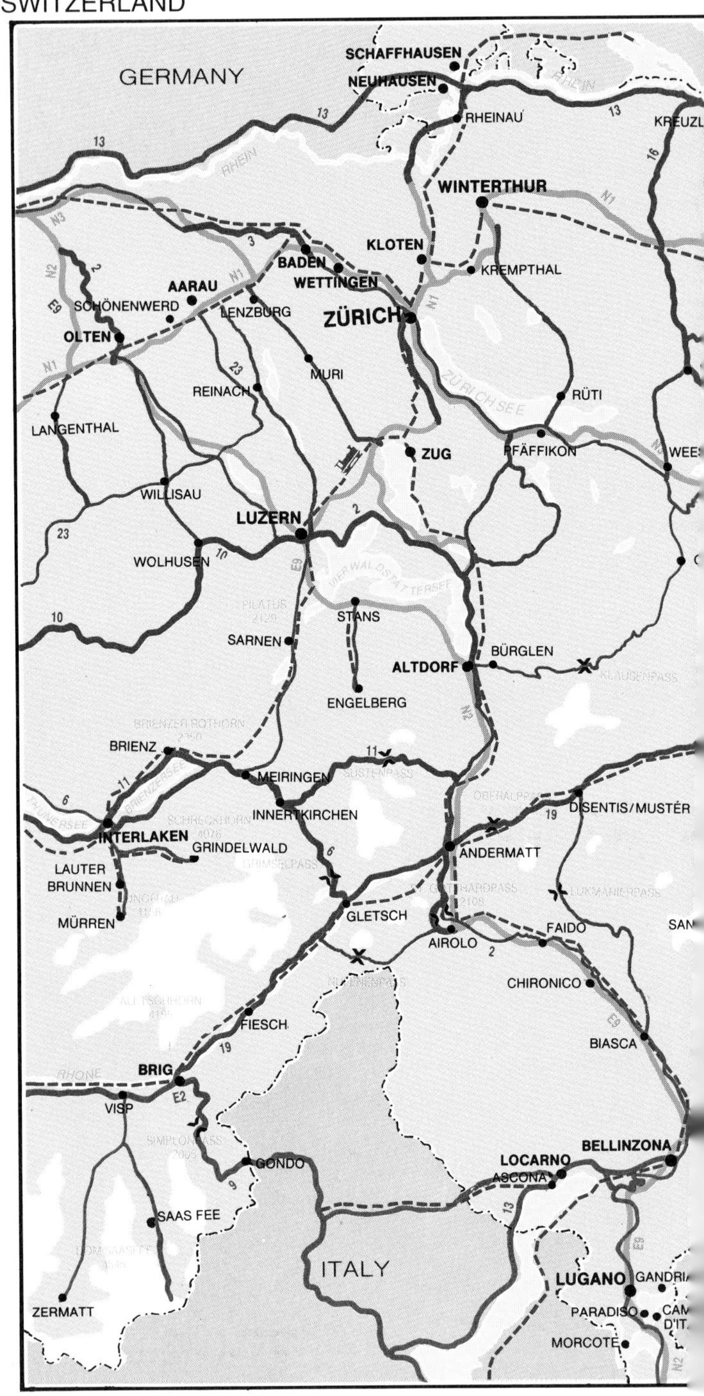

EASTERN SWITZERLAND

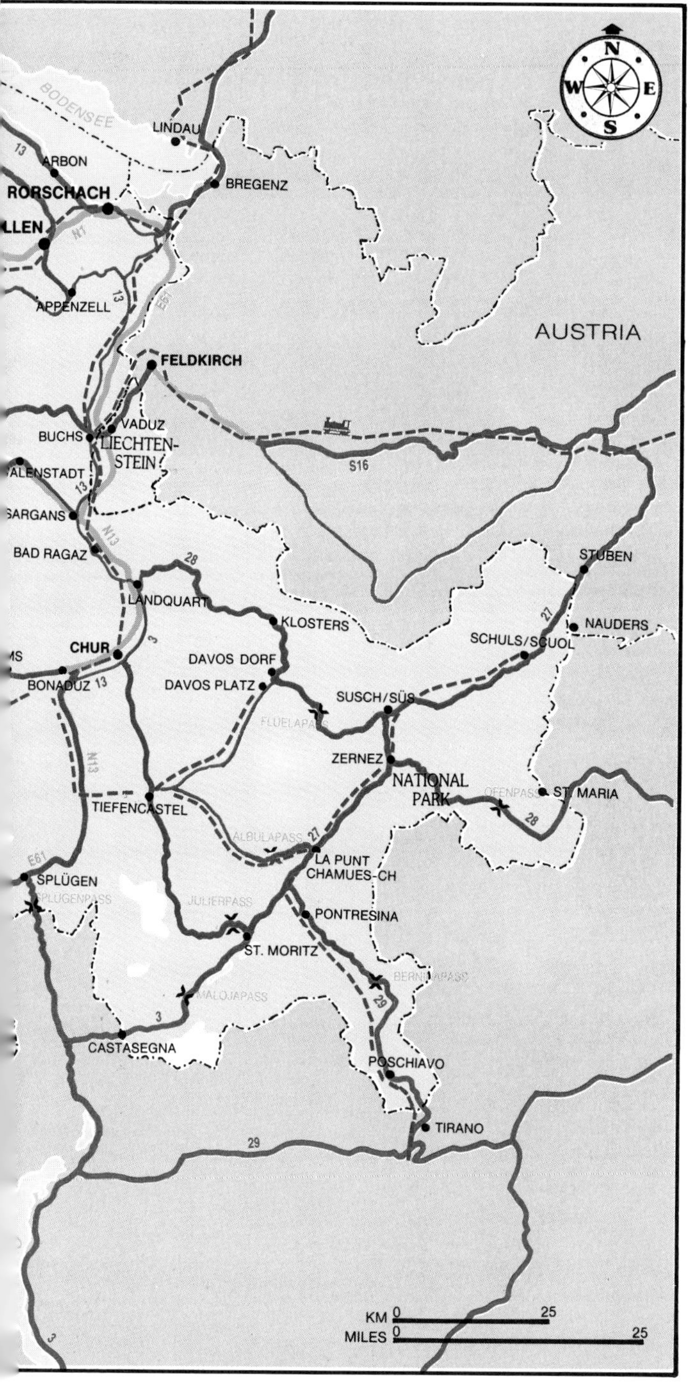
N
W
E
S
BODENSEE
LINDAU
ARBON
RORSCHACH
BREGENZ
LLEN
N1
APPENZELL
13
E61
AUSTRIA
FELDKIRCH
VADUZ
BUCHS
LIECHTEN-
STEIN
ALENSTADT
S16
SARGANS
N13
BAD RAGAZ
STUBEN
28
LANDQUART
KLOSTERS
27
NAUDERS
SCHULS/SCUOL
CHUR
DAVOS DORF
DAVOS PLATZ
BONADUZ
SUSCH/SÜS
FLUELAPASS
ZERNEZ
NATIONAL
PARK
OFENPASS
ST. MARIA
TIEFENCASTEL
ALBULAPASS
LA PUNT
CHAMUES-CH
SPLÜGEN
SPLÜGENPASS
JULIERPASS
PONTRESINA
ST. MORITZ
BERNINAPASS
MALOJAPASS
29
CASTASEGNA
POSCHIAVO
TIRANO
KM 0 25
MILES 0 25

ZÜRICH – A CAPITAL WITHOUT A TITLE

Although Zürich is the largest city in Switzerland, this is not the reason that it is included in the list of major cities of the world. It is not because of size or political importance that is mentioned in the same breath as New York, Tokyo, London, Bonn and Paris, but because of its economic power. The name of the game in Zürich is money.

But don't let this preface mislead you – Zürich is not just one huge exchange hall, big bank or prestigious store; Zürich is also a beautiful, lively city, a cultural center of past and present, and a place where every tourist can find something of interest. Zürich boasts intriguing sights, impressive museums, excellent food and varied entertainment. There is a well-known adage, "wealth shortens the way to happiness"; in Zürich you can test this out.

History

A few archeological remains indicate that, as early as the Stone Age, there was already a primitive settlement on stilts at the spot where the Limmat River leaves Lake Zürich. The protection that the surrounding water provided the place was an advantage to the people of those distant times. Later a Celtic village, evidently primarily fishermen, was founded here. However, the first real historical record of the roots of the city date back to the Roman Era. Toricum was the customs station built by the Romans in the year 15 BC. After a while, they also erected a citadel on Lindenhof Hill (as it is still called today), west of the river, in the center of the modern city.

Zürich – the largest city in Switzerland

The medieval castle which houses the Swiss National Museum

In the third century AD, Christianity reached the residents of the area. As a crossroads on the way to Germany and Italy, the place attracted the attention of conquerors, initially the Alemanni and later the Franks and Carolingians. The kings of this dynasty even chose the city as the location for one of their palaces.

In the mid-ninth century, the importance of Zürich increased when the Emperor, Ludwig the German, established a large, influential monastery here. In 929, Zürich was first mentioned as a city in official documents. In the same period, a self-government was organized which gained power and limited autonomy under the rulers of the country, the Church and the Zähringen nobility.

As a result of these developments, the city was subjected to the direct yoke of the emperorship in the early 12th century, but historically, this concession actually accelerated its recovery. First, it expanded and incorporated the nearby settlements of Neyerdorf, Oberdorf, and Neimarket. Second, in 1336 the first mayor of Zürich, the *burghermaster* Rudolf Brun, created a political precedent when he included the craftsmen guilds (the trade unions) in the government, and added their representatives to the city council alongside the traditional political forces of the wealthy bourgeoisie and the nobility. This was the first step in the growth of the city as an economic center, when the leading industry was production and trade of textiles, particularly silk.

From that point, the road was paved for Zürich to join the Helvetian Alliance in 1351. This was a step that the city had to defend with all its might, against several attempts by the Emperor to put it under siege and force it to return to his rule. These wars ultimately strengthened Zürich, and in the 15th century it grew stronger and added neighboring regions, such as Winterthur and Kyburg, under its jurisdiction.

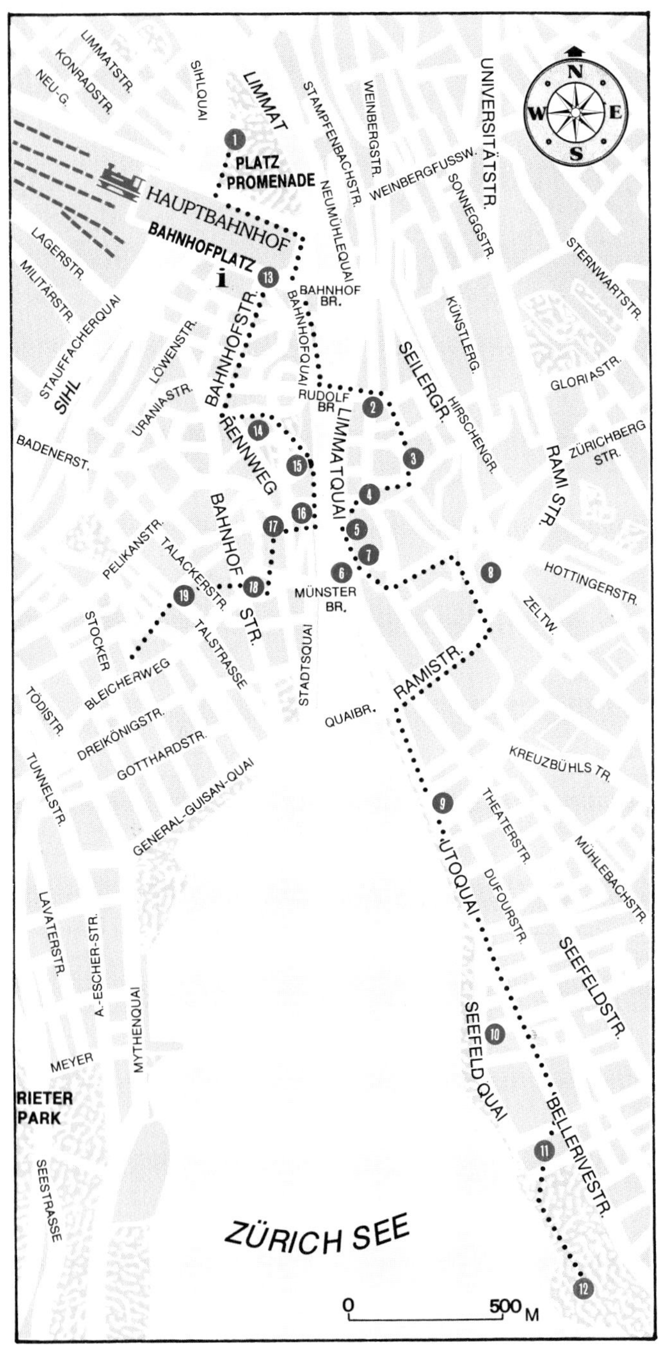
N
W
E
S
LIMMATSTR.
KONRADSTR.
NEU-G.
SIHLQUAI
LIMMAT
PLATZ
PROMENADE
HAUPTBAHNHOF
BAHNHOFPLATZ
STAMPFENBACHSTR.
WEINBERGSTR.
UNIVERSITÄTSTR.
WEINBERGFUSSW.
SONNEGGSTR.
NEUMÜHLEQUAI
LAGERSTR.
MILITÄRSTR.
STAUFFACHERQUAI
SIHL
LÖWENSTR.
URANIASTR.
BAHNHOFSTR.
BAHNHOF
BR.
BAHNHOFQUAI
SEILERGR.
KÜNSTLERG.
STERNWARTSTR.
GLORIASTR.
RUDOLF
BR
LIMMATQUAI
HIRSCHENGR.
ZÜRICHBERG
STR.
RAMI STR.
BADENERST.
RENNWEG
BAHNHOF
STR.
PELIKANSTR.
TALACKERSTR.
MÜNSTER
BR.
HOTTINGERSTR.
ZELTW.
STOCKER
TALSTRASSE
STADTSQUAI
RAMISTR.
BLEICHERWEG
TÖDISTR.
DREIKÖNIGSTR.
QUAIBR.
GOTTHARDSTR.
KREUZBÜHLSTR.
TUNNELSTR.
GENERAL-GUISAN-QUAI
THEATERSTR.
UTOQUAI
MÜHLEBACHSTR.
DUFOURSTR.
LAVATERSTR.
A.-ESCHER-STR.
SEEFELDSTR.
SEEFELD QUAI
MYTHENQUAI
MEYER
RIETER
PARK
BELLERIVESTR.
SEESTRASSE
ZÜRICH SEE
0
500 M
1
2
3
4
5
6
7
8
9
10
11
12
13
14
15
16
17
18
19

In the early 16th century, a social-religious revolution occurred in the city. This was after Ulrich Zwingli, a priest born in Wildhaus, was appointed to serve in the Cathedral of Zürich. Here Zwingli began his work, and eventually became one of the three leaders of the Protestant Reformation, along with Calvin and Luther.

Preaching for disassociation of the local church from the influence of the Pope and the bishopric, Zwingli appealed to the masses and succeeded in realizing his ideas. Among other things, he abolished the sacred ritual, the oaths of the monastery and the priests' life of abstention. He himself married in the city cathedral in 1524. In the end, during the war between the cantons that accepted the Reformation and those who remained loyal to Catholicism, he died in the battle of Capelle in 1531.

Zürich remained Protestant and attracted many refugees of the religious wars, including many professionals who contributed to its development. In the 18th century its prosperity reached a new climax, and it established a name as a cultural center as well.

In 1798, Zürich was conquered by the armies of France and its residents

ZÜRICH

1. *Swiss National Museum*
2. *Niederdorf Quarter*
3. *Central Library*
4. *Old Meat Market*
5. *Rathaus – the House of Representatives*
6. *Helmet House*
7. *Cathedral*
8. *Museum of Art*
9. *Opera House*
10. *Johann Jacobs Museum*
11. *Bellerive Museum*
12. *Zürichhorn Gardens*
13. *Train Station*
14. *Toy Museum*
15. *Lindenhof Hill*
16. *Weinplatz*
17. *St. Peter's Church*
18. *Fraumünster Cathedral*
19. *Historical Museum of Housing*

were all granted full rights, in the spirit of the French revolution. The autonomy of the canton of Zürich, like the others, was abolished under the Helvetian Republic, until 1803. In the early 19th century, when the residents of the city numbered 17,000, the great thrust forward began. In the course of the century, the large university (which today has 6 faculties, teaching more than 18,000 students) and the famous Polytechnic College, the Polytechnicum, were established. Liberal laws were applied which also benefited economic activity: the train line from Basel was laid, and the Zürich Stock Exchange opened in 1877. In the latter part of the century, 12 adjacent neighborhoods were added to the territory of the city, making Zürich the largest city of the Federation. It failed in one thing only – the title of the official capital was bestowed upon Bern, and Zürich has since been forced to suffice with being the unofficial economic capital. In the 20th century, the power of Zürich has grown, as has its influence in banking, commerce, stock exchange (the fourth most important center in the world), international gold trade (the largest center of its type in the world), insurance and textiles, as well as tourism (about 25 million day visitors a year, 85% of them foreigners). Economic organizations throughout the world follow the Zürich exchange closely; large companies cannot afford to disregard it. It is also known as the site of numerous international conferences, and many a diplomatic agreement has borne its name.

A General View

The city of Zürich is situated at the northern end of Lake Zürich. The lake, shaped like a semi-circle, is 18 miles long and 3 miles wide, covering an area of 35 sq. miles, with a maximum depth of 450 ft.

The city, which lies in the eastern part of the Swiss middle-lands, grew in a basin surrounded by hills, where the Limmat River flows out of Lake Zürich, and the Sihl River empties into it from the southwest. The point where the two rivers meet is the center of the city.

The slopes of the hills to the south, west and east were once agricultural areas, most of which have since become urban settlements, some of which have become part of the municipality of Zürich, which today covers some 36 sq. miles.

The city itself is situated at an average altitude of approximately 1,300 ft. above sea level, and the adjacent peaks that dominate it are Zürichberg in the east (2,200 ft. above sea level) and Uetliberg in the west (2,850 ft. above sea level).

Lake Zürich

Zürich is the largest city in Switzerland. Together with its 80 suburbs, the population of the greater metropolitan area is about 850,000 residents. In the canton of Zürich there are 1.1 million inhabitants, about one-sixth of the entire Swiss population.

Due to the extensive international activity of the city, approximately 20% of its residents are from foreign countries. Of the Swiss residents, 80% are German speakers (and Protestants), while the rest speak French or Italian (and are Catholics) and other languages.

Climate

The climate in Zürich is relatively mild. It is influenced by the winds and air currents coming from the Atlantic Ocean, which reduce the impact of its northern location and moderate the climate. Thus, in January the temperatures range between -10ºC and 5ºC, and in June to August, between 10ºC and 30ºC. Statistics show that within a year Zürich receives 45 inches of precipitation, and enjoys 1703 hours of sunshine.

Getting There

Zürich is a Swiss and European crossroads. Convenient, fast *autostradas* lead to it from all directions. From Bern it is 82 miles, from Geneva, 260 miles; from Basel, 56 miles; from Luzern, 36 miles; from Lugano, 140 miles and from St. Gallen, 56 miles.

BY TRAIN

Every hour of the day and evening, rapid trains leave for Zürich from every city in Switzerland and major stations throughout Europe.

BY AIR

Zürich airport is located in Kloten, approximately 7 miles from the center of the city. It serves 130 air routes to 80 countries. The telephone number for airport information is: Tel. 816.40.81.

From the underground train station at the airport you can reach the major cities of Switzerland, or to the city of Zürich itself. A train leaves every 20 to 30 minutes; the ride to the city is only 12 minutes. In order to drive from the airport to the city in a car, take the N1 *autostrada*. By taxi, the average price to the city center is about 45 francs. If you are looking for a more complicated route, you can take bus No. 68 from the airport to Siebach, and from there take Trolley No. 14 to the center.

City Transportation

An efficient public transportation system (VBZ) serves travelers within Zürich. The service operates from 5:30am to midnight, at a high frequency, reaching its peak of once every 6 minutes during rush hour.

You must buy your ticket before boarding the bus or trolley; no tickets are sold on the vehicle (and if you are caught without a ticket, you will be liable to a fine). At every station there is a ticket

machine. Press the button indicating the correct rate and put the amount required in the appropriate slots (the machines do not give change). If you buy a day pass, push it into the slot on the right side of the machine before the first trip in order to stamp the day and the hour.

TAXIS

You can stop a taxi at one of the stations throughout the city, or call one by phone:

Taxiphone, Tel. 271.11.11.

Taxi-Zentrale Zürich, Tel. 272.44.44.

Taxi 2000, Tel. 444.44.44.

CAR RENTAL

All major companies, of course, have special counters at Zürich airport, as well as branch offices in the city:

Avis: 17 Gartenhofstrasse, Tel. 242.20.40.

Budget: 33 Lindenstrasse, Tel. 383.17.47.

Europcar: 53 Josefstrasse, Tel. 155.40.40.

Hertz: 33 Lagerstrasse, Tel. 730.10.77.

If you want a vehicle that you don't have to fill with gas and don't have to worry about parking – you can rent a bicycle at the city railroad station.

PARKING FACILITIES

Public car parks in the city center charge 1 franc per hour. The visitors can also obtain a leaflet from the Tourist Office or the City Police which indicates all multi-storey car-parks throughout Zürich.

Accommodation

As a city that attracts so many – tourists, buyers and business-people – Zürich has the capacity to accommodate its guests, at different standards and varying prices. In total there are 112 hotels in the city, with more than 10,000 beds.

The selection presented below is taken from the list of members of the city's Association of Hoteliers, and their rating is determined according to the criteria of the Swiss Association. All are located centrally, or close to the center, within walking distance from the tourist, shopping and entertainment centers.

FIVE-STAR HOTELS

Eden au Lac: 45 Utoquai, Tel. 261.94.04, fax 261.94.09. On the eastern shore of the lake near the source of the Limmat.

Savoy Baur en Ville: 12 Poststrasse, Tel. 211.53.60, fax 221.14.67. In the Old City on the Banhofstrasse.

Zürich: 42 Neumühlequai, Tel. 363.63.63, fax 363.60.15. On the bank of the Limmat near the mouth of the Sihl.

FOUR-STAR HOTELS

Ambassador: 6 Falkenstrasse, Tel. 261.76.00, fax 251.23.94. Near the outlet of the Limmat River from Lake Zürich.

St. Gotthard: 87 Bahnhofstrasse,

Tel. 211.55.00, fax 211.24.19. Near the main train station.

Pullman-Continental: 60 Stampfenbachstrasse, Tel. 363.33.63, fax 363.33.18. On the eastern side of the Limmat River near the mouth of the Sihl.

Storchen (Zum): 2 Am Weinplatz, Tel. 211.55.10, fax 211.64.51. In the center of the Old City near the river.

THREE-STAR HOTELS

Seidenhof: 9 Sihlstrasse, Tel. 211.65.44, fax 212.01.48. In the center of the city near Bahnhofstrasse.

Sunnehus: 17 Sonneggstrasse, Tel. 251.65.80, fax 252.02.68. East of the river near the university.

Du Théâtre: 69 Seilergraben, Tel. 252.60.62, fax 252.01.54. East of the river near the city center.

TWO-STAR HOTELS

Krone-Limmatquai: 88 Limmatquai, Tel. 251.42.22, fax 251.47.63. In the Old City on the riverfront.

Rothaus: 17 Marktgasse, Tel. 241.24.51, fax 291.09.95. In the Old City near the river.

Villette: 4 Kruggasse, Tel. 251.23.35, fax 251.23.39. In

the Old City, near the outlet of the river from the lake.

Limmathof: 142 Limmatquai, Tel. 261.42.20, fax 262.02.17. East of the river and the main train station.

ONE-STAR HOTELS
Berghalde: 341 Witikonerstrasse, Tel. 381.24.50.

Vorderer-Sternen: Bellevueplatz, Tel. 251.49.49, fax 252.90.63. A tiny hotel, near the outlet of the river from the lake.

YOUTH HOSTELS
Zürich-Wollishofen: 114 Mutschellenstrasse, Tel. 482.35.44, fax 481.99.92. This is the closest youth hostel to Zürich, located in a suburb south of the city, to the west of the lake. A walk here from the main train station can take as much as an hour. You are better off taking Trolley 7 to Morgental station. The hostel is open all year round; the reception desk is open daily 10am-2pm.

CAMPING
Zürich-Wollishofen – Seebucht, Tel. 482.16.12. The closest site to the city, near the youth hostel, on the lake shore. Open May 1 to Sept. 30.

Restaurants

Zürich offers some 1,300 restaurants, in addition to countless snack bars and food stands. Every type of international cuisine is represented: French, Italian, American, Jewish, Japanese styles of cooking, and many others.

It is definitely worth devoting particular attention to local specialties. For instance, try *Züri-Gschnätzelts*, veal with mushrooms and cream sauce with white wine, or *Leberspiesschen*, cubes of liver with bacon seasoned with sage, and served with peas and potatoes. These specialties can be found, among other places, at the following restaurants:

Arvenstübe: 136 Limmatquai, Tel. 251.30.80.

Augustiner: 25 Augustinergasse, Tel. 211.72.10.

Du Nord: 2 Bahnhofplatz, Tel. 211.37.90.

Schwarzer Adler: 10 Rosengasse, Tel. 252.64.30.

Zeughauskeller: 28A Bahnhof strasse, Tel. 211.26.90. In the old arsenal.

Entertainment

Zürich is Switzerland's greatest city in terms of entertainment. As a rule, the night life district of the city is concentrated in the Niederdorf Quarter in the Old City, on both sides of the river, between the main train station and the cathedrals. In this area you will find pubs, night clubs and jazz clubs as well as more intimate entertainment. Some 40 movie theaters show films, usually in their original language with German subtitles.

THEATERS AND CONCERT HALLS

Tonhalle: 5 Gotthardstrasse, Tel. 206.34.40. The city's largest concert hall, hosts famous performing artists.

Schauspielhaus Zürich: 32 Ramistrasse, Tel. 265.58.58. The city's famous theater. Excellent productions performed in German.

Opernhaus: 1 Falkenstrasse, Tel. 262.09.09. Zürich's Opera House.

Theater am Hechtplatz: Tel. 252-3234. Cabaret, chansons and musicals.

NIGHT CLUBS

Byblos: 60 Engelstrasse, Tel. 241.94.16.

Bali Hai: 20 Langstrasse, Tel. 241.59.85.

Kings Club: 25 Talstrasse, Tel. 211.23.33.

Red House: 17 Marktgasse, Tel. 252.11.10.

Longstreet: 92 Langstrasse, Tel. 241.21.72.

BARS

Bellerive Bar: 47 Utoquai, Tel. 251.70.10.

Storchen Bar: 2 Weinplatz, Tel. 211.55.10.

Carlton Pub: 41 Bahnhofstrasse, Tel. 211.65.60 (in the hotel).

DISCOTHEQUES

Candlelight: 14 Marktgasse, Tel. 252.59.40.

Jocker: 5 Gotthardstrasse, Tel. 202.22.62.

City 5: 195 Limmatstrasse, Tel. 42.22.70.

JAZZ

Casa Bar: 30 Münstergasse, Tel. 261.20.02.

Limmatquai 82: Tel. 47.65.30.

FOLKLORE

Börse Restaurant: 5 Bleicherweg, Tel. 211.23.33.

Festivals

February-March – Guggenmusiken: masked balls, carnival bands and parades throughout the streets.

April – procession of the guildsmen in their traditional costumes in the center of the city (Sechseläutenplatz).

June-July, every 3 years – Zürich Lake festival on the river Limmat.

September, the 2nd weekend – Knabenchiessen: a boy's shooting contest, at the Albisgüetli.

December – St. Nicolas Day, celebrated with a traditional "Santa Claus" procession.

Organized Tours

Introductory Tour of the City: This is particularly suitable for getting acquainted with Zürich and developing a basis for getting around on your own. It includes the commercial and shopping districts, the Old City and the lake. This two-hour tour, on buses with multi-lingual guides, leaves the main train station, opposite the tourist office, daily, May to October, at 10am and 2pm.

Tour of Zürich Environs, and Felsenegg Cable Car: The tour, which takes about two and a half hours, includes a marvelous view of the city and lake. The bus leaves the main train station, opposite the tourist office, daily from the beginning of May to the end of Oct. at 9:30am.

Walking tour of the Old City: A tri-lingual (English, French and German) guide leads you through the lanes of the Old City, among the churches, the old homes, the fountains, the bridges and other sights. June to the end of Sept., Tues., Thurs. and Sat. 9:30am-3pm. Leaves from the tourist office at the main train station.

Ride on the Lake: Boats leave the dock at the intersection of Bahnhofstrasse and the shore, daily, Apr.-Oct. A short tour, leaving every 30 minutes.

Ride on the Limmat River: A view from the river of the city and the historic buildings along the bank, overlooking the lake at the charming park of Zürichhorn on the eastern shore. The boats leave the mooring near the Landesmuseum, behind the main train station. Apr.-Oct., every 30 minutes, 1pm-6pm.

Another good possibility is to join the *Zürich Excursions* company which offers city sightseeing tours as well as tours to the regions outside of Zürich. Tel. 462.77.39.

Information and booking are available at the ticket office, Bürkliplatz, Tel. 482.10.33 or at the tourist office in the main Railway Station, Tel. 211.40.00.

Important Phone Numbers

Area code: Tel. 01
Tourist office (at the main train station): Tel. 211.40.00, fax 212.01.41.
Airport: Tel. 816.40.81.
Train Station: Tel. 911.85.11.
Medical first aid: Tel. 255.11.11.
Doctors and dentists: Tel. 261.61.00.
Police: Tel. 117.
Cantonal hospital: Tel. 255.11.11.
Lost and found: Tel. 216.51.11.
Car breakdown service: 140.

Walking Tours

The Eastern Bank

The tour begins behind the city's main train station, on a green triangle which (if you use your imagination) resembles a sort of peninsula, surrounded on two sides by the Limmat and Sihl Rivers, which meet at its vertex. Here, at the location of the first Swiss National Exhibition in 1883, the **Swiss National Museum** (Das Schweizerische Landesmuseum) has stood, since 1893, in a medieval-style castle.

The museum is the most important, the largest and most impressive presentation of the history of Switzerland. 2 Museumsstrasse. Open Tues.-Fri. and Sun. 10am-noon and 2pm-5pm. Sat. 10am-noon and 2pm-4pm. Mid-June to mid-Sept. without an afternoon break. Closed Mon.

The Swiss National Museum

Tel. 218.65.11. Free admission. Trolleys 4, 11, 13, 14 go directly there, to the Bahnhofquai station.

The museum is devoted to a presentation of the history and culture of Switzerland, from the Stone Age to the 19th century. It contains a comprehensive collection of carefully chosen exhibits: weapons, uniforms, battle and celebration flags; works in gold and silver, ceramics, glass; coins, medals, paintings, stained glass, sculpture, furniture, clocks, musical instruments; work implements and many more objects of art and items of daily life. On the ground and first floors you can see prehistoric finds, the Roman collection, and one of the most extensive and splendid collections of the period of the Carolingian Dynasty. The first floor also has rooms completely furnished, down to the smallest detail, with the best of the 16th-and 17th-century household items. There is also a clock collection, with products of the Swiss industry from the 16th to the 19th century.

The hall of weapons and armor of fighting knights, which covers the history of war from the 13th to the 18th century, is overshadowed by the monolithic creation of the painter Ferdinand Hodler, depicting the Retreat of the Confederation Army at the Marignano Battle.

As befitting a city that is the center of the textile industry, the second floor of the museum houses a collection of rural and urban folk costumes of the canton from the past 300 years.

From the museum, the route continues on the bank of the Limmat, leading to the Bahnhof Bridge and across it, and on the eastern bank, to the lovely promenade going south. Opposite the Rudolf Brun Bridge, Mühlegasse St. rises to the left, leading to a 13th-or 14th-century church, **Predigerkirche**, adjacent to the Central Library of Zürich, **Zentralbibliotheke Zürich**. The library is open to visitors Mon.-Fri. 8am-8pm, Sat. to 5pm. Free admission. It contains two and a half million items, books, manuscripts, periodicals, sketches, maps, music books, music notation and more, all from different periods.

The main street of this quarter is the **Niederdorf**, from which the area took its name, or perhaps the other way around – at any rate, this is the most

Soothing harp music by the bank of Lake Zürich

lively district of the city. Crowded pubs with flowing beer, cafés, restaurants, movie theaters, music clubs and other entertainment can be found here. And, when the weather allows, this is the stage for street artists, with their guitars and their collection hats.

Going south from the church library, you come to a street that goes down toward the river, the Rindermarkt. In Zürich there was never a central market. Small markets were held at various points in the quarter, each with its own speciality, like this one, which was for meat. Two famous buildings dominate the area, Bilgeriturm and Grimmenturm, which once served as the residences of nobility and knights, and now house well-known restaurants. The fountain on the street is decorated with a statue of Jupiter, which in the 18th century replaced a medieval statue that stood there. The 19th-century poet of Zürich, Gottfried Keller used to live at No. 9.

Return to the eastern bank of the Limmat, and turn south, towards the Rathaus Bridge, where the historic House of Representatives of Zürich, the **Rathaus**, is located, on the riverbank. The massive neo-Classical style building was dedicated in 1698, and it is situated precisely on the same spot as its predecessor, which served the city in the Middle Ages. Today the city council and the cantonal council hold their weekly meetings here, as announced to all those in the city by the blue and white banner of Zürich that flies above the entrance.

Opposite the house of representatives, at 54 Limmatquai, is **Saffron House** (Zur Saffran), named for the expensive spice, which testifies to its function: it has been the center of the guild of spice dealers since the early 15th century. An earlier wooden building was destroyed and replaced by this beautiful stone building with squared arches in the mid-17th century.

Nearby, on the street by the riverbank, are two more old buildings with an interesting history. No. 42, **Zum Ruden**, is named for a hunting dog, which in the Middle Ages was the emblem on the hunting license. Originally the city mint, in 1348 the building was given by the city council to an association of noblemen. In the 17th century, the building was rebuilt in its present form, and in 1936-1937 is was extensively renovated.

At No. 40 on the same street is **The Carpenters' House** (Zur Zimmerleuten). Originally constructed in 1428 as the center for barrel makers, it later became the home of the guild of wood builders. In 1708 it was destroyed and rebuilt in its present location, with the same design as at first.

A window at the Helmet House reflecting St. Peter's Church

Further down the road is the Cathedral Bridge, which turns right. The bridge was built in 1839 to replace a narrow wooden bridge that stood in the same place. Actually, this was the first stone bridge in the city. Over the bridge, on the same side of the bank, at No. 31, stands an interesting structure, the **Helmet House** (Helmhaus). For many generations this house was the location of the fabric market, and then served as a courthouse. In the late 18th century, the present structure was built, as the municipal library. It now houses a museum with rotating art exhibits. Adjacent to it is the Water Church (Wasserkirche) which, since 1480, has housed the small Gothic church. According to local legend, the guardian saints of the city, Felix and Régula, were beheaded here by the pagan Romans.

The Great Cathedral of Zürich on a festive night

East of this spot – you can't miss it – the **Great Cathedral of Zürich** (Grossmünster) casts its shadow over the entire area. According to tradition, after being executed, Felix and Régula, put their heads under their arms, and walked to the small hill overlooking the Limmat. Here, after many years, a house of worship was built in their memory. Another story says that instead of a prayer house, Karl the Great erected a monastery here. One way or the other, the construction of the cathedral itself began in 1100, the bases of the towers were erected in 1180 and the work continued for a very long time. The southern tower, for instance, was completed only in 1480. The pointed towers that stood high above the cathedral were destroyed in a fire that broke out in 1763; they were replaced with metal-coated wooden domes which became greenish in time, in an imitation of late Gothic architecture. In 1932, Giacometti created new stained glass for the cathedral windows, and in 1938 the artist Otto Muntz added scenes from the life of Zwingli, the 16th-century leader of the Swiss Reformation, over the entrance. You may visit the cathedral daily 10am-4pm, Sun. after prayers, until 4pm.

From the cathedral walk east on Kirchgasse to the **Zürich Museum of Art** (Kunsthaus Zürich). The entrance is on Heimplatz Square. Trolleys 3, 5, 8, 9 and Bus No. 31 come directly here. Open Tues.-Thurs. 10am-9pm, Fri. and Sun. 10am-5pm, Mon. closed. Tel. 251.67.65. Admission fee.

In addition to rotating exhibitions, the museum contains a large and important permanent exhibition of sculpture, painting, drawing and photography. Represented are French and German sculpture from the Middle Ages, Italian and German paintings of the baroque Period and a large collection of Swiss art from the 15th century to the present time, including Hodler, Vallotton, Boüklin and others. French painting holds a prominent position here; there are major works by Cezanne, Renoir, Toulouse-Lautrec, Degas,

The Opera House of Zürich, established on New Year's Eve 1890

Matisse, Utrillo and others. Two outstanding collections lend particular importance to the museum, one of work by Edvard Munch and the other of Alberto Giacometti. A special hall is devoted to 14 works by Mark Chagall.

South of the museum runs Ramistrasse St., which descends west to the outlet of the Limmat River from the lake. There is nothing more relaxing than a walk from here to the south along the riverbank, *Utoquai*, in the marvelous surroundings of lawns, flower beds, trees, the boat mooring and so forth. Further on, to the left of the road, is the **Opera House of Zürich**.

The story of the city opera begins in 1834, when wealthy tradesmen and music-lovers got together, contributed money in return for shares, and established the first opera house. On New Year's Eve, 1890, this hall was destroyed by fire. But those who inherited the stocks did not give up, and they displayed the same volunteering spirit as their fathers had. They collected 2 million francs, and turned to the firm of Fellner and Helmer, who possessed a complete plan, which had not been executed, to build an opera in Krakow, Poland. The plan was executed in Zürich, in less than two years. The luxurious and ornate late 19th-century style can be seen with a walk around the building. Further down the road the shore of the lake makes a turn to the right, to the beautiful Zürichhorn Gardens, where the city's casino is also located. In front of it, at the corner of the shore and Feldeggstrasse, is the **Johann Jacobs Museum**. This is a unique institution, perhaps the only one of its kind anywhere; it is devoted completely to the subject of coffee and its impact on human society. Tel. 388.61.51. Open Fri. and Sat. 2-5pm, Sun. 10am-5pm. Every 2nd and 4th Wed. of the month – public guided tours at 7pm. Admission free. In addition to a library with 1,500 titles on the subject of coffee, from the 16th century to the present day, there are ceramic dishes, silver and other items used for drinking, paintings and drawings. In front of the gardens and the casino, to the left of the bank on Hôschgasse St. (No. 3), is a splendid villa built in 1931 by one of the

Ornamentations atop the Opera House of Zürich

wealthy residents of the city, which now contains the **Bellerive Museum** (Museum Bellerive).

ADDITIONAL SITES

The Bührle Exhibit (Stiftung Sammlung E.G. Bührle): Here you get a peek at an outstanding art collection, acquired between 1934 and 1956, at the beautiful home of the wealthy Zürich industrialist, Emil Bührle. 172 Zollikerstrasse, Tel. 422.00.86. Trolleys 2 or 4 to Wildbachstrasse station. Open Tues. and Fri. 2pm-5pm, Wed. 5-8pm. Admission fee.

Big money has the power to buy the best of fine art. This takes on true significance when you see Bührle's collection – marvelous works by some of the most famous Impressionist masters: Van Gogh, Renoir, Manet, Monet, Pissaro, Gaugin and Degas. There are paintings by other important artists, such as Delacroix (his famous self-portrait), Unger, Corot, the Dutch Ruysdael and Frans Hals, Goya, Guardi and others. In addition to paintings, Bührle was also a fan of religious wood sculpture, and some impressive 12th to 16th-century examples are exhibited here.

Zürich Zoo: One of the nicest zoos in Switzerland, it is smaller than those in Basel and Bern. There are some 2,000 animals of 300 different types, as well as the usual attractions. Watch a beaver family build its tunnels, see a giant deer, giant snakes, a family of Asian elephants, and more. 221 Zürichbergstrasse. Trolley No. 6. Admission fee.

The Johann Jacobs Museum, devoted to the subject of coffee and its impact on society

The Western Bank, along the Bahnhofstrasse

We start this route, at the main train station, where Bahnhofstrasse, the main street of Zürich – and some say of Switzerland – also begins. It was built in 1867, after the "frogs' canal," (which stretched from the train station to the lake), was filled in with dirt. As part of the large project of the time, the wooden train station *(Bahnhof)* was also destroyed, and in October, 1871 the new, present station, (at the time one of the most beautiful and largest in all of Europe), was opened. It

Lindenhof Hill

was considered an architectural masterpiece, and was declared a protected national landmark. The Bahnhofstrasse, which was originally built as a fashionable residential street, gradually changed until it became the prosperous commercial nerve center of Zürich. In the shade of the lovely tilia trees, with maximum comfort for pedestrians, you can bathe your eyes and even purchase the best of products.

There are **shoes**: *Charles Jourdan* at No. 15, *Michel* at No. 98, **jewelry**: *Cartier* at No. 47, *Armin Kurz* at No. 80, **clocks**: *Hofmann* at No. 79, *Gübelin* at No. 36, **men's fashion**: *Day Zürich* at No. 12, *Löw Uomo* at No. 75, **women's fashion**: *Gucci* at No. 36, *Saint-Phil* at No. 20, *Gassmann* at the corner of Paradeplatz; **perfume**: *Schindler* at No. 26, *Lenhard* at No. 39; **department stores**: *St-Annhof* at No. 57, *Vilan* at No. 75, *Globus* between Bahnhofstrasse and Lôwenplatz, *Jelmoli* at the corner of Seidengasse; and, of course, the giant **toy store**, *Franz Carl Weber*.

And while we are on the subject of toys, walking down the Bahnhofstrasse will lead us to a street running to the left, Rennweg, and from it, not much further on, the beginning of Fortunagasse St., on the left. On the corner at No. 15, on the 5th floor (there's an elevator) is the **Toy Museum** (Spielzeugmuseum). Tel. 211.93.05. Open Mon.-Fri. 2pm-5pm, Sat. 1-4pm. Free admission.

The museum houses an entertaining and interesting exhibit of many original items illustrating the history of children's toys from the late 18th century to the beginning of the 20th. There are dolls and doll houses, toy trains, optical and mechanical toys, wooden toys, children's books and more.

Continue on the street toward the Limmat River, to **Lindenhof Hill**. Geologically, the hill is a deposit of glacial rocks – and the spot from which Zürich emerged. This was the site of the ancient Celtic settlement, the fourth century Roman customs station, and a fortress to defend the movement on the Limmat. You can still see ruins of a royal castle from the late Middle Ages here, but for over 500 years this spot has served as a favorite place for meetings, games, competitions and hikes for the residents of Zürich. The fountain of Lindenhof, whose present version was built in 1912, was designed to remind the observer of the heroism of the women of the city when it was under siege in 1292. Inside the wall is the city's first hydraulic pump, from 1666, which brought water to the top of the hill from the Limmat River.

South of Lindenhof is the western end of the Rathausbrücke (Rathaus Bridge). The handsome square next to it is **Weinplatz**, whose name and fountain of vines testify that it was once the square of the wine merchants' market. From the square turn right, to the "old" City Church, **St. Peter's Church**, as it is called. Archeological excavations into its basements have revealed that the church stands in a location that was once a pre-Christian Roman sanctuary. The clock on the church tower was attached in 1534, and is considered the largest of its kind in Europe – 8.7 meters in diameter. The bells of this tower, where, until the 19th century the fire fighters of the city sat, would warn of fires, the greatest fear of European cities in the "wooden era." The central room of the church was renovated from top to bottom in 1705, the first example in the city of Protestant-style architecture. Next to the church area is a stone staircase leading to the grave of Johann Casper Lavater, the well-known preacher, author and physiognomist (interpreter of facial expressions) of the 18th century, and a good friend of the poet Goethe.

St. Peter's Church, whose clock is considered the largest of its kind in Europe

Turn south from the church to the charming commercial street, In Gassen, which runs perpendicular to Bahnhofstrasse, and which until the end of the Middle Ages, when it was built, was actually a winding offshoot of the Sihl River. South of here, on the other side of the street, we come to one of the most beautiful stories and interesting sights in the city, **Fraumünster Cathedral**.

Originally (in the mid-ninth century), a convent for daughters of the aristocracy was built here. Between the 12th and 14th centuries, a church was built adjacent to the convent. The head sister of the convent, who was always a princess, controlled the city and a large rural area, up to the canton of Uri. When the Reformation came to Zürich, the last head sister handed the keys over to the mayor, Hans Waldmann, who was the first man to set foot inside this feminine sacred place. In honor of this, and of his heroism against the Duke of Burgundy in the second half of the 15th century, the people of Zürich erected a statue of him at the exit from the Münsterbrücke.

The church took on its present appearance after general renovations were carried out in the 1830's. Nevertheless, one can still get an impression of the stunning Gothic-style central hall, built in the 14th century. In 1970, the artist Marc Chagall created a set of beautiful stained glass windows behind the choir platform, which integrate well with the general beauty of the place. To the right of the Fraumünster, at 20 Münsterhof

The Fraumünster Cathedral, which stands on the site where a convent once stood

St., is an impressive baroque-style guildhouse, **Zur Meisen**, which housed the Association of Wine Merchants. Built in 1752-1757, its two wings surround a small courtyard closed in by a permanent gate between two posts. In front of this gate, on a dais erected there, Sir Winston Churchill made his famous speech on September 19, 1946, calling for the establishment of a united Europe.

Today the building houses the **Museum of Ceramics and Pottery**, open Sun. and Tues.-Fri. 10am-noon and 2pm-5pm; Sat. 10am-noon and 2pm-4pm. Closed Mon. Free admission. Tel. 221.28.07. Trolleys Nos. 2, 6, 7, 8, 9 and 11, to Paradeplatz.

In addition to touring the handsome 18th-century building, you can also enjoy a fine collection of 18th-century ceramics and pottery made in Switzerland.

From the same square, Parade Square (Paradeplatz), continue on Talackerstrasse and left on Bärengasse, to No. 22. This is the **Historical Museum of Housing** (Wohnmuseum). Open Tues.-Fri. 10am-noon and 2pm-5pm, Sat. to 4pm; mid-Jun. to mid-Sept. open continuously without an afternoon break. Closed Mon. Tel. 211.17.16. Free admission.

Two adjacent 16th and 17th-century buildings, **Zum Schanzenhof** and **Zum Weltkugel**, provide the visitor with a picture of the housing conditions and day-to-day objects from that period until the 19th century. There are three stories of furnished rooms, with all the original furniture and decorations, as well as a basement floor containing an exhibit of the dolls of the 1920s Zürich artist, Sasha Morgenthaler.

ADDITIONAL SITES

Rietberg Museum (Museum Rietberg): 15 Gablerstrasse, Trolley 7. Open Tues.-Sun., 10am-5pm; closed Mon. Admission fee. The museum houses interesting non-European art from India, China, Africa, and other places.

In an attractive park, overlooking the western shore of the lake, stands **Villa Wesendonck**, a neo-Classical style house, which served writers and musicians of the 19th century, among them

Richard Wagner, who spent several years here. The house presently contains the special collection of the Baron Edward von der Heydt.

This is the only large museum in Switzerland devoted to non-European art. It includes works from India – bronze and stone sculpture and miniature paintings; from China – Buddha statues, paintings from the period of the Ming dynasty, vases and ceramics; from Japan – paintings, drawings and wood sculpture; and from Africa – statues made by the Baga, Dogon, Guro, Senufo and other tribes, ritual masks from Zaire, Cameroon and more.

The western bank of Zürich Lake with a view of the Fraumünster Cathedral in the center

FROM ZÜRICH TO THE RHINE WATERFALLS

The N1 *Autostrada* continues east from Zürich and then turns north, toward Winterthur. Approximately four miles before Winterthur, to the east of the road, is **Kyburg Castle**, one of the largest and most splendid of the medieval castles found in Switzerland. It is built like a fortress, with knights' quarters, a church and everything necessary to endure a long siege. It is first mentioned in an historical document from 1027, as the castle of the influential family of the counts of Kyburg. Some time later the castle was inherited by the Hapsburg kings, who because of the castle's fortification, chose to keep their imperial treasures within its walls. In the 15th century, the castle became the property of the canton of Zürich, and the seat of the regional governors.

Today, the building houses a museum containing a very impressive collection of weapons and furniture from different periods. The visitor is also treated to a splendid view of the area. Open to visitors daily 9am-noon and 1pm-5pm, closed Mon. Admission fee. You can get to the castle by the post bus from Kemptthal.

WINTERTHUR

This city is an example of an extraordinary combination of developed industry and a tradition of art and culture. It has major factories for metal products, motors, textile and more, and it holds many festivals of theater, opera and music, including open-air concerts.

One of the wealthy residents of the city, Oskar Reinhart, an art lover and collector, left Winterthur two outstanding museums. The **Oskar Reinhart Foundation**, 6 Stadthausstrasse, is a collection of 18th-20th century paintings by the great artists of the German-speaking countries, including Ankar, Wassman, Böcklin, Culor, Holder and others. In the **Oskar Reinhart Collection**, 95 Haldenstrasse, the best of European painting from different generations is exhibited: Breugel, El Greco, Rembrandt, Poussin, Watteau, Daumier, Fragonard, Corot, Delacroix, Renoir, Van Gogh and Picasso.

Another feature of the city is the *Technorama*, the **Swiss Museum of Technology**, at Technoramasstrasse, which portrays the history of technology and demonstrates research in an exhibition laboratory. Autostrada N4 from Winterthur will take you to the Rhine Waterfalls and Schaffhausen.

THE RHINE WATERFALLS (RHEINFALL)

The waterfalls of the Rhine River are a sight not to be missed, especially in the beginning of the summer, when the snow begins to melt. The river, which is over 450 ft. wide at this location, runs down from a waterfall 76 ft. high. This is the largest waterfall of its type in Europe. It is recommended that you enjoy the view of the falls from **Laufen Castle**, located at the edge of the "elbow" created by the bend in the river. The castle, whose most ancient sections were built 1,000 years ago, also houses a youth hostel and restaurant. You can also get to the castle from Schaffhausen on the postbus, or by walking a few miles.

The Rhine Waterfalls, full of froth

SCHAFFHAUSEN

This city of 34,000 residents, the capital of the canton of Schaffhausen, lies at the mouth of the Swiss land peninsula that juts into German territory. The development of the town is attributed by local tradition to those merchants who had to stop their boats before reaching the Rhine waterfall, continue on land and then return to the river. This point, by force of necessity, became a transit station, and eventually a city. In modern times the river has also helped the city. Industries requiring a cold water current, such as metal, steel and electronics, emerged here. Also noteworthy is the cross street of the quarter, Vordergass with its characteristic painted houses and porches. South of this street is the city church, **All Saints' Church** (Allerheiligen), whose ancient interior sections were originally an 11th-century monastery. Adjacent to the church is a museum, containing a collection of ancient texts, the property of the former monastery, sacred implements and archeological finds uncovered in excavations in the area. Alongside all this, another wing of the museum is devoted to a survey of the industry of Schaffhausen.

The lovely **Citadel of Munot** was built between 1564 and 1585, and its claim to fame has been reserved – it is the only such structure built according to the architectural theory described by the German artist Albrecht Duhrer in his *Essay on Fortifications*, published in Nuremburg in 1527. This is expressed in the building's special beauty, its rounded shape and its round lookout tower, which was seriously damaged in the Franco-Austrian War of 1799 and restored according to the original.

A visit to the citadel is highly recommended, and from there you should take a look at the area and at Schaffhausen at its feet. This is possible from May to Sept., daily from 8am-8pm and Oct.-Apr., daily from 9am-5pm.

Schaffhausen – capital of the canton of the same name

ST. GALLEN – THE HIGH CITY

History

The origins of the city of St. Gallen date back to 612 AD, when the Irish wandering monk, Gallus, companion of the Christian saint Colomban, reached the narrow Steinach Valley, then a dense, uninhabited forest. About 100 years later, in 719, a monastery of the Benedictine order was established in the place where Gallus, who in the meantime had also become a saint of the Catholic Church secluded himself. In the ninth and tenth centuries, the monastery became known throughout Europe as a place of theological, cultural and intellectual development, and its influence was great. In the course of this development, a settlement of farmers and craftsmen emerged near the monastery; this settlement was called *Villa Sancta Galli*, the Settlement of Saint Gallus. In time the settlement grew into a city, today's St. Gallen.

In 1212, the city was recognized by the Holy Roman Empire as a free city with autonomous rights of administration and trade, and this contributed greatly to rapid development and prosperity. In 1454, St. Gallen, and the region controlled by it, joined the Confederation, but as "annexes" only. In 1524, an important change took place, when St. Gallen accepted the Reformation, that is, the Protestant faith, under the leadership of Joachim von Watt, known as Vadian, a scientist and scholar who was elected as mayor. This decision, of course, dealt a serious blow to the Catholic monastery and put an end to its prominence and cultural influence for a long time to come.

In the Middle Ages a textile industry began to thrive in the city. Linen produced in workshops in the monastery and in the city earned a reputation for fine quality throughout Switzerland and other European countries, who

sent merchants to purchase it in St. Gallen. The economic success expanded the industrial base, and a cotton spinning and embroidery industry also developed. The industry expanded throughout the canton, where it is strong to this day.

In 1803, with the end of the short-lived Helvetian Republic, the St. Gallen region became a canton in the Confederation, and the city of St. Gallen became its capital.

A General View

The city of St. Gallen, in which there are some 74,000 residents, the majority German speakers, is the capital of the St. Gallen canton. In the entire canton there are some 400,000 inhabitants, in an area of 785 sq. miles. St. Gallen is the seventh largest city in Switzerland, and it is the cultural and economic center of the region known as Eastern Switzerland – Ostschweiz.

St. Gallen is also the highest city in Europe. Its citizens spend their days at an altitude of some 2,300 ft. In fact, the city is situated in a high valley. To the north lies the large Lake Constance (Bodensee) – the second largest in Switzerland, covering 210 sq. miles.

Southeast of St. Gallen is the small princedom of Liechtenstein, which is economically tied to it. All matters of tourism of the princedom, are handled in St. Gallen.

South of the city lie the mountains. The peak of Mt. Altmann towers at 7,980 ft., and the top of Mt. Säntis, at 8,200 ft. Around the city are hills of varying heights, in the area between the mountains and the lake. The landscape is typical of the Swiss Plateau.

Climate

The characteristic weather of this region of eastern Switzerland is less humid than in other areas, and there are no storms. Temperatures: an average of -7°C in Jan., and of 20°C in Aug.

City Transportation

You can get to St. Gallen by car on the N1 Zürich-Winterthur Autostrada, a distance of 56 miles. Frequent trains run from 5am to midnight between St. Gallen and Zürich, reaching the Zürich airport. The trip takes about an hour. Within the city itself you are best off walking. The commercial district of the city, the Old Quarter and the major sights are all located within walking distance of one another.

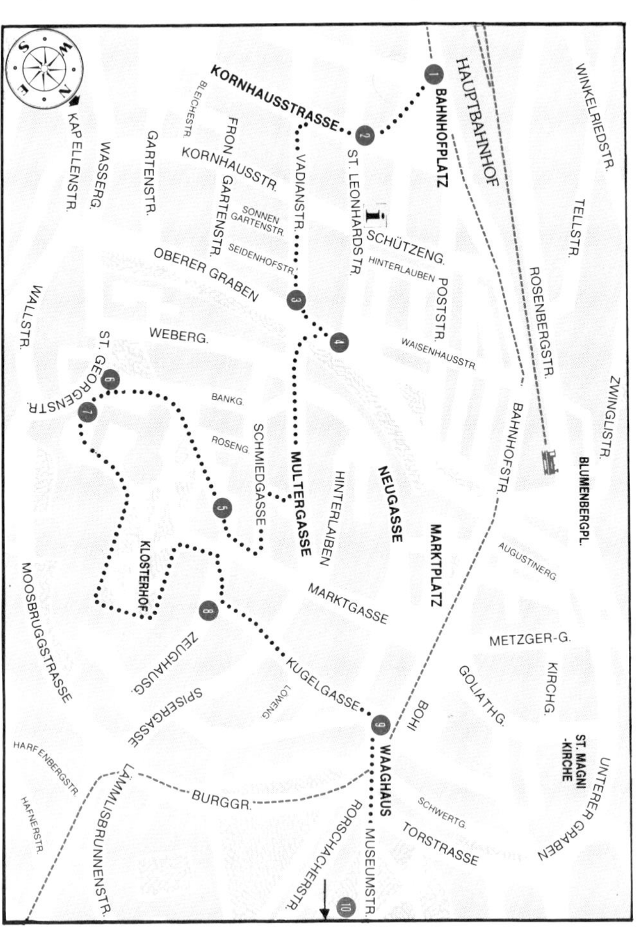

ST. GALLEN

1. Railway Station
2. Tourist Office
3. Textile Museum
4. Broderbrünnen Fountain
5. Cathedral Plaza
6. Cathedral of St. Gallen
7. Monastery Library
8. Church of St. Laurenzen
9. Waaghaus
10. Historical Museum

Nevertheless, there is of course a bus system, and the tickets, as usual, are sold in machines located in the stations. In the stations you will also find maps of the bus routes.

TAXIS

You can find taxis at the train station in the center of the city. You can also ask the hotel clerk, or call one at the following telephone numbers:

Sprenger: Tel. 35.35.35.
Taxi Herold: Tel. 22.27.77.
Taxi Zentrale: Tel. 23.81.81.

CAR RENTAL

For those who wish to rent a car, most of the major companies have offices in St. Gallen. All the companies are found at the Zürich-Kloten Airport.

Avis: 124 Länggasse,
Tel. 25.22.22.
Hertz: 35 Zürcherstrasse,
Tel. 28.84.74.

MOTORBIKE AND BICYCLE RENTALS

You can rent a motorbike or a bicycle at Hauptbanhof: Gepäckbüro, Tel. 23.14.41.

PARKING

Many parking facilities are located a 5-10 minute walk from the Old Town. Here are a few of the parking facilities for private vehicles:

Neumarkt Parking Garage: City Garage AG, Tel. 22.11.14, open Mon.-Sat. 5am-12:40am.

Brühltor Parking Garage: Tel. 24.95.40, open 24 hours a day.

Burggraben Parking Garage: Tel. 22.83.06, open daily 6am-1am.

Oberer Graben Parking Garage: Tel. 22.32.40, open 24 hours a day.

Accommodation

St. Gallen offers its visitors 27 hotels, in the city and the vicinity, in the four-star category and below it. The following is a list of recommended hotels:

FOUR-STAR HOTEL

Einstein: 2 Berneggstrasse, Tel. 20.00.33, fax 235474.

Walhalla: Bahnhofplatz, Tel. 22.29.22, fax 22.29.66. Opposite the city hall, next to the train station.

THREE-STAR HOTELS

Dom: 22 Webergasse, Tel. 23.20.44, fax 23.38.21. In the center of the city on the edge of the Old City.

Im Portner: 12 Bankgasse, Tel. 22.97.44, fax 22.98.56. In the Old City, near the cathedral.

TWO-STAR HOTELS

Elite: 11 Metzgergasse, Tel. 22.12.36. Near the market square.

Vadian: 36 Qallusstrasse, Tel. 23.60.80.

ONE-STAR HOTELS
Sonne: 31 Hauptstrasse, Tel. 31.17.02, fax 31.42.78.

YOUTH HOSTELS
There is a friendly youth hostel at 25 Jüchstrasse, Tel. 25.47.47, fax 25.49.83. It is open most of the year; closed from Dec. 15 to Feb. 28.

CAMPING
There are two camping grounds near the city:

Am Buchberg: Thal, Tel. 44.17.69. Open early May to mid-Oct.

Leebrücke: Bernhardzell, Tel. 38.49.69. Open May 1-Oct. 4.

Restaurants

Some 370 restaurants and cafés await the hungry and thirsty of St. Gallen. You can also adopt the favorite local custom, and bite into the city's famous hot dog – *St. Galler Bratwurst* – at one of the rotisserie grills in front of the butcher shops, where you buy them hot and crispy.

Bahnhof Buffet: 2 Bahnhofplatz, Tel. 22.56.61. The train station cafeteria. Open daily, service until 11:15pm. International, local and Swiss bourgeois cuisine.

Galletto: 62 St. Jakobstrasse, Tel. 25.03.03. A restaurant specializing in Italian food and seafood. Open daily except for Sun., until 11:30pm.

Zum Goldenen Schäfli: 5 Metzgergasse, Tel. 23.37.37. A meeting place for lovers of Swiss cuisine. Open daily, except for Sun., until 11:30pm.

St. Leonhard: 26 Burgstrasse, Tel. 27.90.10. International cuisine, mutton delicacies. Open daily, except for Mon., until 11:30pm.

Important Phone Numbers

Area code: Tel. 071.
Tourist office: 1A Bahnhofplatz, Tel. 22.62.62, fax 23.43.04.
Train station: Tel. 22.00.11, 20.00.05.
Police: Tel. 117.
Medical First Aid: Tel. 111.
Car break down service: Tel. 140.

Walking Tours

A Visit to the Magnificent Library

Start at the city's train station square, going south toward St. Leonhard St., where the city's tourist office stands at the corner of the square and the street. From there take the first turn left, at Kornhaus St., which leads you to Vadianstrasse. At No. 2 is the **Textile Museum** (Textilmuseum)., open Mon.-Fri. 10am-noon and 2pm-5pm, Sat., from Apr. 1 to Sept. 30. Tel. 22.17.44. Admission fee.

This museum, which has been located here since November 1886, is part of a complex including the School for the Textile Arts, the Textile Library, the Swiss School of Fashion and the management of this central industry in the history of St. Gallen.

In two large halls, on the first and second floors, an impressive collection of works of embroidery, spun cloth, woven rugs and wool, as well as various objects related to the subject, are on exhibition. Particularly outstanding are the examples of fashion from different periods, such as the luxurious dress that belonged to the Empress Eugénie, wife of Louis-Napoleon, which took 36 craftsmen 18 months to complete! You can immediately see the work that has been invested. Other admirable works include incredibly delicate lace work from the 16th century to the present day. The museum also exhibits part of the famous collection that belonged to the local textile industrialist, Leopold Iklé, who took the museum under his patronage at the beginning of this century.

From the museum, turn left to Oberer Graben St., one of the streets that goes around the Old City, this one in the shape of an egg. If you look to the left, you can see a square in which there is a fountain, Broderbrunnen Square. The Square was once one of the entrances to the Old City, which was at the time surrounded by a fortified wall.

The Old City of St. Gallen, with its 16th-and 18th-century houses, is enchanting. Wandering through its streets, most of which are restricted to pedestrians only, you will discover decorated building exteriors and balconies (known here by the German word, *Erker*) for which the city is well-known. Wood carving, metal engravings, colored glass, sculpted marble and chiselled stone can all be found here. There is no doubt that a great deal of work and talent have been invested here in past centuries, in order to please the eye. The following is a list of some of the balconies, which you can especially look for:

On Multergasse, at No. 6, a balcony from 1793; at No. 26, a Gothic façade and a balcony from 1600.

On Spisergasse, at No. 3, a wooden balcony from 1700; at No. 11, a house from 1509 with a balcony from 1830.

On Schmiedgasse, at No. 1, a wooden balcony with carved lions' heads, from 1680; at No. 15, a charming 15th-century house with a carved wood balcony from 1707.

The Cathedral of St. Gallen, built in baroque style on the ruins of a 14th century Gothic cathedral

In the southern part of the Old City, the streets open onto a plaza, covered with grass and pebbles. Here we find the **Cathedral of St. Gallen**.

Construction of the cathedral began in 1755, on the ruins of a Gothic cathedral from the 14th century. Undertaken in the period of rule of the church prince Celestin II, the project was designed by architect Peter Thumb. In 1768 the building was opened, with its two 200 ft. high towers. It is one of the few remaining examples of baroque style of that size.

Go into the large hall of the cathedral; you will be absolutely stunned. On one side is incredibly rich decoration, a combination of rococo and neo-Classic ornamentation, in white and gold, while the other side exhibits a marvelous harmony of statues, engravings, colors and furnishings. This is definitely one of the most impressive cathedrals of its type, with its prayer dais, located in the inner part of the hall, surrounded by a metal fence with gold work. In 1983, the UNESCO organization added this cathedral to its list of select sights of beauty and culture in the world.

Opposite the entrance to the cathedral lies a lovely square, Gallusplatz, where there are houses from the 15th century onwards.

To the right of the cathedral entrance, on the other side of the corner of the elongated monastery building, is the entrance to the Monastery Library (Stiftsbibliothek). Tel. 22.57.19. Open Mon.-Sat. 9am-noon and 1:30-5pm, Sun. 10:30am-noon. June-August, Sun. also 1:30-4pm. Closed in November. Admission fee. This library in itself justifies a visit to St. Gallen.

Go to the first floor (sometimes you have to ring the doorbell). The door opens from the inside, and closed circuit cameras follow the visitors' activities. The security measures are strict, as the exhibits are of great value.

Inside the Monastery Library

On entering the library hall, you will have to wear large cloth over-shoes on top of your shoes, so as not to damage the floor. This gives you a feeling of "ice skating" over the smooth, waxed, wooden floor which is rare and beautiful.

After the original ancient (seventh-century) monastery, was destroyed, its library was preserved and moved to a hall specially built in the mid-18th century by the cathedral architect, Peter Thumb. Many consider this hall as a most magnificent example of rococo design. It is rectangular, 32 ft. wide, 110 ft. long and 24 ft. high, two-tiered and decorated with 34 windows. Light pours in through the windows and falls upon the wooden furniture and the splendid floor, which are made of walnut and cherry wood.

An inscription in ancient Greek is displayed above the entrance: *The Pharmacy of the Soul*. On the ceiling is a large fresco, created by the painter Joseph Venemacher, depicting religious scenes. It is hard to decide at first where to look, it is all so impressive.

But the truly great treasure of this place is its book collection – over 100,000 volumes, among them 2,000 priceless medieval manuscripts (mainly from the 8th-12th century), illustrated with paintings and drawings. And as though this was not enough, there are also 1,650 books from the first days of the printing craft.

Among the books and manuscripts on exhibit for visitors, in wooden drawers and under protective glass, is a book from the year 790 – the oldest book written in German in the world. Another marvelous item exhibited here is a Book of Psalms, in Latin, written entirely in gold letters, from the ninth century. On top of all this, in the far right-hand corner of the hall, a gift given in 1824 to the monastery by the nobleman Charles Müller of Friedberg is exhibited: an Egyptian mummy found in Upper Egypt (from the eighth century BC).

Upon leaving the library you can turn left, walk through the passages in the building to the inner courtyard, where there is a small pool, and come out again in the plaza behind the cathedral. The long building to the east is the seat of the cantonal government of St. Gallen. From the northern end of the building the road leads around to Kugelgasse, and then passes by the **Church of St. Laurenzen** (St. Laurenzen-Kirche), which is marked by the monkish simplicity of its interior hall, in utter contrast to the nearby cathedral. The road winds up and crosses the Old City, until it comes to the eastern corner of the market square. Here, on the right, is a strange building, the **Waaghaus**, the weighing station, which as its name indicates once served the merchants.

At lunch (or dinner) time you will be pleasantly surprised to find the *Fondue Beizli* close by, with some of the best menus of the Swiss kitchen (26 Brühlgasse, Tel. 22.43.44; closed on Sunday). Reservations are a must.

Starting at the weighing station and running east is Museumstrasse. Here, at the corner of the municipal park, is the **Historical Museum** of St. Gallen. Tel. 24.78.32. Open June to the end of Sept., daily 10am-noon and 2pm-5pm; during other months, afternoons and Sun. morning only; closed Mon. Free admission.

This modest museum displays a collection of works of art and daily objects, embroidery, tapestries, ceramics and more, from the city's past and from the monastery with which it began. There is also a collection of souvenirs from distant lands brought to the city by merchants returning from their voyages.

Tours in the St. Gallen Area

St. Gallen is a convenient point of departure for a tour or a leisurely trip to many lovely, interesting and intriguing places. For instance, from here you may go to Liechtenstein, the princedom to which we have devoted a special chapter, or to other sights, suggested below:

Rorschach's marina

APPENZELL

Not far south of St. Gallen, at an altitude of 2,500 ft., is the small town that so well exemplifies what is known as "early Switzerland." Appenzell has one main street, on which you will find charming baroque-style houses, shops that sell embroidery and, of course, the famous *Appenzell* cakes. From here you can climb to a marvelous observation point overlooking the mountains and the valley, at **Hoher Kasten**, some 6,000 ft. above sea level.

RORSCHACH

The road from St. Gallen to Lake Constance (about 6 miles) leads to this colorful lake side village, located at an altitude of about 1,300 ft. above sea level. From the local port you can take a ride on the lake, or enjoy water sports.

SARGANS

Travel from Lake Constance via the Rhine Valley and then turn west on the road leading to Lake Walen (Walensee), which takes you to Sargans. A short walk (a few minutes by foot) from the town is Sargans Castle, a medieval fortress from the 13th century, which formerly belonged to Duke Leopold of Austria. Open daily from Apr. 1-Oct. 31. The castle houses a museum of local history and there is a restaurant next door.

A canyon situated not far from Bad Ragaz

BAD RAGAZ

Slightly further south, on the Rhine Valley Road, past the turn to Walensee, lies this charming settlement, at the edge of the Tamina Valley, 1,639 ft. above sea level. As early as the 11th century, Bad Ragaz was already known for its popular thermal baths (37°C). In the winter the city is connected by cable car to the winter sport region of Pizol. Near the town is the Pfäfers monastery, with a beautiful Baroque church.

URNÄSCH

From this pleasant town, in which there is an interesting folklore museum, you can take the road to one of the highest peaks of the Alps ridge (Alpstein), the Säntis, 8,220 ft. high.

The climb up the mountain begins with a tunnel at the bend in the road - Schwägalp. From the upper station of the cableway, it is a short way to a fantastic view: Lake Constance and Lake Zürich together with the Berg and Vararlberg mountains – breathtaking.

Bad Ragaz

LIECHTENSTEIN

St. Gallen is a convenient point of departure for a visit to the princedom of Liechtenstein.This tiny princedom is a sovereign state in every sense, and it attracts many tourists on account of its fame. Actually, Liechtenstein is a remnant of 18th-century Europe.

By car, you can drive northeast toward Rorschach, and then follow the Rhine south, until you are opposite Vaduz, the capital city of the princedom. You can also take a "short cut," through Altstätten, a route recommended especially for those who love winding mountain roads.

By public transportation you can take the train from St. Gallen to Buchs, and from there continue by bus to Vaduz. The Swiss vacation card is valid, in Liechtenstein, as well. Crossing the border between Switzerland and Liechtenstein involves no formalities; there isn't even a border station.

The noble Liechtenstein family, one of the oldest German families, was originally from Mandling, Austria. In the late 17th and early 18th century, a member of the family, Johan Adam von Liechtenstein, acquired two neighboring estates: Schellenburg and Vaduz. In 1719, the Emperor Karl VI granted the status of princedom to the united estates, which were subject to the emperorship.

The castle on the cliff above the city of Vaduz

Initially the princes of Liechtenstein did not live in the princedom itself, but in the family castle in Austria. They were known as courageous military men in the service of the German alliance, and it was only in 1842 that they moved to the castle that stands to this day on the mountain cliff above the city of Vaduz. In 1866, when the German alliance was dissolved, the princedom gained independence. Under the rule of Prince Johan II, the princedom thrived, a progressive constitution was adopted, mandatory army service was abolished (in 1868) and an agreement was signed with Austria for uniform currency – for the purpose of economy.

In 1921, Johan II (who holds a record for his reign – from 1858 until his death, in 1929) decided to introduce Swiss currency in his country. Three years later the ties between the princedom and Switzerland deepened, and agreements were also signed regarding customs, diplomatic representation, postage and transportation.

When Johan II died, he bequeathed his throne to his brother, Prince Franz I, and when he died, in 1938, his son Franz-Joseph II took over. Since 1984, his son, Johann-Adam, has been ruling on behalf of the aging prince.

According to the new constitution of 1921, the Prince is the head of state, and his position is handed down to the male descendants of the family. The prince appoints the judges of the princedom, and represents the state in all ceremonial matters (actually, Switzerland handles Liechtenstein's foreign affairs and security matters). Besides the prince there is a 15-member Parliament, which is elected every four years. The decisions of the Parliament must be approved by the prince, or confirmed by referendum. In Liechtenstein, as noted, there is no army. In the two World Wars it maintained neutrality, like Switzerland. It only has a small police force, numbering a few dozen officers. The population of the princedom today is approximately 30,000; the language of the inhabitants is German, and 90% of them are Catholic (the official religion of the princedom).

The area of Liechtenstein, located between Austria and Switzerland, covers 60 sq. miles (its maximum length is 14 miles; width, 4 miles). Its northern region is flat, situated at the spot where the Rhine Valley widens. In its east are the Alps, and the highest peak in its territory is the Grauspitz, 8,500 ft. high. The economy of the princedom is based mainly on agriculture, tourism and the sale of postage stamps – highly sought among collectors throughout the world. Due to its liberal customs laws and the open system of legal registration, the princedom has also become a very popular place of registration for international financial companies.

Although Liechtenstein's story is lovely, there isn't much to see here. From Vaduz you can go up to the **castle** above, and in the little city itself there are a few restaurants, souvenir shops and a post office that attracts many stamp buyers.

The **Museum of the Art of the Princedom** (Liechtensteinische Kunstsammlungen) in the city, is open daily. Admission fee. On the second floor of the museum is an impressive collection of paintings belonging to the royal family. In the center are a dozen works by Rubens. In the same building there is also the **Liechtenstein Museum of Postage,** which includes a collection of medallions, stamps produced by the princedom and their printing blocks.

For more information about Liechtenstein, call the Tourist Office in Vaduz, Tel. (075) 232.14.43.

Vaduz

THROUGH THE GRAUBÜNDEN CANTON, MOUNTAIN COUNTRY

If you left St. Gallen, and went south to Liechtenstein, you can now continue south, on the N13 *Autostrada*. This is the way to the canton of Graubünden (in French, *Grisons*), which is interesting and unique. First, this is the largest canton in Switzerland, covering almost 2,800 sq. miles. Second, as only 165,000 people reside here, it is the least densely populated canton in the Confederation, with 60 residents per sq. mile. Third, it is the only canton in which the residents speak three languages – German in the north, Italian in the south, and in the center – Switzerland's fourth official language, spoken by only 1% of the population – Rhaeto-Romanic, or Romansch. This is the territory of the ancient Rhaet tribe. Graubünden is mountainous country, the land of Heidi, a region of small remote villages, picturesque wooden cabins and breathtaking landscapes. In this canton you can get in the car and wander around without a planned route. If you follow the route, Road N13 leads to the major city of the canton, Chur.

Chur

Some 31,000 residents live in the capital city of Graubünden, Chur, located in the Rhine Valley. The residents view themselves as citizens of the oldest city in Switzerland, whose roots date back some 5,000 years, to the time of the Rhaets, through the Roman Era, until it became the bishopric and, in the 16th century, the capital. The daily life in the city in those times was also unusual: almost all their income was derived from the food industry.

Chur, the capital city of the Graubünden Canton

A traditional fiesta in Chur

Chur's lovely old city is built around the Cathedral of Notre Dame, next to the bishop's palace. The cathedral was dedicated in 1272; in its central chapel you will find a huge, impressive triptych (a three-part painting), with Holy Mary in the center. St. Martin's Church (1491) is located near the city hall (1464), among the beautiful fountains, old houses and narrow streets.

In the Old City, in the Buol mansion built in the 17th century, there is a museum that commemorates the Rhaets – the **Rätisches Museum**. The museum contains archeological exhibits of the culture of the Rhaets. Open daily, except for Mon. Tel. 22.29.88. Admission fee. Another, less well-known museum, but definitely worth a peek, is located at 11 Reichsgasse in the Hotel Romantik Stern. Here a collection of 19th-century carriages is on exhibition. Open to visitors daily 9am-noon and 2pm-5pm. Ask at the hotel reception desk.

From the city of Chur it is 20 miles to the town of **Arosa**. This is one of the most charming and well-known ski resorts in Switzerland. It is surrounded by forests and small lakes, and hidden by mountains, which allow it many sunny days. The town lies at the foot of the **Weisshorn**, whose peak is 8,700 ft. high. You can get to the mountain by cable car. The top station provides a stunning view of the area.

Traveling south from Chur on Road 3 takes you to a village whose name is immediately associated with money, prestige and the "good life": St. Moritz – the vacation home of Europe's elite.

St. Moritz

The town is situated in the mountainous valley of Engadine, at a height of over 4,000 ft., on the shore of Lake St. Moritz, in an area of legendary beauty: there are 25 mountain lakes, forests, snow-covered slopes and a Swiss record of an annual average of 322 days of sunshine, which has earned the town a reputation for "the climate of champagne." It is blessed with an extraordinary combination of advantages. In St. Moritz Bad, at the southern end of the lake, there are ancient springs of therapeutic water which for generations have been known to relieve the pains of its visitors. It has some of the most beautiful Olympic ski slopes in Switzerland, and St. Moritz Dorf is the location of Switzerland's first school of ski instruction, opened in 1927.

This is a lively place, full of activities intended to entertain and amuse the tourists and vacationers who gather. The horse race held in St. Moritz on the frozen lake is world-famous, and in addition to this, there are golf, polo and many more competitions held here. There is also a museum here, the **Engadine Museum** (Enga-diner Museum), at the southern end of St. Moritz Dorf, where lovely exam-ples of the traditional houses in the area, both small village houses and the homes of the well-to-do, are exhibited. Open Mon.-Fri. 9:30am-noon and 2-5pm, Sun. 10am-noon only. Closed on Saturdays. Tel. 3.43.33. Admission fee.

Accommodation

As a vacation spot with a reputation and a history, tiny St. Moritz has some 50 hotels, and that is understandable. As a place with the aura of wealth and a must for the who's who of the world, it boasts 4 luxury 5-star hotels.

Autumn at the lovely ski resort of Arosa

5-STAR HOTELS
Kulm: Tel. 2.11.51.
Suvretta House: Tel. 3.85.24.

4-STAR HOTELS
Albana: Tel. 3.15.43.
Crystal: Tel. 3.64.45.

3-STAR HOTELS
Edelweiss: Tel. 3.87.40.
Bellevue: Tel. 3.81.63.
Soldänella: Tel. 3.36.51.

1, 2-STAR HOTELS
Bernina: Tel. 3.60.22.
National: Tel. 3.32.74.
Sonne: Tel. 3.03.62.

YOUTH HOSTELS
Bad: Tel. 3.39.69.

CAMPING
Olympiaschanze: Tel. 082/3.40.90.

Ski services

St. Moritz Ski School: Tel. 2.80.90.
Ski rental: Tel. 3.35.76; 6.64.37; 6.54.07.

Important Phone Numbers

Area Code: 082
Tourist Information Office: Tel. 3.31.47.
Engadin Airport: 6.54.33.
Dentists: 2.12.31, 3.40.36.
First Aid: 3.41.41.
Railway Station: Tel. 3.52.52.

From St. Moritz to the Italian Border

From St. Moritz, the train and Road 25 climb southeast along the Bernina Valley to the **Bernina Pass**. The pass, located at a height of 7,600 ft., connects the Engadine and the Italian Valtellina mountains. Four miles later, north of the road, is Pontresina, a winter tourist spot situated between three white towering peaks, one of which can be reached by cable car. Further on is Chunetta Belvedera, south of the road, climbing to a height of 6,800 ft.; you can get to it by a combination of car, cable car, and climbing. The view from the mountain of the valley and the Bernina is fantastic.

Before the last part of the climb to the pass, you should stop at the restaurant at the crossroads, where you can take the cableway to Diavolezza, one of the most famous glaciers in Europe, and where you get a magnificent view of the glacial landscape.

The road from St. Moritz to the Italian border passes through great alpine views

The view from Bernina Pass itself is also one of the region's most beautiful, and from here you can continue down on the cableway to Alp Grum (6,850 ft.). The special route of this cableway takes you to the shore of a mountain lake and to a view of Poschiavo Valley and the Glacier Palu.

Return to the road (or train) and continue the winding route down to the Italian border.

From St. Moritz, along the Inn River, Road 27 leads northeast to the town of Zernez. East of the town lies the Swiss National Park. The idea of the park was born and executed in the beginning of the century, by the Swiss Society for the Protection of Nature, to close off an area from the harm of modern man, and to let nature survive in its natural way. Driving off the roads in the park and picnicking are strictly forbidden, in order to ensure that none of the abundant fauna and flora in the park come to any harm. There are guided tours of the park in the summer. Details at the Zernez tourist office.

From Zernez, Road 28 winds northwest to Davos.

DAVOS

This is yet another special place on the vacationer's map. Davos is a small bustling town, which offers visitors air that "heals the soul and body" as well as many things to see and do. In the winter it is a very popular ski resort.

The two inseparable parts of the city, the northern Davos-Dorf and the southern Davos-Platz, lie in the valley of the Landwasser River. Davos offers its wintertime visitors the largest natural ice-skating rink in Europe. Skiers can ride in its famous mountain train, the Parsennbahn, to the wonderful slopes of Weissfluhjoch (8,820 ft.), or to the Weissflughgipfel Peak (9,300 ft.). For information about bus tours or walking tours, inquire at the local tourist office: 68 Promenade, open daily, except for Sun. 8am-noon and 1:45pm-6pm. Tel. (081) 45.21.21.

An unusual museum is located in Davos-Platz; this is the Berbaumuseum, devoted entirely to the history of mines. There are exhibits of mining equipment, different metals, and so on. Open mid-Jun. to the end of Oct., Wed. 2pm-4pm, Sat. 4pm-6pm.

Since 1971, Davos has become the seat of the annual World Economic Forum, which includes world leaders in the fields of politics, economy, media, science, sociology and culture.

A tranquil walk around Davos

FROM LUZERN TO LUGANO, VIA ST. GOTTHARD

This route, which in map language is called N2, passes through the cantons of Nidwalden and Uri, and then turns south, to the southernmost Swiss canton, Ticino – the Italian section of the Confederation. It follows an old route, through St. Gotthard, one of the most important roads in the history of Switzerland, which served to link the inland area with Italy and the Mediterranean Sea.

STANS

This is the capital city of the canton of Nidwalden, one of the smaller Swiss cantons (108 miles). With a population of 5,900, this is a provincial town in the style of the old Switzerland, with a lovely church in the central square, whose outstanding feature is a 16th-century bell tower. Travelers usually stop here to go up the mountain train and cableway (about a 20-minute trip) to the Stanshorn peak, towering 6,300 ft., where you get a fantastic view of Lake Luzern to the north, and the Alps to the south.

ALTDORF

The capital of the canton of Uri, this town has about 8,200 residents. Historically, or at least according to local tradition, this is where the story of the Swiss Federation began. The residents of the canton of Uri were the first to wave the banner of independence. In honor of this, at the end of the 19th century, a statue of the leg-

endary William Tell, the literary hero of the rebellion, was erected in the central square.

From Altdorf there is a bus to the nearby village of Burglen (east of Road 17) where, legend tells us, William Tell was born. There is now a museum here named after him. This is a 13th-century fortified tower, containing an exhibit of documents and souvenirs, telling the story of the uprising that led to the establishment of the Federation. Open to visitors from the beginning of June to mid-Oct., daily 9am-noon and 2pm-6pm. Admission fee.

On the way to Furka Pass

ANDERMATT

This friendly town serves as a transportation crossroads and a popular winter sports center. Here you can begin the Route of the Three Passes, which also leaves Interlaken and Gletsch. This is 120 miles winding through the Alps and passing by magnificent Swiss landscapes. The beginning of the route from Andermatt brings you to Road 19 to the **Furka Pass**, located 7,970 ft. high, with a splendid view overlooking the Urseren Valley and the villages around it. The route continues to Gletsch, with the Rhône Glacier shining majestically above, and from there northwest on Road 6 which winds some four miles to the Grimsel Pass, situated at an altitude of 8,000 ft. Next to this pass is the "Lake of the Dead" (Totensee), a reminder of the battle between the Austrians and the French that was fought in this area in 1799. The road continues along the Aare River some 16 miles to the Innertkirchen intersection.

Here you can turn toward Interlaken or continue east on Road 11 to the **Susten Pass**. In this pass (7,400 ft.), a tunnel (300 yds.) was dug; it is one of the masterpieces of Swiss engineering. On a gray day it is not worth entering the area, but on a clear day it is recommended that you also get off the train and go up to the wonderful view of the Susten peak in the south, the Titilus in the north, and the Bernese Alps in the west. This marvelous mountain road continues along the river and ends at Gôschenen.

Andermatt is also situated at the entrance to the St. Gotthard mountain pass, which has become a symbol of man's struggle to overcome nature.

The **St. Gotthard Alps Pass** (St. Gotthard Alpenpass): Since the 13th century, when Schölenen Gorges was broken through, this pass has become the most important artery in Switzerland. Historically, the paving of this road is connected to the political awakening of the forest cantons, and to their struggle against the Hapsburg Emperorship, until they gained independence.

In 1830 the pass became a paved road, which enabled comfortable passage for carriages and later for vehicles. In the section between the settlement of Gôschenen and Airolo, is the famous St. Gotthard Tunnel; measuring 10.5 miles. It is the longest tunnel in the world. At the highest point of the St. Gotthard Pass, at an altitude of 6,900 ft., is the historic transit station. This is also the geographic entrance into the Italian culture of the canton of Ticino. From here on, as the names of the towns indicate, it is all Italian.

It is best to visit here between June and October, when the heavy snows have melted. There is a **house of worship** from the 14th century, which was built in memory of the German saint, Gotthard, after whom the pass is named. There is a restaurant, a snack bar, a roadside hotel, a youth hostel and a post office. There is also a unique museum, the **National Museum of St. Gotthard.** Various documents, reconstructions, weapons, uniforms, antique vehicles, pictures and much more tell the story of the road, the struggle of man

against the elements of nature and his eventual success in creating the pass.

The marvelous mountain road continues south. Caution: we warn drivers of the temptation to catch a glimpse of the magnificent mountains while driving. It is better to stop once in a while at one of the many charming towns on the roadside, for a good look.

FAIDO

This is a beautiful vacation center, with hotels, surrounded by forests, waterfalls and old homes. On a nice sunny day you can stop and rest at one of the cafés in the center.

GIORNICO

An enchanting town on the bank of the Ticino River, with ancient bridges and a church, Giornico is well worth a visit. The 12th-century St. Nicholau Church is an example of an unusual design, influenced by Lombardic architecture.

BIASCA

This is another lovely town on the crossroads, and it also has an interesting church, St. Pietro, with a 12th-century mural of Jesus.

BELLINZONA

Although it is not the largest city in the canton, Bellinzona is the capital of Ticino. About 17,000

Enjoying greenery and fresh air in the Bellinzona vicinity

people live in this city, which has always been of top strategic importance, as it controls the roads through the Alps. For this reason, the city was strongly fortified when it was built, and there are three impressive castles here to this day. The first, the Great Castle (Castel Grande), is the oldest, and was built where there had formerly been a Roman fortress. The place is mentioned in texts referring to the war between the Franks and the Lombards in 590. It dominates the section of the road leading to the St. Gotthard Pass. Today the castle houses the cantonal offices, whose towers are open to visitors Apr. to mid-Sept., daily 9am-noon and 2pm-5pm.

The second, **Montebello Castle** (Castello di Montebello), was built around the year 1300. At the beginning of this century, it was extensively renovated. Today it houses the **Museum of History and Archeology of the city**. Open Apr. to mid-Sept., daily 9am-noon and 2pm-5pm, closed Tues.

The third, Sasso Corbaro Castle (Castello di Sasso Corbaro), was built in the year 1400. Today it contains the Museum of Folklore of the Canton of Ticino. All three fortresses fell in the early 16th century to the army of the Confederation, and were made the seat of the regional governors, the representatives of the ruling cantons. Dating back to that period, they also each have a second name: Uri Castle, Schwyz Castle, and Unterwalden Castle.

The tourist office of Bellinzona is located at Palazzo Municipale, Tel. (092) 26.05.11, 26.05.13, fax (092) 25.38.17.

From Bellinzona going south, the road splits – on the right, Road 13 leads to Locarno; on the left, Autostrada N2 takes you to Lugano.

LOCARNO

The 35,000 residents of the second largest city in the canton are lucky enough to enjoy an abundance of sunshine (by Swiss standards, of course). Locarno boasts 2,286 hours of sunshine on average a year (in comparison to 1693 in Zürich, for instance). The pleasant climate is complemented by the city's location on the banks of the beautiful Bay of Lake Maggiore (which has only its northern end in Switzerland, the rest is in Italy).

In 1925 the representatives of the European states gathered here with the representatives of Germany, and signed mutual agreements known as the "Locarno Contracts." In 1936, these contracts became meaningless pieces of paper when Hitler ignored them and led Europe into the World War II.

A view of Bellinzona, the capital of Ticino

In Locarno you should take long walks along the city's promenade, breathing in the fragrance of the flowers and the view of the scenery. In addition, there are two sights here that are worth a visit. The first is **Visconti Castle** (Castello Visconti), located at the end of Via Luini (the road runs from the lake west, into the city). This is a fortified palace in medieval style, with a lovely inner courtyard decorated with arches, that was built by the aristocratic Visconti family in the 15th century, and became property of the Federation when they captured the region in 1513 from the Milano dukedom. From that time until 1803, when the canton became independent, this was the seat of the governor and the garrison. Today there is a museum of archeology, history and art in the palace, which contains several marvelous halls preserving the spirit of the times when the palace served as a military base. Open to visitors Apr. to late Oct., daily 9am-noon and 2pm-4pm, closed Mon.

The second sight is **Madonna del Sasso Church and Monastery,** located on the offshoot of a mountain overlooking the city. You can get here comfortably on the cable train from the center of the city (near the tourist office). The monastery was built in the late 15th century, with a fantastic view of the city and the lake below.

Next to the church is the cableway that climbs up to a height of 4,420 ft., to **Cardada**, a favorite skiing spot of the area residents, and from there even higher, on the chair lift to the Cimetta peak, at 5,475 ft., for a great view of the surrounding area.

The tourist office of Locarno is located at 2 Via F. Balli, Tel. (093) 31.03.33, fax (093) 31.90.70.

ASCONA

On the other side of the delta created in Lake Maggiore by the Maggia River, opposite Locarno, is Ascona. Originally a fishing village, Ascona has evolved as a very attractive spot for tourists. In the past generations, it has become particularly popular among artists, writers and musicians who come here and impart a special character to the town. The Ascona Music festival which is held here every September also adds to the cultural atmosphere. The church of Ascona, Notre Dame de la Miséricorde, is famous for its 15th-century murals.

For more information contact the tourist office of Ascona: Tel. (093) 35.00.90.

The marvellously decorated Madonna del Sasso Church

LUGANO – THE ITALIAN CORNER

"The Queen" is what some call the city of Lugano, and not without reason. The city boasts a comfortable climate, a magnificent landscape, mountains and a crooked lake which meet at the shore under the forested slopes.

Lugano – known also as "The Queen"

Lugano is one of the top names on the vacationer's map of Switzerland and of the world; its long-standing tradition of tourism is a central feature. In the city and its vicinity you can enjoy a perfect combination of recreation, rest, nature walks and visits to interesting sights and museums. The social and recreational life of the city is centered in its Old Quarter, around the Piazza Riforma. It is particularly popular in the summer and fall, and its winter advantages outnumber those of many other places.

History

Archeological ruins uncovered in the Lugano region indicate that there was a settlement here in the Roman Era. Later the city was part of the territory under rule of the Lombards, before they were assimilated into the Italian population. In the early Middle Ages, Lugano was governed by the church prince of Kum, and in the late Middle Ages, in the storm of the regional wars and exchange of territories, it became subject to Milan. The duke, who recognized the importance of the place, established a fortified castle there, on the shores of the lake, in 1498.

But the castle and the garrison of the dukedom could not stand up to the Swiss conquest, and in 1512 the city became part of the area annexed to the Confederation. Since then, although the city waned in terms of political independence – economically and culturally it flourished. The *Feira*,

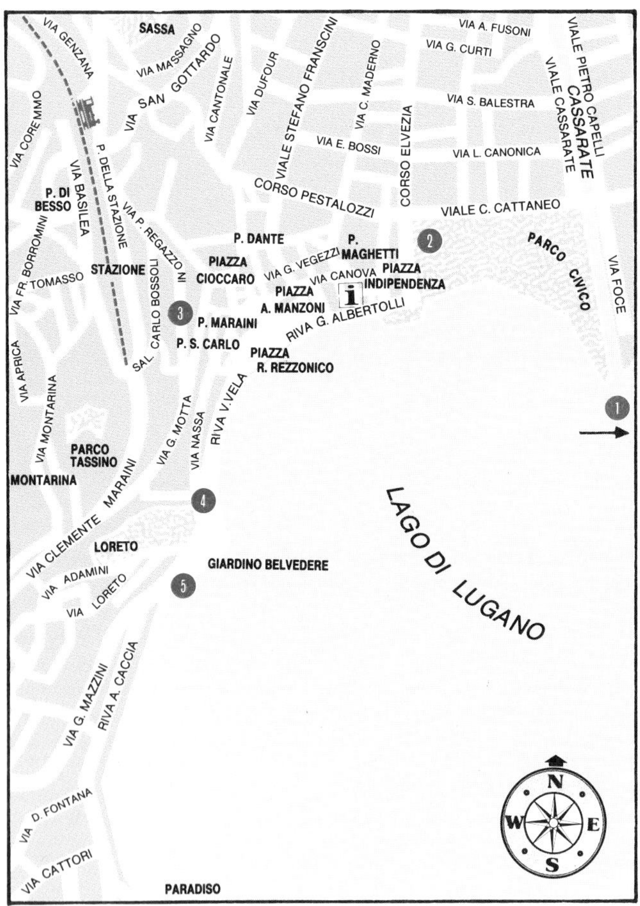

LUGANO

1. Villa Favorita
2. City Park and City Museum
3. San Lorenzo Cathedral
4. Santa Maria degli Angioli Church
5. Belvedere Gardens

the large fair held there every fall, transformed it into an important crossroads of trade between Italy and Switzerland.

This also led to a building boom in the city, which included mansions for the wealthy, large churches, the famous Collège of Pères Somaschi, and in the 18th century, a very active print shop which printed many books and gave the city its name in the cultural and educational world of Europe. The riots that followed the French Revolution shook the political tranquility of Lugano, again. The city became an autonomous entity, first as part of the short-lived Helvetian Republic, and later as part of the new Italian canton – Ticino – which was created in 1803.

In the 19th century, Lugano became known, among other things, as a political refuge, for those forced to flee the political upheavals and struggles in Italy. The opening of the St. Gotthard train line gave a great boost to the development of the city, which became the most important crossroads before the Alp pass.

A General View

Lugano, with 29,000 residents (52,000, including the suburbs), is the largest city in the canton of Ticino. The large majority of the city's residents are, of course, Italian speaking. The city is situated at the edge of the Swiss "finger" that juts into Italian territory at the northwestern tip of Lake Lugano. The lake winds around in a semicircle, and its southern end turns sharply to the west. This is the smallest of the three lakes in the regions, after Lake Maggiore and Lake Cumo. It covers 20 sq. miles, and is 22 miles long, with a maximum width of two miles, and maximum depth of 945 ft. It sits at an altitude of 900 ft. above sea level. Two-thirds of the lake is located in Swiss territory, and a third in Italy.

The lake was created in a dent made by the movement of the Alps glaciers, and its beaches are the result of glacial erosion. The wild beauty of the area is a result of the mountains that close it in from three sides – east, west and north – with steep offshoots that run down to the water, the highest of them (some 3,300 ft.) in the north. In the southern part of the lake, between Melide and Bissone, where the water is relatively shallow, an embankment was constructed, with a road and a railroad track, connecting with the St. Gotthard route and shortening the distance to Italy.

Climate

Lugano's climate is one of the city's strongest points. The annual average temperature is approximately 12°C, the summer is hot, the fall is pleasant and in winter, temperatures only rarely drop below 0ºC. Some examples of the

range: Jan.-Mar.: 6.4ºC to 12ºC; Jun.-Aug.: 23.7ºC to 26.4ºC.

Generally, the city enjoys blue skies. The average rate of cloudiness is 43% annually, in comparison to 77% in Zürich.

Getting There

The city of Lugano, which is situated on the St. Gotthard Road, benefits from convenient access from the north and the south. From Luzern a railroad track and Autostrada N2 lead to Lugano; from Milano, Italian Route N9.

Internal Swissair and Crossair flights connect the city daily with Bern, Zürich, Geneva and Basel, as well as Nice in France, Venice in Italy and more. Flight information is available at Tel: *Swissair*, Tel. 23.63.31, *Crossair*, Tel. 50.50.01.

Boat lines offer frequent service between the city and the settlements around the lake, and the cableway connects it with the nearby mountain settlements. Within the city and its environs, the ACE local public transportation company operates trolley buses (buses run on an electric cable) and buses. There are 10 lines in total, running from 7am to 11pm, at an average frequency of once every 10 minutes. Tickets can be purchased from the machines in the stations, which also indicate the price of the trip according to distance.

A cable-car connects the center of the city with the Railway Station; it is pleasant and panoramic.

TAXIS

Taxis can be called by phone, from the following companies:

AABC: Tel. 51.91.91.
Europa: Tel. 54.59.59.
Tele-Taxi: Tel. 51.21.21.

CAR RENTAL

All major car-rental companies have offices at the airport:

Avis: Tel. 59.54.59.
Budget: Tel. 59.57.57.
Hertz: 59.58.93.

BICYCLE RENTAL

Bicycles can be rented at: Hotel la Perla, Agno, Tel. 59.39.21. Hotel Cadro Panoramica, Cadro, Tel. 91.45.01.

Accommodation

The climate in Lugano, the therapeutic powers attributed to its fine air and its marvelous scenery all help to attract tourists. The city offers a wide range of them with plenty of rooms.

FIVE-STAR HOTELS

Grand Hotel Eden: 7 Riva Paradiso, Tel. 55.01.21, fax 54.28.95. On the lake shore, in the Paradiso Quarter in the southern part of the city.

Principe Leopoldo: 5 Via Montalbano, Tel. 55.88.55, fax 55.88.25. In the Montalbano Quarter, west of the lake, on a hill south of the city (1,250 ft. high).

Splendid Royal: 7 Riva Antonio Caccia, Tel. 54.20.01, fax 54.89.31. On the lake in the southern part of the city.

Villa Castagnola au Lac: 31 Viale Castagnola, Tel. 51.22.13, fax 52.72.71. On the lake, east of the city center, near the Lido bathing beach and the city park (Parco Civico). Lines 1, 2 from the center.

FOUR-STAR HOTELS

Admiral: 15 Via Geretta, Tel. 54.23.24, fax 54.25.48. It is located in the Paradiso Quarter, not very far from the lake, with easy access to the city center by Buses Nos. 1, 2, 9, 10. For those who are interested, there are dietetic meals.

Excelsior: 4 Riva Vela, Tel. 22.86.61, fax 22.81.89. On the lake close to the city center.

Dulac: 3 Riva Paradiso, Tel. 54.19.21, fax 54.61.73.

THREE-STAR HOTELS

Ceresio: 19 Via Serafino Balestra, Tel. 23.10.44, fax 23.79.30. North of the center of the city, close to Parco Civico.

Continental Beauregard: 28 Basilea, Tel. 56.11.12, fax 56.12.13. Located near the city center, behind the train station of Lugano.

Cristallo Centro Hotels: 9 Piazza Cioccaro, Tel. 22.99.22, fax 22.09.55. In the city center, at the foot of the cableway to the train station.

Romantik Hotel Ticino: 1 Piazza Cioccro, Tel. 22.77.72, fax 23.62.78. Center of city, at the foot of the cableway to the train station.

Walter au Lac: 7 Piazza Rezzonico, Tel. 22.74.25, fax 23.42.33. In the center of city on the lake and promenade.

TWO-STAR HOTELS
Flora: 16 V. Geretta,
Tel. 54.16.71, fax 54.27.38.

San Carlo: 28 Via Nassa,
Tel. 22.71.07, fax 22.80.22.
In the center of the city, on a street parallel to the promenade.

ONE-STAR HOTELS
Montarina: 1 Via Montarina,
Tel. 56.72.72, fax 56.12.13.
Close to city center to the east.

Rosa: 12 V. Landriani,
Tel. 22.92.86.

Restaurants

The local cuisine is, of course, Italian – pizza, pasta and so forth, but with a cantonal touch. International tourism has introduced many types of cooking – French, Chinese and more – but you should take advantage of the opportunity and try on the Italian-Ticino dishes.

A typical place for this is *Sayonara*, in the center of the city, in Piazza Cioccaro. Warm meals are served daily until 11:30pm. There are also two other places in the nearby square, Piazza Riforma, the restaurant *Gambrinus*, which is a well-known meeting place for beer-lovers, as well, and the pizzeria-café-bar, *Federale*.

Another, very interesting pizzeria is *Da Franco*, located in the Cassaate Quarter, east of the center, at 12A Via del Tiglio. Lines 1 and 2 take you to the area. In the center, at 4 Via Aristo (corner of the main street, Via Pretorio), is a pizzeria-grill, *Commercio*.

And if you must, there is a *Burger King*, offering the familiar menu, in Piazza Riforma.

Important Phone Numbers

Area code: Tel. 091.
Tourist office: 5 Riva Albertolli,
Tel. 21.46.64, fax 22.76.53.
Train station: Tel. 157.33.33.
Post office: Tel. 21.90.11.
Public transportation in the city:
Tel. 20.72.24.
Police: Tel. 117.
Medical first aid: Tel. 58.61.11.
Ambulance: Tel. 22.91.91.
Lost and found: Tel. 23.93.26.

Walking Tours

Villa Favorita: Tel. 52.61.52. Open mid-Apr. to mid-Aug., Fri.-Sun. 10am-5pm. Admission fee. Lines 1, 2.

In a three-story villa, built in the 17th century, is one of the most outstanding private art collections in the world. It became famous in 1988, when British Prince Charles visited here and offered to buy the collection for a huge sum, in order to exhibit it in London. the offer has been cordially refused, for now.

The collection belongs to Baron Heinrich Thyssen, the German steel tycoon, who in 1920 began acquiring paintings and works of art for considerable sums. His intention was to acquire a collection that would represent the development of European painting in all schools and periods. The Baron became the owner of a collection that, when first presented to the public, in 1930 in Munich, was awarded high praise by art critics and the public at large.

In 1932, the Baron purchased Villa Favorita, in order to hold his creations. When he passed away, in 1947, the collection was handed on to his son, Hans-Heinrich, who continues to collect today.

What can you see here? Over 250 paintings, in 20 exhibit halls, of the great European artists from the 13th century on. Among the works are some

Exhibits at Villa Favorita

The lovely interior of the Santa Maria degli Angioli Church

of the best pieces of art in the world: Titian, Raphael, Memling, Van Eyck, Rembrandt (a self-portrait at age 37), Rubens, Ruysdael, Holbein (his famous work, the portrait of the British King Henry VIII), El Greco, Velázquez, Goya, Watteau and others. The museum also includes exhibits of French impressionism, German expressionism, cubism, surrealism, early American painting, and modern Russian painting, as well. Not everything is on view to the public, due to lack of space. In addition to paintings, there are also many sculptures, antique furniture, carpets, tapestries and jewelry on show in the villa.

The City Park (Parco Civico) is located close to the city center, at the northern tip of the bay. Lines 1, 2, 9 and 10 go there. This is undoubtedly one of the most beautiful parks in Switzerland, and perhaps in all of Europe. It is colossal and offers innumerable pleasures to the visitor: rich, cultivated sub-tropical plants, a rose garden, sculptures, including the favorite Socrates, made of white marble in 1971 by the Russian sculptor Antokolsky, ancient fountains spouting jets of fresh water, an animal reserve with birds and deer, and in the summer, open-air concerts almost daily. In the eastern section of the park is the cantonal library and a natural science museum (not particularly special; admission is free).

The **City Museum of Lugano** is also located in the park, in a beautiful classic palace, the Villa Ciani. It was built in 1839 for the brothers Giacomo and Fillipo Zianni, then famous politicians, who contributed greatly to Ticino's establishment as an independent canton. In 1912, the city of Lugano purchased it from their descendants for a huge sum – 1,775,000 francs. One part of the palace belongs to the adjacent modern congress building, and the other houses the museum. Paintings and sculpture from the 15th-20th century are exhibited. At the present it is closed for restoration. Enquire at the tourist office for details.

Another possibility is the **Cantonal Art Museum** in 10 Via Canova. It houses a rich collection of 19th and 20th century art, by local artists such as Cisari, Genucchi, Huber, as well as by Old Masters: Degas, Renoir, Klee, and others. Tel. 22.79.43. Open Wed.-Sun. 10am-5pm, Tues. 2-5pm. Admission fee.

San Lorenzo Cathedral: Located between the train station and the center of the city, this is an excellent place from which to view the city and the lake. The exterior of the cathedral, built in 1517 in Renaissance style, is very impressive.

Going south from the center toward the Paradiso Quarter, along the promenade on the lake front, you quickly arrive at two sights that are definitely worth a visit.

Santa Maria degli Angioli Church: The square in which this church is located is named after Bernardino Luini, the Lombardic artist. Construction of the church began in 1499. In 1529, three years before his death, Luini painted two murals in the church; many come here especially to see the picture of the Madonna and son with John the Baptist, and that of the Crucifixion, which are considered his best works. Very popular in his time,

Lunch with a view on the San Salvatore peak

Luini was greatly influenced by Leonardo da Vinci, and he decorated many churches, particularly in Milan. Many of his works can be seen today in museums in Paris, London and Florence.

Beyond Santa Maria degli Angioli Church lies **Belvedere Gardens** (Giardino Belvedere), with its palm trees, olive trees, camellias, roses, lilac bushes, mimosa and more. Among the flowers are 12 modern statues, which were commissioned by the city of Lugano from different artists.

Tours in the Lugano Area

The area around Lugano offers many wonderful sights. The possibilities are varied. Guided tours on foot, or in horse-drawn carriages, are organized several times a week in the tourist season. For details, contact the local tourist office, 5 Riva Albertolli, Tel. 21.46.64.

Bus tours for getting to know the city and the area are operated by the *Danzas Company*, during the tourist season. Details and tickets are available at 2 Guisan, Tel. 54.17.76.

You can ride a cable car to the nearby peaks and get a view of the scenery. From the Cassarate Quarter, the **Mont Bre** cableway climbs to a height of 3,060 ft. (trolley bus rides leave every 30 minutes from 9am-11:45am, 1:40pm-6:15pm). From the Paradiso Quarter there is another cableway, to the **San Salvatore** peak, 2,990 ft. high rides leave every 30 minutes from 8:30am). On the peak you can find a good restaurant and a self-service cafeteria. The best outing is to sail on the lake and stop at the villages on its shores. The boats leave Apr.-Oct. from the Lugano mooring, in the center of the city at Maraini Square. You can get off the boat, wander as much as you like and board another one. The following are some of the places we suggest you visit.

GANDRIA

An ancient fishing village at the foot of Mount Bre, situated on a rocky shore near the slope, until 1935 Gandria could be reached only via the lake. You should wander through the enchanting narrow lanes, among the old houses. Near the dock are a restaurant and a cafeteria. The road to the right from there leads to the small local cemetery. Here you are reminded of the local saying about the density of the village's population: the only place a Gandrian resident can find to rest his body is in the cemetery! Another saying refers to the steepness of the village: the local chickens have a pocket like a kangaroo, for if they didn't, their eggs would roll down into the lake. Opposite Gandria, on the other shore, in Cantine di Gandria, is the **Swiss Customs Museum** (Museo Doganale). This entertaining museum illustrates the history of the struggle of the customs officials against smugglers, and among the exhibits are smuggled objects that were caught, from weapons to salami. Open May 6 – October 23, daily 1:30pm-5:30pm. Free admission.

At Gandria

CAMPIONE

This village is a unique phenomenon in itself. Located southeast of

Lugano is situated on Lake Lugano

Lugano, on the opposite shore of the lake, this is a Swiss village in Italian territory. That is, the currency, postal service and telephone service are all Swiss, but the area on which it stands is Italian territory. This is a European political anachronism. The debate, by the way, has always been whether this is a Swiss village on Italian land or an Italian village on Swiss land! Whatever the case, it is a charming place, with a famous casino that attracts many gamblers. The losers can recover while looking at pleasant 13th to 17th-century wall paintings of the Church of Madonna dei Ghirli. Tel. 68.79.51.

MELIDE

This is a small village, some three miles south of Lugano on the lake shore, best known for the special museum near it: **Miniature Switzerland**, a local version of Disneyland. There are sights, buildings, squares, castles, cathedrals, landscapes, rivers, and much more, from throughout Switzerland, all accurately reduced 25 times of the original sizes. There are also trains, mountain trains, boats, and the like, all tiny and operating marvelously. Open mid-Mar. to the end of Oct., daily 9am-6pm; mid-July to mid-Aug., until 10pm. Every June-Sept. the village of Melide holds chamber music concerts. Enquire at the local tourist office, Tel. 68.63.83.

MORCOTE

Located some six miles south of Lugano, this historic fishing village situated on the side of the mountain, has expanded because of its beauty and has become a popular tourist sight. Its old buildings with arches in front, its charming alleyways and restaurants make it a great pleasure if you come on a day when it is not too crowded. A climb up the narrow lanes and ancient steps leads to the **Church of Santa Maria del Sasso**, where you can see beautiful 16th-century murals and a handsome 17th-century organ. Nearby is a cemetery with impressive gravestones, situated on steps, on a slope. In **Scherrer Park** (Parco Scherrer) near the village, there are sub-tropical trees and plants, and classical buildings. The park is open Mar.-Oct.; guided tours on Tues. and Thurs. at 10am, 1:30pm, 3:30pm. Other days open 9am-5pm.

CAPOLAGO AND MONTE GENEROSO

One usually comes to the little village of Capolago (by boat or by train from Lugano) in order to climb up to the highest mountain in the region, **Generoso**, 6,000 ft. high. Take the mountain train to the peak, where a breathtaking view awaits you of the Lombardic plain and a panoramic view of the Alps and Lakes Cumo, Lugano and Maggiore.

At Miniature Switzerland, where sites are reduced 25 times their size

THROUGH THE RHÔNE VALLEY, FROM LAKE LÉMAN TO ANDERMATT

The valley through which the Rhône River flows, cutting through the Alps from west to east, is the oldest paved road in a mountain area. This is the upper Rhône, with its source at a height of 7,300 ft., in the glacial region of Gletsch. It runs into Lake Léman, and comes out the opposite side in Geneva. Most of the river is located in the French canton of Valais, and a small part of its western end is in the canton of Vaud.

Here we describe the route from west to east – against the current of the river. You can connect it to the route described in the chapter, "From Lausanne to Bern," which leads to Sion Castle, near Montre. On the map this route is marked N9.

Aigle

This small city is situated at the intersection of the Rhône Valley, a section of the Grande Eau mountains, and the point from which Road 11 turns north to Interlaken. The city is a center of the wine industry, and at the nearby Aigle Castle you will find the Museum of Wine (and salt). The castle itself, built in medieval style beginning in the 11th century, once belonged to the family of the counts of Savoy. The museum houses an exhibit of the wine-making process and its development in the last 400 years, including different tools, grape strainers, barrels, bottles, old labels and so forth. In the other part of the museum is an exhibit of the history of salt production, including many items from the 16th century on. The museum in open May-Oct., Sat. and Sun. 10am-5pm. Admission fee.

From Aigle, or from the town of Bex which is southwest of it, you can get to the Sex Rouge Peak – 9,900 ft. high. This spot offers an extraordinary view of the Swiss Alps, and the Diablerets Glacier. North of here the road continues to the famous ski resort, Gstaad, where all the who's who – movie stars, members of royal families and simple millionaires – gather to enjoy the snowy slopes.

St. Maurice

Not to be confused with St. Moritz, the vacation resort in Graubünden canton, this little city was originally, in the Roman Era, the most important center of the region. It also played an important role in the history of Christianity, because of the massacre near here (by the Romans themselves) of the Roman army commander Maurice and his African legion, who adopted the belief in Jesus and abandoned the Roman gods. Maurice became a saint of the church, and in the early sixth century a monastery was established in his name. Today not only Christians come here to visit and see, among other things, the monastery's treasures, collected over the generations, including gifts from kings and princes, valuable acquisitions, jewelry, religious works of art and more. The true jewel of the collection is a ninth-century drinking vessel, which is said to have belonged to the Emperor Karl the Great. These treasures, which are invaluable, can be viewed only on guided tours, held Nov.-Apr., daily (except for Sun. mornings and Christian holidays) at 3pm and 4:30pm; May, June, Sept. and Oct., also at 10:30am; Jul. and Aug. also at 9:30am and 2:30pm.

Martigny

This important crossroads of the Rhône Valley is the first major stop north of the St. Bernard mountain pass. On a cliff overlooking the city stands the round tower of La Batiaz Castle. It was

The great dam of Mauvoisin

built in 1259 by the Bishop of Sion, and a few months later was captured by Pierre II, King of Savoy. Today, only its impressive ruins remain, and from here you can look down at the city and the area. On the way from the castle to the city you pass Notre Dame de Compassion Church, built in the 17th century. From there cross a covered wooden bridge to the city. In the center of the city, in the 19th-century city hall building, is a great and special artistic creation, a huge, 55 sq. yard stained glass window, illustrating the Rhône and the Drance. In the city there are also remains of the Roman settlement uncovered in archeological excavations, and a Galli-Roman museum, where the findings are exhibited. Among the exhibits are statues originally from a temple dated somewhere around the first century AD.

From Martigny, as noted, Road 21 turns south, toward the historic Grand St. Bernard mountain pass. The first part of the road goes through the beautiful valley created by the Drance Mountain, descending from the mountains to the Rhône Valley. A short distance after it begins, road N506 breaks off from it, leading to the French border and to Chamonix, the ski resort at the foot of one of the most famous mountains in the world, Mont Blanc. In order to get to this marvelous place you need a visa to France, but the effort is undoubtedly worth it.

Further down the road, some eight miles later, another turn to the left in the direction of the village Verbier, leads to the giant dam of **Mauvoisin** (Barrage de Mauvoisin). This is a prime example of the harnessing of water for use by man. The dam, some 800 ft. high, stops tens of millions of cubic yds. of water running from the mountain peak, gathers it in a lake and releases it to generate many kilowatts of electricity.

The Grand St. Bernard Tunnel connects the Swiss Rhône Valley and the Italian Aosta Valley all year round. The tunnel is the result of cooperation between the two countries, in the late 1950's and early 1960's, aimed at solving the problem of crossing the mountains, which are covered with heavy snow six months a year. The tunnel is four miles long; those more interested in touring than in transportation should use the old road, which takes you to the historic St. Bernard hospice.

Grand St. Bernard

On the Swiss side of the Italian-Swiss border, 8,000 ft. up, is the **hospice** of the St. Bernard order of monks. For some 900 years they have lived here, despite the difficult conditions. They devote their time to extending aid and assistance to visitors in the mountains. One person who came through the pass and needed no help from the monks was Napoleon Bonaparte, in 1800, leading an army of 40,000 soldiers on their way to surprise the Austrian coalition in the battle of Maringo. An inscription on the wall of a roadside inn, a few miles north of the pass, declares, *Napoleon stopped here, asked for, received and drank a glass of milk, and paid 5 francs.*

In the hospice itself, the tradition of hosting guests continues, and those passing through can sleep in the rooms of the monastery for a small sum, according to their ability to pay. A roadside cafeteria offers a light menu and drinks, and in the back of the hospice is the local museum. Open mid-June to the end of Sept. 8:30am-6pm. Admission fee. The museum tells the story of this place and the struggle against the difficult mountain conditions through documents, paintings, drawings, maps and other items. Below the museum are the kennels of the famous St. Bernard dogs – those big, beautiful, sad-eyed animals who used to carry alcoholic drink around their necks and were sent to rescue those lost in the snow. Today, in the age of rescue helicopters, these lovely canine rescuers have become a thing of the past.

A street in Brig

Return to the Rhône Valley Road, going east, to the city of Sion.

Sion

The capital of the canton of Valais, Sion has about 23,000 residents. It earned its central place in the history of the region in the fourth century AD, when it became the bishopric; the settlement developed around the monastery that was built here. In the Middle Ages, the Bishop of Sion became an important political figure and the Church Prince. In that period two impressive sights were also constructed in Sion. **Tourbillon Castle**, situated on a cliff north of the city, was built in the 13th century by a bishop who wanted a secure place for himself and his men to live. The castle endured the wars and many days of siege until it was damaged by fire in 1788. Only ruins are left, but these are very impressive to this day. Nearby is the fortified church of Valère. In the Roman era this was the location of a military fortress and a pagan temple. The fortified church was built in the 12th and 13th centuries, and it demonstrates the fortification of churches in the days when they had to confront military struggles. The early 15th-century organ here, is considered one of the oldest in the world still in use.

Zermatt – a vacation and ski resort that offers wonderful conditions for vacationers

In the museum of Valère you can see exhibits from different periods, including a very impressive bull's head uncovered in archeologic excavations at the Roman site of Octodorus in Martigny, and a collection of Roman and Gothic boxes. There is also a section devoted to the folklore of the Valais canton, which includes many traditional costumes. You can visit the church and the museum in the summer, 8am-noon and 1:30pm-7pm; in the winter to 5pm only, closed Mon. Admission fee.

From the area of the castles, turn west to the ancient city of Sion. Here we pass by the Castle of Maggiore, the modest cantonal museum of fine arts, and the cantonal museum of archeology.

A typical alpine scene of mist and mountains

Further on is the beautiful 17th-century city hall, with its doors decorated by magnificent wood-carvings, and a council room which is definitely worth a visit. Nearby is also the **Notre Dame du Glarier Cathedral**, a 13th-century building with a Roman-style tower that was constructed in 1100. In the Lombardic Quarter south of the cathedral, the **Supersaxo House**, built in 1505, is also worth a visit. On the second floor is a central hall with a splendid ceiling of artistic wood carvings depicting, among other things, the birth of Jesus.

TOURS IN THE AREA

The Underground St. Léonard Lake: From Sion the Uvrier-Sion bus goes on Road 9 to the lake, four miles northeast of the city. Not far from the parking lot is the entrance to a **stalactite and stalagmite cave** and **St. Léonard Lake**. Boats sail in the lake, passing by the fabulous sights of the stalactites and stalagmites illuminated with electric lights. The height of the water in the lake is maintained with a pump that works continuously.

Grand Dixence Dam: About 10 miles south of Sion is this huge dam, the largest project of its kind in Switzerland, with a fantastic wall 950 ft. high. Built in 1966, the dam's hydroelectric center has the capacity to produce nearly two billion kilowatts a year. A special bus comes here from the Sion train station.

Sierre

Sierre enjoys a lot of sunshine and a mix of French and German culture. In the city center, on the ancient and charming street, Rue du Bourg, you will find the impressive 17th-century city hall. The interior of the building is full of mural paintings, stained glass windows and works of art, and it also houses a **Museum of Tin Implements** from the 17th-19th century. There is also a beautiful hall dedicated to Rainer Maria Rilke, the Austrian-Czech writer and poet, who lived in Sierre until his death in 1926. You can visit the museum Mon.-Fri. 8am-noon and 2pm-5pm. Free admission.

Enjoying the special tranquility of Zermatt

Near Sierre there are two well-known vacation towns. One is **Crans**, where you can take a cable car to the peak of **Bella-Lui** mountain, a magnificent panoramic observation point at 8,400 ft. The second, **Montana**, is a small town situated on a sort of "balcony" overlooking the lakes and the mountain landscape, which enjoys a clear climate, attracting many tourists who want to ski and benefit from the sun at the same time.

Leuk

Long ago this small city was already a favorite of the bishops of Sion, and they chose to build castles here for themselves and their staff. From the city a road leads north (about 9 miles) to the hot springs of **Leukerbad**, at a height of 4,500 ft., which have been known since the 19th century for the relief of rheumatic ailments.

On the way to Brig lies the town of **Visp**, where the road turns south to the village of Täsch. Leave your car in Täsch, and take the mountain train up to Zermatt.

Zermatt

One of the best known vacation and ski resorts of Switzerland and of Europe as a whole, Zermatt has attracted generations of mountain climbers, captives of the legend of the conquest of the Matterhorn, which towers above the town in the southwest. The story of the triumph over the Matterhorn, in the middle of the last century, is accompanied by blood-curdling tales of mountain climbers who plunged to their death from a height of 3,000 ft. and the like – the legend has always encouraged tourism. Modern Zermatt offers wonderful conditions for vacationers: a special tranquility, a street of hotels, restaurants and souvenir shops, the Alps Museum – which as you would guess, depicts the conquest of the Matterhorn – and a cableway for safe passage up to the surrounding peaks.

The hot springs at Leukerbad are known for their relief for rheumatic ailments

Matterhorn

Climbing to the towering (14,700 ft.) Matterhorn Peak is a professional project for experienced mountain climbers only. The tourist office, Tel. (028) 67.10.31, can help and advise you regarding Alpine matters. The average tourist can go up the *Kleine Matterhorn* (12,700 ft.) on a series of cable cars that leave the station at the edge of the

Picturesque Brig

town. The breathtaking view from the little peak includes the Theodule Glacier and the Italian Alps.

Gornergrat

This peak (10,300 ft.) is situated to the east of the Matterhorn and can be reached on the open mountain train, on the highest such track in Europe. The view from the train and the mountain (one of the most beautiful in Switzerland) includes the pointed Matterhorn, its higher neighbor (15,300 ft.) to the south – Monte Rosa – and the glaciers surrounding the Gornergrat. (You can continue after this on the cable car to another peak of the Stockhorn mountain).

Brig

The city of Brig is an important crossroads located at the beginning of the Simplon mountain pass. Its train station connects Switzerland with Italy. The central figure in the city's history is Senior Kasper Stockalper, who was in charge of the Simplon pass in the latter half of the 17th century and knew how to exploit his position for prosperous business ventures. Stockalper invested much of his money, between 1658 and 1678, in building the castle which is considered the largest home of nobility in Switzerland – Stockalper Castle. It is indeed magnificent. In 1948 the city of Brig purchased the castle, and opened it for guided tours, daily 11am-1pm and

2pm-5pm, tour every hour on the hour; closed Mon. Admission fee.

From Brig, as noted, Road E2 continues to the **Simplon Pass** to Italy, toward the city of Domodóssola. Simplon is a magnificent mountain pass with a story. In the days of the "trustee" Stockalper, the road was established, two hospices were built there and protection against road robbers was organized. Afterwards, Napoleon contributed to local development. Because it was convenient to get to his war campaigns through Switzerland, and the cantons agreed (or were forced) to supply him with 16,000 soldiers and logistic assistance, he decided in 1800, while he was still only the first consul of France, to cultivate Simplon. Shortly after going through the steep St. Bernard route with his army on his way to the battle of Marignano, Napoleon ordered that a road be paved in Simplon that would allow the French artillery units to get through quickly with their heavy equipment. The road was paved, but Napoleon never used it.

Between 1895 and 1906, in an extraordinary engineering feat for that time, a tunnel was dug northeast of the Simplon Pass for the railroad track. This was the longest train tunnel in the world, stretching 8,000 yds. Between 1912 and 1922 another tunnel was dug, enabling two-way railroad traffic, and measuring 18,107 yds. Since the tunnel was created, it has served as an inspiration for many detective stories; the long dark

train trip through tunnel has been the setting of many a mysterious crime.

The road of the Simplon Pass is open to traffic Apr.-Oct., more or less. In the winter, it is closed because of the snow and the strong wind storms; at that time cars can cross to the other side on special railroad cars.

Aletsch Glacier (Aletsch-gletscher): From Brig, a trip north to the largest glacier in Switzerland is highly recommended. Known as the Great Aletsch, the glacier covers approximately 45 sq. miles, and is 14 miles long. This "small" example of the prehistoric glacial age arouses the imagination regarding what it was like at the time when,

Aletsch Glacier

according to some scientists, the dinosaurs froze to death.

From Brig, Road 19 runs northeast, continuing the trip toward **Andermatt**.

On the way, there is another mandatory stop: **Gletsch**. This is a high winter sports town (5,500 ft.) from which you can get to the **Rhône Glacier** (Rhône Gletsch), which is 6 miles long. On the glacier awaits a cool adventure, an **Ice Cave** (La Grotte de Glace), cut into the ice. Open to visitors daily, June-Oct., daylight hours. Admission fee.

(From Gletsch you can take the route of the Three Mountain Passes – see "From Luzern to Lugano").

INDEX

S

T

U

V

W

NOTES

NOTES

NOTES

QUESTIONNAIRE

In our efforts to keep up with the pace and pulse of Switzerland, we kindly ask your cooperation in sharing with us any information which you may have as well as your comments. We would greatly appreciate your completing and returning the following questionnaire. Feel free to add additional pages.

Our many thanks!

To: Inbal Travel Information (1983) Ltd.
18 Hayetzira St.
Ramat Gan 52521
Israel

Name: ______________________________

Address: ______________________________

Occupation: ______________________________

Date of visit: ______________________________

____

Purpose of trip (vacation, business, etc.): ______________________________

____

Comments/Information: ______________________________

____

____

____

____

____

____

____

3/95

INBAL Travel Information Ltd.
P.O.B 1870 Ramat Gan
ISRAEL 52117